W9-DCN-529

The U.S.A. Up Close

**GIULIO
ANDREOTTI**

The U.S.A.
Up Close

*From the Atlantic Pact
to Bush*

*Translated from the
Italian by Peter C. Farrell*

NEW YORK UNIVERSITY PRESS
NEW YORK AND LONDON

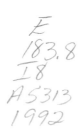

E
183.8
I8
A5313
1992

FLORIDA STATE
UNIVERSITY LIBRARIES

SEP 14 1992

TALLAHASSEE, FLORIDA

Copyright © 1992 by New York University
All rights reserved
Manufactured in the United States of America

Library of Congress Cataloging-in-Publication Data
Andreotti, Giulio.
[USA visti da vicino. English]
The U.S.A. up close: from the Atlantic Pact to Bush / Giulio
Andreotti : translated from the Italian by Peter C. Farrell.
p.   cm.
Translation of: Gli USA visti da vicino.
Includes index.
ISBN 0-8147-0604-5 (cloth)
1. United States—Foreign relations—Italy. 2. Italy—Foreign
relations—United States. 3. United States—Foreign
relations—1945–1989. 4. Andreotti, Giulio—Journeys—United
States. 5. Visits of state—United States. 6. Visits of state—
Italy. I. Title. II. Title: USA up close.
E183.8.I8A5313   1992
327.73045—dc20   91-38248
                                                   CIP

New York University Press books are printed on acid-free paper,
and their binding materials are chosen for strength and durability.

Contents

Foreword

No Italian leader has made a greater contribution to the postwar history of his country than the author of this volume, Giulio Andreotti. Prime minister six times, member of cabinets for twenty-three of the last thirty years, he has been so inextricably related to the Italian political evolution that no adult Italian can remember a government that Andreotti did not either head or shape. And every U.S. secretary of state since Dean Acheson and every president since Truman has had to deal with this extraordinary statesman. These assertions run counter to many American stereotypes which cast Italian governments in a mold characterized by a high degree of instability marked by frequent changes of cabinet and elections perplexing to an electorate used to a two-party system.

The reality of Italy is in fact quite different. No European country has made more dramatic economic progress since the end of World War II than Italy. None has had a basically more stable government. This is why Italy has triumphantly overcome huge handicaps. There was the legacy of thirty years of fascism and of military defeat in World War II, while possessing the sparsest natural resources of any of Europe's major powers. Totalitarianism and defeat had sharpened the differences between North and South Italy that reflect nearly a thousand years of separate development. Western Europe's largest and most disciplined Communist party threatened its nascent democracy. Italy's industrial plant was devastated even though it had not achieved international competitiveness even before the war.

Today, Northern Italy may well be the most dynamic and inventive economy in Europe. Italian democracy has surmounted the challenges of both communism and terrorism. And no country has been a steadier supporter of the North Atlantic Alliance. Refuting the views of some Gaullist advocates of European integration, Italy has proven that Atlantic partnership is compatible with devotion to European unity, indeed that both sides of the Atlantic gain through such a partnership. No government has more consistently backed European federal institutions and economic integration than Italy's.

The assertion that Italian governments are fundamentally stable may strike American readers as odd, given the frequent rotation of Italian prime ministers. But if one compares the composition of American and Italian cabinets over the past thirty years there is much more continuity in the Italian government. For the core group of Italian leaders tends to alter only very gradually. The same personnel appear in successive cabinets even while their posts are changed from time to time.

The Italian political system permits the expression of many different shades of view represented in various political parties, most with around 10 percent of the total vote. The largest democratic party—the Christian Democrats—oscillates between 30 and 35 percent but it is composed of many factions, almost as independent as political parties, which permit it to adjust to dominant currents by only slight shifts in leadership. The Communist party, with around 25 percent of the vote, has so far been outside the system.

This is the politics of an ancient country grown wary from many shattered illusions, grown skeptical from having watched empires rise and fall on its very soil, cautious of excessive enthusiasm, but tenacious in pursuit of its values which, given the Italian character, will always be judged by their human quality. No people prizes the individual more than the Italian; hence the insistence on translating high-sounding claims to propositions relevant to family and day-to-day experience. Americans seek the limitations of governmental power in constitutional guarantees. Italians bring it about through a common sense, matter-of-fact endurance which makes it nearly impossible to enforce any law contrary to fundamental popular instinct.

This is why Italian politicians are as different from the American as night and day. American political figures operate in a system that believes every problem has a solution and that in turn those solutions are reflections of individual leadership. Hence, the overwhelming emphasis on self-assertion and the dramatic. Italian political figures on the other hand operate in an environment ever suspicious of charismatic claims and reluctant to accept any hint of a personal tour de force. Italians derive their reassurance not from star quality but from a performance that makes the individual leader dispensable. This produces an emphasis on anonymity, on skillfully operating the system, not on transcending it.

Giulio Andreotti has been the most durable and in many ways the most brilliant of this type of political leader. Meeting him for the first time, Americans might be amazed that a personality so unobtrusive in appearance and conduct could have dominated Italian politics for close to three decades. Nor would they immediately comprehend his low-key, almost antidramatic style. They would not be familiar with a political code that insists on always doing more than you claim and, above all, being far more powerful than you appear.

But closer acquaintance would leave no doubt about Andreotti's significance. He has been prime minister six times; no cabinet has been formed without his blessing for at least two decades. He has been closely identified with Italy's postwar achievements ever since he served as the secretary to the great Prime Minister De Gasperi in the late forties when Italy's postwar democracy fought off a Communist onslaught.

Giulio Andreotti has achieved this dominance because he possesses one of the sharpest and subtlest minds of his generation. His understated behavior reflects his conviction that a policy based on brilliant analysis needs no fanfares. Americans have reason to be grateful that in Andreotti high intelligence is clearly related to commitment to Western values and friendship with the United States.

This book gives American readers an opportunity to meet one of Europe's most interesting men. It deals with Andreotti's relationship with American leaders over most of the postwar period. As already mentioned, he has known every president since Truman and every secretary of state since Acheson. Characteristically, Andreotti tells his story in a series of vignettes describing in the main common efforts and a few disappointments, including sketches of Americans that impressed him, and of Americans that puzzled him. He was disappointed when America in the Kennedy administration withdrew without warning missiles from

Italy that the Italian government had placed there at great domestic cost. But he puts that in the context of a previous ten years of close cooperation that sustained Italian democracy.

Twenty years later—in the Reagan administration—America invaded Grenada, once again without telling its ally, then on a state visit to Washington. But Andreotti is not pejorative; he considers impulsive moves dominated by domestic politics an American idiosyncrasy, more than compensated by the staunch friendship of an indispensable ally.

Andreotti tells his story neither with gloating nor with self-pity. His pithy portraits of American leaders are invaluable. In the end, one is reassured to know how America looks to a subtle, complex friend and feels fortunate that the partnership on both sides of the Atlantic was in such good hands.

HENRY A. KISSINGER

Preface

Last year when I finished putting together my impressions of forty years of both occasional and regular contacts with the Soviet world in the form of a book, I was sure the editor was going to ask me to do the same for the other superpower (the twinning exercise now seems quite obvious). This second effort at synthesis is all the more arduous due to the intensity of the relationship in terms of quantity and quality. Therefore, I have had to make a selection of persons and events, and this introduces a certain measure of omission as regards a complete chronicle of that relationship. On the other hand, completeness is neither my intent nor, perhaps, is time ripe enough to pursue such an objective.

Leaving aside the three major subdivisions of that continent extraneous to our present field of interest, when we say "America" we are referring to the "United States," an extremely varied reality with at times contradictory features. In a situation marked by deep friendship and admiration, being objective even about something which strikes you as being not entirely correct represents, in my opinion, a sign of mutual freedom. This is a manifestation of the fraternal affinity with all Americans, not just the twenty million of Italian descent; it has deep roots dating far back in time and is not something created with the Atlantic Alliance.

This reconstruction of my American diary is not limited to political relations and is based on three distinct periods of public life, with an introductory part dedicated to indirect observation in the shadow of Alcide De Gasperi: 1. the eight years as minister of defense; 2. relations as president of the Council of Ministers; 3. the years of responsibility as minister for foreign affairs.

The paramount lesson De Gasperi taught us was a great sense of dignity in dealing with other nations, even though he was aware of Italy's absolute need for the assistance of others at that time and realized it was impossible for others to attribute to fascism alone the blame for the war lost by the country. In a world where, after the defeat of Hitler, the Anglo-Russian-American coalition became a thing of the past and split asunder into two-sided cold war between democracy and Stalinism, Italy's place was logically on the former front, even if this was to inflict upon the country a wound to be healed by time and steadfastness alone.

Using the records of discussions in the Council of Ministers (I was its secretary from 1947 to 1954) to retrace the stages of our reincorporation into the international scene is always a very useful exercise for me from two viewpoints. First of all, the actual documentation confirms how only the patience and courage of a few enlightened minds were behind the groundwork necessary for the global reconstruction of Italy. The masterpiece of De Gasperi, Sforza, Saragat, and a few others was their understanding of the exact point of convergence between Italy's interests and those of the great democracies. At the same time, however, it was necessary to begin a process of decantation, above all in order to bestow credibility upon our role as allies. With almost half of all Italians devotedly lined up on the other side (Nenni being honored with the Stalin Award was an expression of that fact), what type of military security could we have had or offered in the tragic case of a third world war?

De Gasperi did not live long enough to see the coming together of the two Italys, but his clear vision of the Atlantic Alliance as much more than a military pact shed light on subsequent developments and is still a source of guidance for us.

The Western ministers of defense, together with their colleagues in foreign affairs, are the statesmen who meet most frequently with Americans. During my term of office it was customary, among other things and besides the ministerial-level meetings of the Atlantic Alliance, to be invited on a rotation basis to visit the installations overseas with itineraries quite different from the normal tourist trails. To those trips I owe a knowledge of parts of the United States which not even most Americans have an opportunity to visit in their lifetime. From Louisville,

Kentucky, to Phoenix, Arizona; from San Antonio, Texas, to the submarine bases in New England; from Colorado Springs to Omaha in Nebraska; from the airports of the Pacific to Cape Canaveral in Florida, and to other bases and states. My thorough visits to these places really make me feel like a very privileged person. I returned each time with a renewed confirmation of something written about Mussolini: if he had gone to the United States only once, had seen the power of its industrial base, and had grasped its indissoluble bond with democratic Europe, he would never have ventured into a suicidal conflict.

During my first two terms of office as president of the Council of Ministers (1972–73 and 1976–79, I will not refer to the one just begun), relations with Washington unfolded within two distinct scenarios according to the differing domestic and international situations. As part of the general critical reassessment of what had been done under Presidents Kennedy and Johnson, the Nixon administration deemed imprudent any American interference in Italian politics geared to stimulate the creation of center-left governments (in the biographies written by Kennedy's closest aides immediately after his assassination there were—just how opportune I really don't know—detailed descriptions in this regard), and all the more so since the Socialists were once again mixed up "de facto" with the Communists in fierce opposition to the cabinet over which I presided together with Deputy Malagodi. In my official visit to the White House, which in truth I had not requested, I had to set the score straight on these comments to make sure people would not consider Italy in the throes of democratic uncertainties (not the case at all). Nixon and Kissinger pursued a policy of broad international openness, accomplishing the master stroke of establishing relations with the People's Republic of China while maintaining excellent relations with Moscow, and they didn't want the Western front to come apart at the seams and thereby endanger their maneuver. In fact, it wasn't and still isn't very easy to explain the subtleties of our domestic life to people abroad. I just hope I was able to illustrate why the precarious state of my government (threatened day after day by those who used secret ballots to shoot down the official party line and who, fifteen years later, would become the same people who decry secret ballots as the devil's handiwork) by no means whatsoever implied instability in the major lines of Italian policy.

When I returned to Palazzo Chigi (the office of the prime minister in Rome) in 1976 it was easy for me to demonstrate the truthfulness of this assumption since it was then supported by the compact Italian front against terrorism and by the public acceptance of NATO by the Communists. Therefore, I came down very hard on the unfounded and unfair warning of danger for democracy in Italy issued by the quadrumvirate Ford, Schmidt, Callaghan, and Giscard d'Estaing at the summit meeting of the seven most industrialized countries in Puerto Rico.

And yet, there was an impending danger in financial terms (we only had foreign currency reserves to cover requirements for no more than one week) and we needed an expression of confidence. This was the reason why I went to see Gerald Ford despite the fact he had lost the elections and was about to hand over the helm to Jimmy Carter who, in a gesture of great importance, sent the incoming secretary of state Cyrus Vance to meet with me in Washington.

During the Carter presidency the only disturbing note was the petulant habit of having the ambassador in Rome, without any real enthusiasm on his part I believe, issue imprudent and entirely unnecessary bulletins opposing the entry of the Communists into the Government coalition.

There is no doubt that Ronald Reagan's personality stands out above the crowd. I had met him in Rome during the trip for his international debut when he was still the governor of California and what had struck me the most was the frank way he admitted being unacquainted with the issues not covered in the file cards prepared for him by the State Department. When he became president those cards were a customary support in his discussions where his degree of dependence on his staff was quite evident. He didn't try to hide it. Quite the contrary, he seemed anxious to get the file card reading over with so he could become an engaging host and draw from his vast store of jokes and amusing stories. However, it would be completely incorrect to consider him a mere spokesman for the apparatus. This was true of the mundane and small-scale matters, but when it came down to the major decisions he really didn't play it according to anyone else's script. I recall his staff's discomfort when he pulled a piece of paper out of his pocket at a small meeting on the eve of the 1985 encounter with the Soviets in Geneva and said it was the result of two days' solitary meditation: "I do not know," it read, "if Gorbachev really wants to continue in his courageous and new course, but before history and our own conscience none of us must have remorse for not having helped him."

In Reykjavik he realized that the turning point had come. He dismissed everyone and reached an agreement with Gorbachev. When briefing us on the outcome a few hours later, George Shultz declared that the president was exceptional because he had ventured into unfamiliar territory on his own. Fortunately . . .

Certainly, the transition from the excommunication of the empire of evil to the policy of a constructive smile with Moscow was very bold. And yet, the declared ambition to free the world from the nightmare of a nuclear holocaust stood firmly in the background as the basic source of inspiration.

While other political aides did not live up to expectations and messed things up, George Shultz progressively assumed his own distinct identity at Reagan's side. I can write about him in a very familiar way because we met on numerous occasions and had an exchange of correspondence on the critical events of the none-too-distant past which is all in the archives and will help to shed light on decisive points of contemporary diplomacy.

George Bush and James Baker are now faced with the difficult task of being original while ensuring continuity. Neither one of them wants to be or even appear to be the tail end of the Reagan-Shultz comet and that is why they have asked for a few months' period of grace. However, with Shevardnadze's most recent meetings in the United States with Baker and Bush, the policy of broad cooperation has once again spread its operational wings and everything seems to be moving in the right direction.

Public life in the United States most certainly rotates around the president. For a long time, however, I have been convinced that the secret behind a long-standing political relationship also involves close relations with Congress where, despite elections to the House of Representatives every two years and to the Senate every six years, key people remain in office for a long time as eminent reference points. Those of Italian descent on Capitol Hill are now numerous, influential, and represent a very important link with us.

I fail to understand why so few people in Italy, even among those at the highest level, share this point of view. The glamour of a White House reception seems to be the focal point of all aspirations, without notice even being taken of the protocol-decreed ritual behind certain ceremonies. In addition, whoever writes the welcome speeches doesn't really go that far out of his way to change the words. He most likely just checks the files and changes a few words. For example, for someone like me he underscores the "lengthy experience," while for novice prime ministers most worthy of praise is their "youthfulness."

I remember one occasion when Henry Kissinger, who by the way was always very affable with me, expressed the wish to see "new faces" coming from Italy (he actually said "fresh faces" but the exact translation of that into Italian could give rise to misunderstandings). Most likely the episode was due to an unconscious expression of irritation toward a political system such as ours which is more stable than theirs. Whenever I inquire about some of my past colleagues on the NATO Ministerial Council, I ordinarily receive puzzled looks or total silence as a reply. During one of my latest visits to Washington I was speaking to someone at a very high level about a secretary of state for whom, when he was in office, I had had the highest regard, Dean Rusk. I was the one who informed the person that the ninety-year-old professor at the head of the University of Georgia in Athens, Georgia, was precisely that elderly diplomat.

Henry Kissinger is still very well known, but he owes it more to his numerous professional activities and appearances on TV than to any sustained echo of his albeit remarkable period of government service.

America, however, is not just Washington or people in government. In my notes you will find quite significant passages on my contacts with the pluralistic world of religion, trade union leaders, universities (four of which have conferred honorary degrees upon me), movieland, the fascinating world of racing, and most of all, with people of Italian descent whose presence has increased and is so gratifying.

I really wouldn't be scandalized at all if the average reader finds such pages more interesting than the other ones. In fact, I'm sorry I wasn't able to make them even longer. They are very much alive in my heart and mind along with experiences such as high-level political talks in the White House or Congress; the hospitality of the late Francis Cardinal Spellman in New York; the invitation to the home of Jimmy Stewart in

Los Angeles to celebrate his wedding anniversary; the evenings spent in the company of Msgr. Alberto Giovannetti with the families of friends whose names are not necessarily in the social register; the hours spent in the Disneylands on both coasts; an afternoon in the deafening din of a ball park; and the breathtaking neon spectacle of Las Vegas.

Man does not live by politics alone.

Introduction

This book, *The U.S.A. Up Close,* now being published in the United States with quite a flattering foreword by Henry Kissinger, has met with favorable reviews and success among readers both in Italy and in a number of Spanish-speaking countries in the wake of its immediate translation in Mexico. By no means do I claim to have . . . discovered America. All I meant to do was to put together piecemeal impressions from different times and experiences which, from a political viewpoint, are interlaced with an ever-present ingredient: the strong link which connects the two shores of the Atlantic and which must remain the cornerstone of international politics.

Frequently in good faith, and for individually valid reasons, there are those on both sides of the Atlantic who believe this link is bound to become weaker since the prospects of European union may perhaps place greater emphasis on security, and because some circles in America consider it neither right nor just that the United States, almost fifty years after World War II, should still invest so much money and manpower in shouldering the burden of the Old Continent's "defense." Others would prefer to focus on the Pacific rather than on the Atlantic, ever mindful of growth in that region looked upon with just as much admiration as fear of competition. I know the White House is not party to the waning of interest toward Europe, and that statements by individual congressmen or senators do not voice the opinion of Congress as a whole, and less so of the nation.

In 1936 Franklin Delano Roosevelt called upon Americans to experience the glory of *interdependence* after having tasted the fruits of independence. He was referring to the two American continents, but in my opinion, the same wise doctrine led the United States in the '70s to participate in the Helsinki process which, in December 1990, was sanctioned anew during the Paris Conference and in the documents signed by President Bush and Secretary of State Baker. Much the same is happening with the Atlantic Alliance as it adjusts its strategies—and not only the military ones—in the face of the radical changes sweeping through the nations which have shaken off communism.

The United States and Canada *are* Europe. Far-removed and out of date is George Washington's warning that the United States had to remain aloof from any permanent form of alliance with any foreign power. This was right in 1796, but not now. A reporter in New York recently asked me if one day the United States of America and Europe might become one. Aside from the fact that the latter has yet to become a reality, I feel our task at present is to strive in a resolute and realistic way towards the success of NATO and CSCE which are so closely linked together.

After my book was published and I was once again chosen to head the Italian Government (August, 1989), I had numerous contacts with the Bush administration, including more than customarily frequent relations in writing, by telephone, and in person with the president of the United States. As minister of foreign affairs before that time, I had established a good relationship with Jimmy Baker whom I regard more and more as a person whose financial acumen is coupled with strong principles of justice heightened by a profound religious spirit.

I would add in passing that his predecessor George Shultz and I are still good friends. In fact, George invited me, along with other European leaders, to join a consultative committee on the foreign policy studies which he coordinates at Stanford University. He called me to extend this invitation while I was engaged in a debate at the senate on the Gulf crisis, and I thought he was calling to express his own views on the issue (just as Henry Kissinger had done). Not at all. He seemed happy to bear no active responsibilities at such a complex time, and only spoke to me about his work at the university. We all have wonderful memories of George. Gorbachev told me he had been so pleased to see him during his visit to California, and reiterated his appreciation of the work George had done for détente and for peace as part of the Reagan team.

I have returned to the White House three more times, one of them as president of the European Community during the semester of Italian presidency, and on that occasion I was accompanied by Jacques Delors, the head of the EEC Commission. This was a new and very positive change. His presence was quite useful since I felt that the American president had not been properly briefed by his staff about the EEC's actual position in the Uruguay Round negotiations (GATT). The common agricultural policy of the 12 EEC member countries can be criticized, and in fact we ourselves have decided to adjust it in a gradual way. The fact remains, however, that total EEC imports of foodstuffs from the United States far outnumber our exports to America.

We sought to leave lasting traces of our six-month presidency of the European Economic Community. During our previous term of office we had brought the negotiations on the enlargement of the EEC to Spain and Portugal, which had lasted for seven years, to a positive conclusion. In 1989 we endeavored to finalize a meaningful and standing protocol of political understanding between the EEC and the United States. I was particularly pleased with it.

I have already mentioned the solemn meeting in Paris for the signing of the European Charter on Security and Cooperation. The East European countries had already been party to the earlier version of Helsinki in 1975, but at that time they had come under the Communist banner. In fact, numerous columnists had found it easy to wield irony over the contradictory position held by Brezhnev, who subscribed to the joint commitments while continuing to apply the doctrine of *limited sovereignty* in order to keep member countries bound to the Warsaw Pact. In reply to similar comments made by American friends at meetings of the Interparliamentary Union I said that Brezhnev would pass while the winds of liberty unleashed by Helsinki would bring decidedly positive effects with them. I must confess, however, that I never thought communism in Europe would be swept away so swiftly. In Paris, the USSR of Gorbachev and Shevardnadze was radically different from the USSR of Brezhnev and Gromyko. The presence in Paris of Albania, notably absent from the 1975 meeting, was highly welcome. As part of a progressive evolution from its long-standing position of rigid isolation,

Albania has now resumed diplomatic relations with the United States, and we Italians are more than happy to relinquish the comfortable American embassy in Tirana that we had agreed to occupy in order to spare it from expropriation by the old regime.

The annual Summit Meeting of the Seven Most Industrialized Countries of the West was also held in Paris. As it coincided with the Bicentennial of the French Revolution, the relative and most stately celebrations perhaps had more of an impact than the summit's political substance. Yet, ever faithful to its *grandeur,* France somehow always keeps Europe's colors flying. George Bush, however, needn't fear the threat conjured up by his predecessor James Monroe that the American continent may be colonized by a European nation.

Incidentally speaking, there is one area of interest in Europe—particularly in Mitterrand's France—where signs of touchiness and concern are quite evident: the movie industry. Just as in the years immediately following World War II, American productions dominate the scene in movie theaters and on TV screens. Some protectionistic trends are surfacing in the EEC (shares of airtime reserved to European movies, for example, and similar norms), but I believe a more balanced exchange would be preferable. This, however, can only be achieved by dubbing a larger number of foreign films which would otherwise be confined to no more than a few "art houses" in the United States. Such an initiative would have more than just economic and financial implications. The American interlocutor has long been Jack Valenti who, I would recall, was close to President Johnson.

The 1990 Summit of the Seven was held in Houston. Bush was "the host with the most," and prior to the session itself he organized a rodeo in honor of the participants. Unfortunately both Helmut Kohl and I had to miss this enticing Texan evening because the final game of the World Soccer Championship was being played in Rome at the same time. The Italian team was not on the field as it had been eliminated by Argentina in the semifinals, but it would have been inconsiderate of me not to attend the game along with the German delegation which—one step ahead of unification—was headed by the presidents of both the FRG and the DRG.

I traveled all night long and upon my arrival in Houston I found a thoughtful gift from President Bush, which made up for my forced absence from the rodeo: a cowboy outfit complete with silver-studded boots and a Stetson . . . my grandchildren would love it.

Our discussions focused on an analysis of the situation in formerly Communist Europe. The political will to support a democratic development in those countries was widespread, but many maintained that aid should be linked to a sound program of appropriate measures to redress and modernize both their economies and their political systems. Bush told us that Congress was adamant on this point. Even Mrs. Thatcher, who in a way had been Gorbachev's Western "godmother" with the warm hospitality extended to him before he became the number one man in the USSR, was now quite cautious.

A working group was formed to evaluate the programs being prepared by the Soviets. The input from the World Bank and the International Monetary Fund should appease a certain category of Anglo-Saxon public opinion, while the participation of Jacques Delors' team will ensure a balanced judgment.

Drug abuse was also discussed in Houston, with special emphasis on its unchanged—if not growing—threat over past years. The launching on the market of a low-cost narcotic (crack) is triggering new waves of alarm, and President Bush is once again particularly active on this issue.

During an interval in our proceedings each one of us was asked what we would like to see. On two previous trips to Houston I had enjoyed visiting, respectively, one of the major heart surgery centers and the NASA Space Exhibition. It was quite natural that I would ask to see another renowned medical institution, the M. D. Anderson Cancer Center at the University of Texas.

Most striking for me were not just the technical and scientific briefings and all the information on results obtained or pursued, but the human approach underlying all the work done by those scientists. Among other things, they showed me a small self-regulated unit for home-care chemotherapy which is electronically programmed for one month. It looks like a small portable radio, and a person can carry it in a pocket as he goes about his ordinary activities. Dr. Irwin Krakoff introduced me to some patients who were there for their monthly "recharge," and I noticed they didn't have that despondent look about them that is typical of such patients. I was informed that if psychological depression can be kept at bay, even certain negative consequences of this therapy, including the disheartening loss of hair, can be at least partially avoided. In another ward Dr. Lester Peters showed us the radiotherapy technology used in the operating room.

At the end of the visit I extended my heartfelt congratulations to the director of the center, Dr. Charles A. Le Maistre.

The American administration was very diligent in the follow-up to the Houston summit. Not even a week had gone by when I received a message from George Bush on the steps taken towards the USSR both to inform them on the readiness to support their efforts, and to prepare the framework for sound and sustainable assistance from the Seven. When I went to Moscow on July 26 I noted Gorbachev's satisfaction over the full support he was receiving for his reform policy, with hopes for prompt and positive results. Both with me and during the press conference, Gorbachev repeatedly stressed the importance of the role the United States should continue to play in Europe.

On August 2 Saddam Hussein swept into Kuwait and declared the annexation of the Emirate to Iraq. He most likely expected that the United Nations would do nothing more than pass a resolution of condemnation as it had always done in the past, and his misdeed would go unpunished. However, he had not reckoned with two important circumstances: the change in U.S.—USSR relations which had put an end to the tradition of crossed vetoes in the Security Council, thus endowing the United Nations with a potentially veritable authority; and the reaction bound to be triggered by the fear that temptations to overpower weaker neighboring countries might become contagious. Furthermore, governments such as the ones in Cairo and Ryad were very disappointed over the about-face on the part of the Iraqi leader on whom they had relied both during and after the war with Iran.

Only history will tell whether Saddam Hussein really did plan, after Kuwait, to continue his drive towards some Saudi Arabian provinces. Such a hypothesis was justified by the massive forces he had fielded, and all the more so since the Emirate had been taken almost without firing a shot due to its well-known lack of military potential. The countermove was immediate. The European Community's protest carried considerable political weight, and the determination displayed by the UN Security Council was quite significant, with the backing of a request for a resolution on military intervention submitted by King Fahad and by the Emir of Kuwait who was in exile in Saudi Arabia. A strategically impressive maneuver brought droves of American, British, and French troops into the desert theater while the Allied fleets took up positions to ensure compliance with the punitive embargo decided in New York against the Iraqi invader.

The international community sought to send a clear message of political determination with the combined thrust of the naval blockade and the deployment of ground and air forces ready to take action if the embargo did not succeed in liberating Kuwait.

Throughout the Gulf crisis there were repeated contacts, by telephone as well, among the heads of state and government concerned, and always in full respect for the primacy of the United Nations in restoring the terms of violated international legality. I must say that for us—but also for other countries, I believe—the UN platform represented the key point supported by all political and parliamentary groups.

Some problems were created by the Kuwaiti regime itself: in 1986 the Emir had dissolved the elective assembly (which in any case only represented part of the population) and Parliament had remained closed even though the national Constitution stipulated that it should be reinstated if and when new elections were not held within a minimum lapse of time. In the past I had had an opportunity to attend one of the sittings of the assembly and many of us at the bi-annual conferences of the Interparliamentary Union had admired the high level of their parliamentarians. Therefore it was necessary to make it quite clear to world public opinion that the reaction to Saddam Hussein's attack was a question of principle and did not merely aim at protecting the Emir. I said so to George Bush, and he agreed. In any case, a more democratic system in Kuwait had to be discussed after and not before the Emir's return to his country.

Saddam Hussein made a quite cunning move to confuse the issue by implying that he would be willing to withdraw from Kuwait if Israel returned the occupied territories of the West Bank and Gaza. The idea that the UN couldn't apply two weights and two measures was supposed to divide the international front and, in any case, turn Baghdad into the focal point for support to the Palestinian cause. Hence the allegiance declared by the PLO which paradoxically led to Arafat's virtual isolation from almost all the Arab-Islamic world.

Saddam, however, had set his sights much higher. Relying on the presence of Soviet experts, he thought he could split the positions of the United States and the USSR and thus force the Security Council into a stalemate. I readily admit that I found this aspect more disquieting than all the rest because it would have meant losing ground in the transition from the Cold War to peaceful East-West coexistence.

What was the real degree of compliance with the commercial sanctions? The UN had set up a monitoring unit, but no official data was forthcoming; in addition, the press and the intelligence services seemed to circulate little more than contradictory information.

In the meantime the Baghdad Government refused to allow foreigners to leave the country and issued a stream of statements to let the whole world know that the "guests" (as the hostages were called) would be moved close to probable targets for air attacks as a deterrent against such attacks.

George Bush and Gorbachev decided to meet in Helsinki.

On September 5, I received an urgent and confidential message from Washington in which George Bush, referring to his forthcoming meeting on September 9 in Helsinki with Gorbachev, illustrated for me the objectives he intended to pursue: continued Soviet support to the efforts of the anti-Saddam Hussein coalition; a clear sign of ongoing U.S.—USSR cooperation to emphasize the importance of the new relations which had been established following the end of the cold war; the issues relative to the reduction of conventional armaments and to European security; first-hand information on the Soviet domestic situation and on progress in economic reforms.

He stressed the importance of such meetings as a way to maintain and further bolster East-West dialogue, and highlighted the need for us to keep in close contact. He concluded by saying he would be grateful for my thoughts or advice.

I thought it best to answer in writing, and did so the following day.

Dear George,

In reply to your letter of yesterday, I would venture to offer a few thoughts on the eve of your important meeting in Helsinki.

1. It is important to confirm, even visually, that East-West political cooperation has by now become a firm point destined to progressively strengthen security and peace throughout the world.

2. The new relationship between Washington and Moscow affords the opportunity to bestow an effective peacemaking role upon the United Nations which so far has almost always been paralyzed by crossed vetoes within the Security Council. This is an added reason why it is crucial for Saddam Hussein's initiative to be doomed to failure. Were it permissible to occupy and even annex another State, any reference to the rule of law would be meaningless, and might alone would govern international relations.

3. Kuwait must therefore be returned to its sovereignty.

4. Since this is a matter of principle, Saddam Hussein has no right to advance the justifications he seeks to propound when referring to Israel's failure to honor the UN resolutions on the *occupied territories,* or the enormous riches in the hands of the families of some Arab heads of state. It is essential for world public opinion to clearly see the difference between the question of principle (mandatory withdrawal from Kuwait) and all the rest.

5. Strict compliance with the embargo voted by the United Nations (and previously by the EEC) is a sine qua non condition for compelling the government in Baghdad to retrace its steps as is its duty.

6. I take the liberty of making a suggestion which might enable the Iraqi government to save face, if that's the issue at hand. I recall that Paragraph 8 of UN Resolution 598 to put an end to the Iran-Iraq conflict reads as follows: "... moreover calls upon the secretary general, in consultation with Iran and Iraq, *and with other states in the region,* to examine measures which would strengthen the security and stability of the region." This excerpt from the resolution of July 20, 1987, could serve as the starting point for an international conference on the Gulf.

7. Having reiterated the fact that withdrawal from Kuwait cannot be subject to any conditions, in no way to be ignored is a widespread movement of social discontent among the populations of many Arab states. The aspiration to enjoy the benefits of the oil resources currently monopolized by only a few families in a few states is fanning the flames of rebellion. In the Maghreb countries, which are closer to us, I witness with concern a growing rapprochement between masses of *integralists* and *anti-integralists* which is conditioning governments. A word of understanding from Helsinki would be desirable, together with a reference to the need to enhance representative systems

wherever they exist, or to promote such systems where they do not exist.

8. It must be repeated that Western solidarity, even in military terms, pursues no colonial aims and, *for the amount of time strictly necessary*, seeks to guarantee that no outrage be maintained or perpetrated among the countries in the region.

9. Lastly, it should not be forgotten that China too has the right of veto in the Security Council. The U.S.A.-USSR encounter should not give rise to reactions in Beijing, and an act of consideration—however formal—would be necessary.

Dear George, that's all I wanted to say about the Gulf. I am pleased to learn that in Helsinki you will also be discussing the other major issues on the table at present. It is vital for the disarmament talks and the preparations for the Helsinki Two Conference (CSCE) to regain their due momentum and resonance. In particular, I feel it is most urgent to reach a conclusion on the ban on chemical weapons. We could have had this two years ago, and it is the only way to set up an appropriate international system of control. Thank you for your offer, but I will not take any more of your time by calling you. However, should you wish further elucidations, I'll be happy to hear from you.
With best wishes and regards.

Giulio Andreotti

The meeting in Helsinki was successful. There was complete agreement on the unconditional withdrawal from Kuwait, the restoration of the legitimate government, and on security and stability in the Persian Gulf.

Would Saddam Hussein get the point?

Unfortunately messages from Baghdad gave no inkling of it, despite the pressure and advice flowing in from literally half the globe. Many pilgrims of peace passed through Rome which was also a meeting point for representatives of the non-Islamic religious hierarchies of Iraq—beginning with the Chaldean Christian Patriarch Bidawid—who sought to establish a channel for mediation.

While there were still hopes that Sadam would eventually give in, the deployment of forces to cover the opposite scenario continued with due efficiency. One hundred twelve thousand eight hundred and twenty-nine American troops transited through Rome's Fiumicino airport alone. On numerous occasions, both on the phone and in person, George Bush voiced the hope that all of this would serve as a deterrent to avoid the clash.

And since authoritative voices were raised in Congress against the use of force, the Iraqi government most likely mistook this deep-seated hope to avoid war (shared by Bush no less than others) for a signal announcing that the use of arms would not be authorized.

Upon the request that the Italian Air Force and Italian navy vessels join the Allied forces (several Arab states were also present in varying degrees), the Italian government submitted the matter to Parliament for decision and met with broad consensus. In reply to some objectors who felt free to say the Americans were taking action only because oil resources were at stake, I forcefully recalled that in the 1944–45 war to liberate Italy from Nazi-Fascism, 90,475 Americans had sacrificed their lives and many more had been wounded.

And Italy didn't have any oil then, nor does it have any today.

To those who renewed their concerns over the future of the Palestinians I was able to say that last October in New York I had heard George Bush declare his firm commitment to tackle the two crucial problems in the Middle East (the Palestinians and Lebanon) as soon as Kuwait had been liberated. I was even able to show select friends a copy of the minutes of the meeting between Baker and Tarek Aziz when the secretary of state had given assurances that the two aforementioned Middle East problems would be approached with the same determination that had been applied to Kuwait. We had received the text from reliable Arab sources. Israel's non-response to Iraqi missile attacks was an additional element which could only be ascribed to Washington's good advice.

In December Saddam Hussein suddenly announced that the guests—hostages were free to leave the country. Among the reasons for this decision he also mentioned how important Christmas is for Christian families, and this fanned hopes that he was coming to his senses. It should not be forgotten that strong emotions had been raised in the United States by the Saudi Arabian denial to allow copies of the Bible to enter the country for American troops. In this regard, during those weeks I frequently ventured to point out that the Gulf crisis had to come to an end before Ramadan (even though the Prophet had waged battle during the fasting period) and, in any case, before the annual pilgrimage to Mecca.

The Security Council gave Saddam Hussein a forty-five-day deadline to leave Kuwait; and it was peculiar to speak—as some people did—about an ultimatum expiring after a month and a half.

Efforts to bring pressure to bear were intensified. The former president of Nicaragua Daniel Ortega crossed the ocean three times with the former chancellor Don Miguel d'Escoto, and all to no avail. I saw them after their third attempt, and they were quite vexed because Saddam had appeared even more unyielding than before, rejecting even the slightest hint at withdrawal.

Colonel Ghaddafi maintained a straightforward attitude throughout the crisis, and shared his disappointment and annoyance with me over the phone. By now we were approaching the forty-fifth day, and what were already dim hopes that war could be avoided were fading away. Incurable optimists were still waiting for a spectacular last-minute move (for example, a message from the Prophet in a dream) which would enable Saddam Hussein to sidestep the tragedy.

Gorbachev was one of those who didn't want to give up, and after the veritable "shuttle diplomacy" conducted by his envoy Primakov (who later published a very interesting diary on this experience) he decided to make a last-ditch attempt to persuade Saddam Hussein.

The usual troublemakers saw this effort by Moscow as a sign of divergence. This was unfair, particularly in the light of the unflinching loyalty displayed by the USSR throughout the discussions at the Security Council. As a matter of fact, the alleged dissent had to do with the conditions imposed upon Saddam Hussein: Did withdrawal from Kuwait suffice, or was it necessary to neutralize the residual military potential of the Iraqi regime? Quite naturally, public opinion was excited over the idea of a second Nuremberg trial, or something like that.

When the zero hour struck, the military solution was inevitable, and, for our part, the Italian parliament approved it by a large majority. Our Tornado pilots actively participated in the bomb attacks, striking at key targets in accordance with an extremely precise master plan. How long was this somewhat preparatory phase to last? An endless stream of American troops—some of them stationed in central Europe—were flown in, and people came up with all kinds of forecasts based on the moon's cycles and on other such factors. Equally intense was the succession of predictions on how long land operations would take, while grim reports circulated about studies conducted by American research centers on the many thousands of fellow citizens who were to perish in battle, and for whom body bags had allegedly been procured for their bleak return home.

I need not dwell upon the lightning course of that formidable military operation called Desert Storm. From the moment the land attack was launched to Saddam Hussein's capitulation it took forty-five hours and thirty minutes.

The American forces quite tactfully let Arab units of the coalition be the first ones to enter Kuwait City.

During the 1939–45 war I heard an elderly and wise professor of mine say that while we were experiencing tough times, far more difficult would be the post-war period. That professor has passed away, but his theory still applies even to the post-Gulf war period.

My latest trip to the United States in May 1991 was for reasons alien to politics, even though, due to the presence of our president of the republic, Francesco Cossiga, it also included an invitation to the White House. Ever since 1957, as a sort of sideline activity, I have been involved with the Center For Ciceronian Studies, which is responsible for the publication of the *Opera omnia* of that great orator and author of ancient Rome, and every two years convenes a conference attended by Latin scholars from all over the world.

In 1989 we had met in Warsaw and the topic selected for the conference was a most timely one, both there and in all the other countries where constitutions were being drafted to mark the demise of lengthy communist dictatorships. It was not by coincidence that President Jaruzelski, who attended the inaugural session with Francesco Cossiga (a most faithful Ciceronian), asked me if the concept of state which I had addressed in my speech had been meant for him personally and not just for the gathered scholars. During this conference in Poland, Professor Maristella Lorch, an Italian-American, launched the idea that the 1991 colloquium be held in New York at her Columbia University. The suggestion was received with unanimous enthusiasm which was not dampened in the least by the logistical complications made all the more difficult by the distance factor. And so, on May 6, 1991, five hundred foreign guests met in the vast rotunda of Columbia University, along with professors and students from universities all over the United States, to begin a four-day round of scholarly disquisitions on one aspect of the immense Ciceronian cultural heritage: namely, his influence on the legal system and educational policy of the United States.

On the previous day, Sunday, the guests had been received in St. Patrick's Cathedral by His Eminence John Cardinal O'Connor, Archbishop of New York, who did not fail to express his deep satisfaction with the efforts to uphold the Latin language, which has always held a place of honor in the Catholic Church (John Paul II had even said that the way Latin studies were being neglected was *disgraceful*).

In her welcome address delivered in consummate American style, Maristella Lorch began by saying she had been asked the most peculiar questions when she had spoken about our forthcoming conference; for example, what did *this* Cicero do in life, had he ever come to New York before, what was his family background. One lady who had just returned from a trip to Rome and Florence thought it was a convention of tour guides (who in Italy are called *cicerone*). In my turn I attempted to lighten my ponderous introductory speech by showing a one-dollar bill where there are no less than three inscriptions in Latin, including the motto *E PLURIBUS UNUM,* which was selected by the Founding Fathers to embody the aspiration to unity on the seal of the nation.

Among the statements delivered, highly successful was the one by Professor Witold Wolodkiewicz (University of Warsaw) who substantiated the specific influence of Ciceronian texts in the Constitution of the United States of America, drafted by men who were quite familiar with classical studies, or who, when not so in their own right (like Jefferson, it seems), chose their advisors from among people with a sound background in European universities.

The Ciceronian Colloquium was a success. Among other things, it revealed the extent to which many American universities in addition to the ones in New York (including Boston, Portland, Washington, and elsewhere) conduct in-depth Latin studies. No less gratifying was the social program of excursions, particularly for many of the participants who were setting foot in the United States for the first time, since professors' salaries more or less everywhere do not leave very much room for savings. Many indeed were the eyes brimming with tears of joy over the charms of the Metropolitan Museum, Lincoln Center, the Guggenheim Collection, and the trip on the Hudson River. And the resounding applause reserved for saxophone player Gerry Mulligan by these stern personalities would probably have astounded their students, who would hardly suspect them of being so in tune with their times.

Concurrent with this *colloquium Tullianum* was the opening of the Italian Academy of Advanced Studies set up by joint agreement between our government and Columbia University (President Michael Sovern and Provost Jonathan Cole). When adding to this the inauguration of new premises for the Italian School in New York (with a very original curriculum and matching Italian-American participation), May 1991 scores high marks on the report card of Italy's relations with America as it prepares to celebrate the quincentennial of Columbus Day.

The sudden news that President Bush had been taken ill and admitted to the hospital made us think for a few hours that our visit to Washington would be canceled, but the reports issued soon afterwards were so reassuring that it seemed the mass media had overplayed the facts. Nonetheless, I was struck by the punctilious reconstruction of George Bush's medical history, beginning with ordinary childhood diseases and narrated with a wealth of details which certainly did not deserve such attention. In the United States, a man in public office is in the limelight far more than in any other country.

I traveled to Washington with Cossiga and we found the president in fine shape, ever ready to joke about the heart monitoring unit which his physicians (who remained in the next room just in case) made him wear for control purposes. At the same time extensive lab tests were being conducted on the thyroid of the first citizen of the United States.

In addition to being proud of his service record as a navy pilot, George practices at least five sports: those forced marches called jogging (which Americans have spread all over the world almost as much as Coca Cola), golf, fishing, squash, and tennis. Being a rather sedentary person myself, I feel uncomfortable by comparison to him, but after all I'm not in bad shape for someone just over 72.

Compared with the last time, I noticed the president let Jimmy Baker do more of the talking, but this made sense since the secretary of state was briefing us on his complex mission to bring peace to the Middle East. We encouraged him, of course, recognizing that the U.S. contemporary history looks like the revenge of defeated communism: here, as in the Soviet Union and Czechoslovakia, centrifugal forces are giving rise to concerns. Everyone should contribute to calming down the inflamed spirits, convincing them that self-government can come about only in a gradual way and on the basis of consensus. The White House is faced with legal difficulties in responding to Soviet requests for credit to purchase wheat, but the political will is present, and there is hope that the secretary of agriculture will find a way to overcome the obstacles.

Having reiterated our warmest wishes for political success and the best of health, we hastened back to New York. Cossiga went to St. John's University to receive an honorary degree (welcomed by Edward Re with his customary warmth) and I joined my Ciceronian colleagues.

In the following weeks George Bush briefed me directly on the positive developments in global negotiations with the USSR, and also on an important peace initiative for the Middle East based on a substantial armaments reduction and on a commitment to be undertaken by all producing nations to discontinue the supply of arms and munitions to countries in the Gulf and in the rest of the area. This is a challenge against the mercantile attitude of the weapons industry, and George knows he can count on our full support.

We're now looking forward to seeing him again in London at the Summit of the Seven in July, and hopefully in Rome at the NATO Council meeting in the fall.

G.A.

1 | *That Difficult "Ph"*

My first contact with America dates back to my childhood and was a rather unusual experience. Our concierge, Laurina Volpi, was a good-natured woman from the Marche region who hadn't been subject to the rigors of compulsory education as a child and every so often she would come upstairs to have my mother read her the letters she received from relatives who had emigrated to Pennsylvania. By way of compensation for my mother's good deed I was given the envelopes and was very happy to have the foreign stamps. And yet those envelopes fanned my unquenchable curiosity: why did Philadelphia have to be spelled with a double "ph"? I also listened most attentively to the contents of those letters full of ordinary news about the daily life of a working family whose standard of living, certainly higher than what it had been originally, left me practically spellbound. Both reader and listener became ecstatic, involving me as well in their feelings of admiration, when they learned, for example that the laundry over there was washed in machines which eliminated those cracks inflicted upon the hands of my mother and of the kind doorkeeper by the European way of doing the "wash." Fifty years later when I heard people criticize consumerism and household appliances in general I was careful to remain aloof precisely on account of my childhood memories. America for me was the civilization of physical respect for housewives.

I wouldn't say they taught me very much about America in elementary school. Especially in the fourth and fifth grades our teacher was so imbued with self-sufficient nationalism that everything non-Italian was worth little or nothing in his eyes. He used to tell us quite often that Christopher Columbus had happened upon the new continent by mistake and only recently had the efforts of Europeans over there been crowned with success in their fight to abolish slavery. The only person he really had anything good to say about was President Lincoln, and perhaps even that was done out of malice since he used to stress the point of his violent death at the hands of one of his own fellow citizens.

When in high school I received some more direct information at the playground built by the Knights of Columbus on the outskirts of Rome and kept in excellent condition for use by the city's children. It was there that I first met an American and his name was Fr. Francis Spellman. Always courteous and with a ready smile, he was treated with utmost deference by the playground attendants. Apparently nothing more than an occasional encounter, it was actually the beginning of something very important in my life.

Another memory from my youth. Just as in the case of the flight to South America in 1931, I was intrigued by all the news about the flight to Chicago and New York by Italo Balbo and his officers two years later. Most striking of all were the pictures of festive groups of Italian immigrants with vivid descriptions of their patriotic enthusiasm over the daring feat. What was not made public, however, was what I heard in my local parish. The Italian postal authorities had issued a special stamp entitled "Return Flight" which couldn't be used and was therefore destined to become, as it was "improperly" called, a prefab rarity.

With the onset of the war I was declared physically unfit for admission to the Officers Candidate School and served my time in the armed forces in the Office of Legal Medicine, a turn of events that had three advantages: I was able to attend lectures at the university and received my degree; I had a half day free each week to dedicate to my work in the offices of the Federation of Catholic University Students with Aldo Moro; and I got to know many renowned physicians who had been called up from their respective clinics or hospitals. These officers, perhaps because of their professional background, harbored the greatest admiration for their American colleagues and their scientific discoveries. They were not shy about their feelings since in no way were they conditioned by what they called a "temporary wartime parenthesis."

From the point of view of this general outlook, I am very thankful for that period of my life as well.

When the landing took place at Anzio on 22 January 1944, without the slightest German counterattack by land or air, we all thought our liberation was only hours away. However, almost five months went by and during those months our admiration for the Allied troops experienced moments of disappointed irritation. It took years for us to understand the strategy behind keeping the Germans tied down in Italy and preventing them from retreating northward before the definitive landing in Normandy, and I received confirmation of this from Dwight D. Eisenhower himself.

During the long waiting period, the parties in the National Liberation Committee had prepared detailed plans for the exercise of power after the war. As we say, however, they counted their chickens before they hatched because they overlooked the fact that any effective authority would be in the hands of the Allied military government. Despite the participation of the Italian armed forces alongside the Allies immediately after the armistice, the government of Salerno was in the same position as titular bishops in the Catholic Church who exercise authority over ancient dioceses which have disappeared and whose exact location is known unto God alone. When Badoglio and his ministers came to Rome to transfer the powers of government to the political parties, they had very little to hand over. In addition, the ceremony was held in a secluded alcove of the Grand Hotel which was packed with English and American officers who were the very center of every attention on the part of the hotel staff. Ivanoe Bonomi and the ministers didn't even receive permission to remain in Rome and had to make their own difficult way back down south.

The Palace of the Corporations on Via Veneto was the headquarters of the Allied officers in charge of press relations, which entailed the supply of printing paper to newspapers and the exercise of policy controls. At times there were some rather strange episodes. One day I saw a person in uniform moving around the place as if he owned it. The Fascist authorities had sent him off to a concentration camp on charges of dealing in drugs and it was rumored that he had sent the Japanese minister of foreign affairs Matsuoka on such a "trip" that his audience with Mussolini had been delayed by 48 hours. Since the Allies had found him in a place of Fascist punishment they had set him free with all possible honors and given him the keys to the medicinal drug locker of the Fifth Army because there was a reference to drugs in his personnel file. In brief, that is the story of his triumphal return into the city. His name was Max Mugnani and his official occupation involved importing champagne from France.

At a lower level, the relations with our liberators were quite varied in nature. There were those who received candy bars and K-rations, and those who experienced close encounters with tipsy GIs on the streets, especially at night. When we finished making up *Il Popolo,* the daily newspaper of the Christian Democratic Party, at the printing press in Palazzo Sciarra at 2:00 A.M., it was always an adventure getting home . . . on foot, naturally. However, everyone was still imbued with the euphoria of the liberation and even some of the eccentric things done by the governor, Charles Poletti (who had announced his intention to introduce Romans to the existence of soap) were accepted good-naturedly by the population.

The problems of "the day after" began with the return of the civilian government to Rome (with strenuous negotiations to wrestle even an iota of authority from the man at the top of the Allied hierarchy, Admiral Ellery W. Stone) and that period was quite different from the dreams on the eve of armistice. The city of Rome was literally overflowing with refugees who had to be fed, no matter whether the direct responsibility lay with Bonomi or Stone. Legendary is the outcome of a late evening telephone call from De Gasperi to the mayor of New York, Fiorello La Guardia; some ships already on their way to other destinations were rerouted to Italy and the people in Rome and Naples didn't have to go without the few ounces of bread they could get with their ration cards. A truly disgraceful propaganda move on the part of the Allies helped make the widespread pangs of hunger all the more acute. For two days after the liberation they had distributed white bread made out of real flour and people thought that the horrible stuff we were used to eating was gone for good. I raised this point with the officer in charge of the Psychological Welfare Department, but he dismissed my objections by saying everything had been planned by centers of research on human behavior which "back home" were much more advanced than anything we fanciful Latins had.

Living side-by-side with De Gasperi I was able to share his daily concerns over the big problems to be solved as well as his anxiety in striving to cope with the much more important issue of the day-to-day food supplies. I began to appreciate the Western solidarity which warded off even worse perils on the Eastern front where Marshal Tito's troops, in perfect harmony with the Soviets at that time, made more than one move against the city of Trieste. In an interview some time later, Secretary of State Dean Acheson said De Gasperi never gave him a moment's respite because of "his" Trieste.

In order to help the younger generations understand what the situation was like for fledgling democratic Italy, I would venture to mention a photograph circulated in the international press showing Secretary of State James Byrnes shaking hands with De Gasperi at the Peace Conference. Together with a sort of weak smile from the Brazilian minister of foreign affairs, Jan Neves de Fontoura, that was the only friendly gesture on a very cold day in Paris. Everyone else considered the representative from Italy as a loser who had to be punished.

With the defeat and demise of both Hitler and Mussolini it was immediately evident that the curtain had also been drawn on the understanding between the Soviets and the other Allies. I obtained confirmation of this fact through the Vatican. During the height of the war Roosevelt had asked the pope to substantiate the thesis that nazism was more dangerous than communism because, while the former based its expansion on military occupation, the Soviets were just (!) propagating their ideas. Drafted by Msgr. Domenico Tardini, the Vatican's reply was as sharp as a knife.

The pontiff was very prudent in his pronouncements in order not to confuse principles with wartime activity, yet there was no way to condone a conceptual attenuation of persecuting and atheistic communism, and the same applied to the condemnation of the Germans' racial paganism. I would also mention the numerous reservations voiced at the U.S. State Department over Roosevelt's decision to send a personal representative of the president of the United States to the Vatican. It was looked upon as a domestic electoral ploy to win the votes of the Catholics, while the Protestants were told it was a temporary and very informal measure. As Msgr. Tardini noted: "It was the American President who had approached the constant teaching of the Pontiff in explicit terms and not the Pope who was siding with the Wall Street bankers."

Once each ally had returned to his own natural way of doing things, the White House—counterorders, my friends—asked the pope to accentuate the reprobation of communism. The reply to President Truman, once again written by Msgr. Tardini, was as follows: "The Church is not at all interested in a new ideological crusade, but rather in reiterating those principles which are fundamental and unchangeable in defense of the human being and civil society as Christianity has always conceived them. . . . The Pope wanted to stress the need to eliminate the many social, racial, and religious aberrations existing precisely among those peoples and those groups who boast about being Christian." When the director of the *Osservatore Romano*, Dalla Torre, wrote an editorial calling for a deeper understanding of certain aspects and requirements, Msgr. Tardini clarified that for the State Department the condemnation did not concern Russia as such, but rather communism "wherever it may be, no matter whether in power or striving to get there."

With a true sense of responsibility and despite certain outbursts of nationalism displayed by Vittorio Emanuele Orlando, the Constituent Assembly ratified the signing of the peace diktat drawn up in Paris by the twenty-one winners. Neither a government nor even a regime can permit conditional forms of acceptance in such cases since, for better or worse, they do represent the continuity of the nation.

We were comforted by the American assurances that the United States would not claim reparation, while the Soviets demanded the dismantling of our fleet right down to the very last ship. This news, delivered by Ambassador Clement Dunn, was not unexpected to De Gasperi because I had been able to inform him ahead of time, thanks to confidential information from Francis Cardinal Spellman who had gone to Washington a number of times to plead the Italian cause. There may not be any traces in diplomatic archives of the work done by the archbishop of New York, but it was most valuable for us on more than one occasion.

Italy's political future still depended upon us at that time, however. We, too, bore the full brunt of the world's bitter division into two blocs. Our western propensity has been ascribed to a financial and economic need which could only be resolved by moving in one direction. This, however, is a very partial explanation. The crux of dissent was objective freedom, with an aggravating factor in the sense that a Communist victory would have sacrificed freedom without alleviating the material difficulties. What might have been open to question at that time turned out to be true as the collectivistic models evolved and fell to pieces. Nowadays not even Stalin's relatives try to defend him or his system. Even though we cannot exclude the fact that Italian leaders would have opposed resistance to "Stalinization" if the Red front had won the day, there is no way of knowing if they could have safeguarded the national identity other countries are only now striving to attain in the wake of changes in the USSR.

De Gasperi went to the United States in February 1947 and made a very favorable impression, not only on the politicians, with a very dignified and realistic presentation of the prospects for Italy. He obtained an initial loan for the reconstruction work and plenty of encouragement to keep thinking positively in the midst of the enormous difficulties faced by a destroyed and divided country. With a poor sense of timing explainable only by subservient obedience, at that same time Togliatti, founder of the Italian Communist party and its leader until his death in 1970, wrote an anti-American editorial entitled "How Stupid They Are."

This turned out to be the proverbial straw that broke the camel's back with such devastating effects. The government of the National Liberation Committee came apart at the seams. However, there could have been a split between Socialists and Communists, since three years earlier Togliatti's party had broken the joint-action pact and had joined the second Bonomi government, while Nenni and his friends had adopted a contentious position and remained on the outside. In 1947–48, however, Nenni and the vast majority of his party set their sights on forming an alliance with the Popular Front in the belief that together they could beat the Christian Democrats and their allies in the first elections after the founding of the Constituent Assembly, aiming first and foremost at the Social Democrats who had based their split from the Socialist camp on the sides formed on the international scene.

The electoral battle of April 18, 1948, was a decisive one. America sent a kind of capillary-action assistance in the form of hundreds of thousands of letters from past emigrants to their relatives and friends in Italy with an appeal to safeguard the democratic institutions. In more specifically political terms, on March 20, England, France, and the United States issued a solemn declaration restoring Trieste to Italy. In contrast to these forms of support, the Soviets disclaimed the rumor spread by the Italian Communist party that they were prepared to forgo reparation from Italy for wartime damages. Moreover, Moscow and the other "socialist" capitals looked with a rather wary eye upon the Italian Communists who were actually being tried under charges of having allowed themselves to be thrown out of the government.

The great Democratic victory of April 18, 1948, has become part of history. The American press reported it in a rather interested and friendly way, exalting the figure of De Gasperi. What came across between the lines, however, was a certain degree of coolness toward the Christian Democratic party; maybe because over there Christianity is something supposed and not confessed or because of a recurrent vein of antipapal feelings. Nor would I exclude the rebound effect of Italian influences on the part of those who did not deny the determining importance of the Christian Democratic party but, with a deep sigh, considered it a necessary evil.

The defeat of the communists and their bedfellows also helped to dispel some rather curious suspicions about Count Carlo Sforza. As a political exile in the United States he was expected to underwrite a pledge of neutrality on institutional issues in order to return home after the fall of fascism. The unlawful request for such a pledge was lawfully disregarded and this aroused the spite of certain American circles where the Republic—in Italy—was tantamount to a dangerous left-wing adventure. Those same circles also harbored numerous reservations on an issue where Sforza and De Gasperi had adopted a very resolute stance: in order to avoid giving rise to Teutonic revanchism anew, perhaps this time with a shirt of a different color, Germany was not to be humiliated. The Americans still had vivid memories of the anti-Nazi reaction fanned by years of propaganda to support the human and financial effort to prevent Hitler's conquest of Europe. Luckily at that time they didn't even dream that the two losers, Germany and Japan, would become the economic and industrial driving powers in the world.

What prevailed in the end was the involvement of the Federal Republic of Germany in any and all planning for our old continent, and I'm sorry Adenauer, who was well aware of the facts, didn't extend due recognition to the Italian government in his memoirs.

Those were the golden years of the Marshall Plan and the Atlantic Pact. With just as much energy, however, De Gasperi launched a domestic policy of real reform with the distribution of underutilized land or parts of large estates and a development plan for southern Italy. At a later stage we will see how this innovative insight triggered the reactions of the prosperous property owners who had supported the democratic coalition in the elections out of fear of the Popular Front but were not prepared to make sacrifices in the name of justice. Since these classes had more opportunities than others for frequent contacts with Americans, a climate of mistrust on the staying power of the Christian Democrats crossed over to the other shore of the Atlantic. The disgruntled people quite naturally refrained from expressing their hostility by speaking openly about their own affected interests (also because reforms and social justice were encouraged in the United States) and just insinuated we were not doing enough to combat communism in Italy.

The outcome had no effect on our "blue chip" rating relative to the clarity of our international policy, but De Gasperi's prestige lost ground following claims about his supposedly lukewarm stance against communism. McCarthy with his witch-hunt was not the only one to get entangled in this reactionary spiral. In various ways and without even realizing it, also involved were many convinced believers in democracy.

2 | *Eisenhower*

I never had any personal relations with Presidents Roosevelt or Truman and in the latter's case my only recollections are limited to De Gasperi's favorable impressions after his return from the White House. He had told me that President Truman, customarily defined as commonplace to distinguish him from the striking qualities—in social policy as well—of his predecessor, in fact had a very resolute personality and a willpower well known to his cabinet and staff. While the New Deal had earned a place in the history of mankind for Franklin Delano Roosevelt, the courageous decision by Truman to unleash the atomic bombs in order to subdue Japan and bring the war to an end is not one of those decisions that leaves no traces in history.

The field is obviously divided between those who approve the decision and those who condemn it. The fact is that public opinion in the United States was behind the president, and perhaps this was due to the underlying rancor over the surprise attack on Pearl Harbor. In addition, and looking at the figures, the two years experts considered it would take to end the war would have cost many more human lives. Then there was the likely risk that German scientists would have come up with the bomb somewhere else in the world. Moreover, the American nuclear potential helped to dissuade the Soviet bloc from taking advantage of its marked "conventional" superiority in Europe during the period of postwar Stalinism.

The first president of the United States I met in person was Dwight D. Eisenhower when he came to Italy on a state visit. Our paths had crossed briefly during an earlier trip he made to Italy as NATO commander in chief and I had really been impressed. On that occasion De Gasperi had referred to him as a "humanistic general."

The arrival of a president of the United States was a major event and not even the inclement weather conditions were able to put a damper on it. My memories of Eisenhower's visit border on a nightmare, heightened by the added element of a downpour rare for our capital city. Ever since then I have been pleading for the installation of mobile awnings at Ciampino Airport to shield official visitors and members of the armed forces from the annoying showers they suffer while the inspection of the honor guard takes place; it looks like we may get them for the third millennium of Christianity. On that morning the strength of American paper earned my full respect because the general was able to read his formal statement with each sheet of paper practically reduced to a liquid state. Vernon Walters, the interpreter, had no problems and impassively translated by memory as the rain beat down upon him and ran off the host of medals and ribbons testifying to his wartime prowess.

The weather at the Tomb of the Unknown Soldier the next day was even worse: we practically had to "swim" through the ceremony. Since umbrellas clash with military uniforms, I too as the party accompanying Eisenhower had to feign indifference as the wind and water seemed to herald the oncoming universal flood. Therefore, except for snatches of conversation in the car, upon our return to the Quirinale Palace, the official residence of the president of the republic, we were not able to hold the talks on defense issues ordinarily following such a ceremony. Nonetheless, I did ask him what was really on my mind: "Why did the Allies leave Italy on its own on 8 September 1943, and why, a year later, did it take them so long to travel the few kilometers from the Anzio landing zone to the capital?"

Eisenhower replied that the Italian General Staff was responsible if the announcement of the armistice had not been followed immediately by the planned airborne landing of an American division at an airport near Rome.

My later enquiries confirmed the existence of a dispatch transmitted that same evening from the Ministry of War. Drafted by Col. De Francesco (who was later to become a three-star general and commanding general of the *"Carabinieri"*), but most certainly conceived and approved at a much higher level, the dispatch informed the Allies that the airport in question was still in German hands and not "secure." A very reputable act indeed, but since it was a wartime operation I considered it somewhat absurd to cancel the planned military support without even having identified or pinpointed an alternative option.

I also received an equally convincing explanation for the delayed liberation of Rome in 1944 after the undisturbed landing at Anzio. Apparently it was necessary to keep the German troops tied down in Italy. Otherwise, they would have pulled back toward northern Europe and would have bolstered the defenses against the final operation of the Normandy landing.

Eisenhower struck me as being quite pleased with the opportunity to talk about the moment of his life he considered more important than the albeit notable feat of having been elected president.

During the official luncheon Eisenhower spoke very warmly about De Gasperi, saying that he was one of the most impressive statesmen he had ever met, and referred to some of his statements at the NATO Ministerial Council.

3 | *August 1954:*
The First Trip

The minister of the merchant marine, Fernando Tambroni, extended a certain number of invitations for the maiden voyage of the large ocean liner *Cristoforo Colombo*. He was very kind to include my name on the ministerial list even though a few months earlier I had ceased any government-related responsibilities after seven years as undersecretary to the Prime Minister's Office and a few days as minister for internal affairs in the Fanfani government which never received parliamentary ratification. I did not accept the invitation because I was busy organizing my life as a member of parliament and was intent on setting up a small group within the Christian Democratic party in preparation for a convention with every sign of being all too much of an experience in . . . compulsory togetherness. De Gasperi encouraged my efforts publicly by giving his name (it was still possible then) to our miniticket called "Springtime" as well as to the dominant group under Fanfani-Scelba. Moreover, I had no qualms about saying I wasn't really attracted by the "high society" climate customarily characteristic of maiden voyages. In addition, my wife had her hands full with four small children and wouldn't have been able to accompany me.

However, after our party's convention with the speech-testament of its leader, De Gasperi, who had been nothing short of heroic considering his very precarious state of health, already beyond hope of survival, I was pleased to accept the second invitation from Tambroni to sail from Naples to New York on the *Andrea Doria* and to return on the *Colombo*. Italo Gemini and Vincio Delleani were my traveling companions.

Gemini, the president of the Entertainment Association, had been very helpful when I was working on legislation specific to his field of interest and I had been able to appreciate the extent of his exquisite discretion; he had withdrawn from all his engagements for the opening of new theaters precisely to avoid any incompatibility with his (unpaid) role as a ministerial consultant. Delleani and I had gone to the same school and he was the director of Cinecittà. In brief, my two traveling companions were far removed from the world of politics.

Our departure was set for August 24 and I had no way of knowing the period was going to coincide with De Gasperi's funeral. He passed away five days earlier, dashing our hopes that the air of his mountains would prevail over all the catastrophic diagnoses which for some months had decreed the worst possible outcome for him in no uncertain terms.

Shortly before his death De Gasperi sent me a note of congratulation on the publication of my book entitled *A Meatless Lunch for the Cardinal*, on the letters of Pius X reprimanding the archbishop of Bologna for his role at the reception for Vittorio Emanuele III. In the same note De Gasperi referred to my planned trip to New York and expressed his disappointment over what he felt to be the Americans' incomprehension of his person and his position.

In order to understand the sense of this disheartened reference we have to return to the previous year, when the De Gasperi government had been soundly whipped in Parliament due to the defection of the coalition allies and the prime minister's own resolute decision not to accept compromises with the opposition (Nenni had even told him not to worry about the Atlantic Pact, which was "just another piece of paper like so many others"). In addition to a certain and unfortunately customary lack of interest in losers, some American circles were suspicious about what they considered De Gasperi's excessive pro-Europe position. There had already been symptoms of this when the Coal and Steel Community was established and even though the American administration had been in favor of the European Defense Community, at least part of the Pentagon (persistent distrust of Germans?) had made no mystery of its perplexity. Moreover, in her personal assessments not always shared by the diplomats, Ambassador Clare Boothe Luce sang the praises of Pella as a strong person in comparison with the accommodating posture of De Gasperi. The lady in question had not been of the same view at the beginning of the Pella government when she criticized an excerpt of his inaugural address rejecting any taint of parliamentary discrimination. However, when Pella stood on the Campidoglio (Rome's City Hall and the official residence of the mayor of Rome) and threatened to declare war on Yugoslavia, his forthright resoluteness had a winning effect on the ambassador, who said she was convinced communism would be swept away by this democratic leader with an iron fist in a velvet glove. And yet this lady's enthusiasm didn't help the Pella government to remain in office for more than six months. Once Saragat's passive collaboration came to an end, the four-party coalition was reformed under the leadership of Mario Scelba.

I very much appreciated, however, the gesture on the part of Mrs. Luce who was on vacation in the United States when De Gasperi passed away and returned immediately to Rome to attend the funeral.

I went to Naples by train to board the ship and I was still under the emotional effect instilled by the deep affection shown for De Gasperi by the immense crowds along the streets as the funeral procession went from the Church of Jesus to the Verano cemetery. On the train I traveled in the same compartment with former Head of State Enrico De Nicola. Even though he attributed his unsuccessful reelection to De Gasperi and not to himself, he reminisced over some very special moments of De Gasperi's career and was adamant in stressing how he had gone to the airport in person to welcome the prime minister upon his return from the United States in February 1947.

Fernando Tambroni was very kind to come and see us off on our trip. I was grateful to be able to get away from Italy for a while because, without De Gasperi, I felt a point of reference was missing in Italian politics. I also regretted not having done something in the Chamber of Deputies for the ratification of the European Defense Community which De Gasperi had urged of Pella and Scelba in vain. Well founded was the prediction of nonratification by France, but De Gasperi felt that Italian approval would have given a substantial psychological impulse to its supporters in the French Assembly.

Confirmation of France's refusal to ratify the EDC reached us in mid-Atlantic. Our government had used the hands of others to remove a stumbling block, but Europe was at a fearful standstill.

Now that people can fly to America in only a few hours the trip by sea may well seem a useless waste of time and, in fact, regular ocean liner service has become a thing of the past. On the other hand, it was an excellent way to do some deep thinking, get in some reading, and even do a bit of exercise. During such a moment of personal depression I was most grateful for the experience. Then there is the slow approach to the Statue of Liberty in the first light of a new dawn, with the onrush of feelings and impressions which Concorde passengers can't even imagine as they proudly check their watches to make sure it is three hours earlier than the time of their departure from London or Paris.

I wanted my visit to be private and far removed from the realm of politics in order to avoid any interference in government matters, and I had left the relative logistics up to Cardinal Spellman (he sent one of his auxiliary bishops, Msgr. Joseph Pernicone of Sicilian descent, to greet me on board) and to Gemini and Delleani's "movie mogul" friends. I received a very warm welcome from Ms. Della Grattan whom I had met in Rome during the visit of the preceding mayor of New York, Vincent Impellitteri. Della wanted to take me to meet the new mayor of New York, Robert Wagner (whom I would meet only years later as the "personal representative" of the president of the United States to the Holy See), while I also declined an appointment at the State Department with the assistant secretary for European affairs, Livingstone Merchant, so kindly proposed by our ambassador, Alberto Tarchiani. I didn't know what the position of the Scelba government would have been after the fall of the EDC and, moreover, I had no matters to discuss with the American administration.

Since that trip I have crossed the Atlantic at least one hundred times and never again have I had entire days at my disposal just to visit New York City: its museums, ball parks (baseball was a new sport for me and I was entranced more by the frenzied fans in the bleachers than by what happened on the field), the excursion around the bay on the yacht of the president of Paramount, Balaban, who tickled my curiosity when he explained the complicated mechanisms applied in order to use such a business expense for tax deduction purposes.

Balaban himself arranged a premiere viewing of the movie *White Christmas*, shot in what was then the new Vista-Vision system. Christmas was also the inspiration for a gigantic musical in New York City, where to my great surprise I saw people standing for hours in a seemingly endless line at the advance booking window.

A top executive in another American movie company invited us to his country house in Connecticut, less than an hour's drive from Manhattan in a delightfully green area, and cooked the steaks himself on a very original barbecue. In addition to Italo Gemini's presence, I owed this hospitality to the contacts established with this branch of American industry during my seven years as undersecretary to the Prime Minister's Office (the Ministry of Entertainment didn't exist yet). At the beginning those magnates had done their utmost to lobby against legislation promoting the Italian movie industry which, among other things, set aside a share of total projection days for domestic movies. They then realized the need for a compromise. As a result, they agreed to pay 2.5 million lira (1950 lira) for each of their films dubbed into Italian, but there was no way to get them to accept the right of reciprocity in dubbing. Despite earmarking revenue from dubbing to the launching of Italian movies in America, the impossibility of dubbing into English (as they said, for . . . cultural reasons) actually reduced the circuit for our movies to a few specialized theaters.

I had earned a certain degree of respect by cleaning up the foreign currency black market. During the years prior to the promotional legislation, close to 80 percent of global proceeds from Italian theaters went to American movies. Pursuant to a monetary agreement they had to invest half of their Italian earnings in economic activities or in charity. This led to the creation of a network of pseudo-assistance; small amounts of money were given to very needy shelters and orphanages in exchange for receipts indicating ten or even one hundred times those amounts. I understood the extreme state of need of the beneficiaries, but it was still a very grave practice for Italy's image as well.

Once legality had been restored many other projects were financed in complete transparency and one of them was the large North American College on the Gianiculum Hill. The American bishops were very pleased ("You helped us to save a bundle," Cardinal Strick told me in the inimitable street Italian he had picked up in Trastevere) and so were we, since the presence of bishops in the world who have studied in Rome is by no means a negligible fact. For example, the Italian soldiers shipped off to POW camps on distant continents found it very comforting to be assisted by priests and bishops who spoke Italian.

But let's go back to the trip in 1954. The fever for video tapes was growing in the movie industry. With the regular theaters feeling the pinch of TV competition, people thought entertainment had moved into homes and that the show had to go on without intermediary TV services. The statistical estimates bantered about did not turn out to be entirely correct and, at least over here, many video tapes circulate on the black market clearly to the detriment of movie companies' legitimate interests and authors' copyrights.

Before leaving and, as I mentioned earlier, after having avoided a visit to Washington, we went on delightful trips to New Jersey and Niagara Falls, the latter reached by plane from New York. We then crossed the border and spent a few "Canadian" hours in Toronto. The falls were just like we had seen them in the movie *Niagara*. We picked our way along a winding catwalk in yellow rain gear and then, in black rain gear, sailed up to the main fall practically spellbound by the scene and by our emotions.

Once back in New York I was taken on a visit to one of the large department stores (Macy's). On the fifth floor there was an exhibition of dairy cows who seemed very much at home under the same roof with appliances, sporting goods, and ready-to-wear clothing. Everything over there comes off the assembly line and women don't seem to be fazed if four or five of them show up at a reception wearing identical dresses. Quite the contrary, they congratulate each other on their good taste.

I went to say goodbye to Cardinal Spellman who had been my host on numerous occasions during the week in New York. He spoke to me about De Gasperi in words I found very moving, and briefed me on the operations of his Curia, which had a budget only slightly lower than that of the Italian state (and without a deficit). Schools, hospitals, social work, libraries, assistance to the members of the armed forces—Cardinal Spellman was also the military Ordinary—and everything run according to professional management criteria. With almost a tone of coyness in his voice, he told me about a problem absorbing much of his attention: he had launched a collection among the faithful for the construction of a new seminary with an estimated expenditure of eighteen billion lira and he had surpassed the target by almost six billion lira.

Cardinal Spellman invited me to return in October to attend the annual charity dinner in honor of a great benefactor, Al Smith. He said he expected to have Umberto of Savoy as the guest of honor, but that wasn't my reason for declining the invitation; a special trip just for the occasion struck me as somewhat exaggerated. Ever since then I have always sent my contribution to the Al Smith dinner, but have never been able to attend it in person.

"In any case, remember, America is not only New York and you must get to know it in depth because, whether you like it or not, we are important." Those were the cardinal's parting words as I left his Madison Avenue residence with the understanding we would soon meet again in Rome.

As I was leaving, one of the nuns in the cardinal's household wished me the best of health, but I thought she had done so in an overly emphatic way. Cardinal Spellman was quite amused and explained why Sister Mary thought I was quite ill; at breakfast she had seen me eat only a bit of milk laced with coffee and a couple of cookies.

During the return voyage we made brief stops at Las Palmas in the Canary Islands and at Lisbon, and I had the distinct impression of having broadened my knowledge of new skies and new lands. Against the background of deep sadness over De Gasperi's death, it was an unforgettable experience. I felt as if I had been orphaned for the second time, but this time it was worse because I had never known my natural father.

4 | *The Ambassador's Slipup*

During the last year of De Gasperi's life there was already a great deal of tension within the Christian Democratic party due to a monopolizing tendency which left very little breathing space for the pluralism indispensable in a political party such as ours. In particular, I recall an all-night meeting of our parliamentary caucus early in February 1954 when high-voltage electricity filled the air, while a very intense discussion took place between Fanfani and Gronchi which culminated when the chairman, Giuseppe Cappi, fainted. I was so absorbed in the proceedings that I forgot my wife had been rushed to the delivery room. Only hours later did I find out I had become a father for the fourth time. My wife chose the name Serena for our daughter and I liked it because it seemed in such perfect contrast to the turbulence which prevailed on the night she was born.

De Gasperi's death inevitably heightened the malaise within the party because no one stood out as "the" successor and especially because the failure to realize that such a statesman's mantle could only be worn by the entire group of his followers led to a lot of confusion and many erroneous moves. In addition, May 1955 marked the end of Einaudi's term of office as president of Italy and it was easy to imagine the way domestic political life was to rotate around the presidential elections.

During that same period I received an unexpected invitation to lunch from Mrs. Clare Boothe Luce who said she was alarmed over a possible Italian shift leftwards and wanted "to know my viewpoint on the situation." The third and only other luncheon guest was a young diplomat,

Mr. Wells Stabler, whom I would meet again years later as ambassador on the Iberian peninsula and even later as an official of an important American agency.

I had met Mrs. Luce before she became ambassador when I helped organize a conference at the University of St. Thomas in Rome with two main speakers: her husband Henry Luce, the renowned publisher of *Time, Life,* and *Fortune,* and Alcide De Gasperi. On that occasion I had the opportunity to appreciate both the beauty and the intelligence of this most elegant lady in her forties (already co-director of *Vogue* and *Vanity Fair*), together with her Catholic fervor so typical of a convert from Episcopalianism. However, aside from formal events and a meeting arranged by Cardinal Spellman to support the Italian cause for Trieste, our paths had not crossed again.

In the course of the private lunch Madam Ambassador told me quite clearly how people in America were very concerned over the confused situation in Italy, plagued as it was by discord between the political parties and clashes among the Christian Democrats. If the Scelba government were to fall, clouds of doubt could well descend upon everything and she considered such an eventuality to be quite disturbing. It was not up to her to interfere (just what people say when they do interfere) in Italian domestic affairs, but she felt some of the positions assumed by Gronchi, the speaker of the Chamber of Deputies, were out of line.

Courtesy in speech must never be to the detriment of clarity, and I found it easy to reply that the search under way for new balances both inside and outside the Christian Democratic party was not to be looked upon as a trauma or as an abrupt change in course.

A country as complex as Italy may seem fragile in the daily quest for points of convergence between vastly different positions and interests. I reminded her of what De Gasperi used to say quite often about Italian politics: it needed medicine, but not surgery. Even the proportional voting system, harshly criticized by Madam Ambassador in the Roman parlors of select social circles, as everyone knew, constituted the best possible way to appease spirits and gradually lessen the gap between positions. The slight majority correction rejected by voters in 1953 would have been useful, but the reactions it had triggered at that time illustrated the psychological delicacy of such electoral systems. More than dutiful was our vigilance regarding the communists, but not to be forgotten were Italy's regular compliance with its Atlantic Alliance obligations and the total absence of acts of sabotage. When her predecessor has hastened to the Viminale in a state of maximum alarm after a declaration by the CGIL (left-wing trade union) that American weapons would never be unloaded in Italy, De Gasperi had told him not to be worried because the civic sense of Italians prevailed over everything else (the CGIL secretary, Giuseppe Di Vittorio, had asked me the evening before to reassure De Gasperi that the stevedores in Leghorn had never refused to handle any type of cargo).

I also made it a point to add, with a touch of malice, that strong governments are not the ones that flex their muscles or fill the air with threats.

Even though quite attentive to my line of reasoning, Clare Boothe Luce didn't seem very convinced. By way of example she referred to a recent session of Parliament where criticisms had been raised over the vote against the admission of continental China to the United Nations. With marked emphasis on each word she said it had to be clear to everyone that the U.S. Senate would never recognize communist China.

I explained the considerations of Western solidarity behind our negative vote in New York and, after some subtle irony over the reference to the Senate and not the House of Representatives where Mrs. Luce had served two terms, I ventured to say it was somewhat risky to use the word "never." In any case, leaving one-fourth of mankind outside the United Nations might be a temporary remedy, but it wasn't an eternal dogma.

When speaking about this episode only a few months ago at a luncheon hosted in my honor by Ambassador Maxwell Rabb (the ambassadors from the People's Republic of China and the USSR were among the guests) I learned from our former ambassador to the United States, Egidio Ortona, that sometime after my conversation with Mrs. Luce, she had said Italy should be a bridge between the Chinese and the Americans. Was such a reconsideration of her position linked to our exchange of views? I don't think so, but it is worthy of mention.

Before seeing me to the front door of Villa Taverna Mrs. Luce asked me very indirectly if there was any truth in the rumor that De Gasperi had sought to prevent her appointment to Rome despite the intransigent position assumed by Eisenhower. As far as I recalled, but I didn't tell her, Secretary of State John Foster Dulles was the one who had practically solicited our government's "nonagreement" to her appointment. I don't believe he did it under the impulse of antifeminism, but because of lobbying by the most obstinate Protestant circles.

I have no idea if Mrs. Luce reported our conversation to the State Department. I'm sure, however, she considered me a sort of disappointed leftist and was quite irritated over the advice I had given her about the election of Einaudi's successor. It was not wise, and I told her so, to count on any of the possible and quite uncertain results, despite the predictions circulating among her favorite social contacts. And in fact this advice altered her disposition toward me. In the midst of the frenzy over the presidential elections, further complicated by the error of not presenting a most willing Einaudi for reelection and by what many of us considered an unacceptable statement by the government that the next president should not be a Christian Democrat, Mrs. Luce advised Washington on what she considered the only firm fact: the speaker of the Chamber of Deputies would not be elected. Twenty-four hours later Giovanni Gronchi was elected president of Italy and the U.S. Embassy in Rome cut a very poor figure.

She remembered my words of advice, even though it was too late, and was very fair in admitting it to me. Yet, for reasons of policy coherence, she had to continue depicting the start of Gronchi's term of office in very dark colors. Later on she was most courteous to me on numerous occasions (she also invited me to spend a vacation with my family at her villa in Honolulu) and I responded by always being the first to send her Christmas greetings and by congratulating her on the success of her play on Broadway.

A recent article written by Ambassador Mario Luciolli offers an in-depth illustration of a thesis I consider somewhat farfetched. His appointment at the head of the diplomatic office of the Quirinale was supposedly determined by the need to sort of keep an eye on the freshman president who was reported to be rather lukewarm in his relations with Americans and to have a benevolent propensity for the socialists and beyond. In fact, an influential columnist like Joe Alsop had predicted the fall of Italy into communist hands within six months.

Gronchi himself was aware of these biases and prefaced the publication of the speeches delivered during his visit to the United States in February 1956 with the following words: "The consensus I encountered during the trip turned out to be neither occasional nor ephemeral and, in public opinion and the press not only in Italy, the repercussions of my general approach to political and economic problems had and continue to have an impact which cannot be denied by an attentive and objective observer."

When thinking about all this with the hindsight of today, I can come up with no truer reason than this: he somehow interpreted and expressed, in a sort of coming of age of the times, a state of mind latent yet conscious and widespread in all sorts of countries. I use the words "in a sort of coming of age of the times" because this state of mind was already perceptible even in the distant past in the comments and statements of politicians and journalists with overtones of perplexity and profound concern. However, it seemed circumscribed to a rather small minority. In people's minds these were most responsible yet theoretical precursors of international or supranational solidarity and intellectual circles, always prone to nonconformism and therefore rejected by moderates as affected by a mania for criticism quite deleterious to an orderly democratic-party system. In fact, the situation of malaise and exasperation was further aggravated by the presence of other political groups. However, they excluded themselves from exercising any possible influence due to their preconceived position of integral and dogmatic negation of anything said by the West.

At least during the initial period of Gronchi's presidency, the perception of Italian policy was also clouded by the evident suspicion toward the Quirinale harbored by the minister of foreign affairs, Gaetano Martino and other illustrious Christian Democrats.

Mrs. Luce remained in Italy for more than a year after Gronchi's election, despite certain difficulties in her relations with members of the government.

There were even some comical episodes during that time. One evening she arrived unannounced at the Quirinale and, once ushered into the president's office, confessed she had come to the wrong palace because she was actually supposed to see Prime Minister Segni. Was it due to a lack of collaboration on the part of her embassy staff? All the more serious were the doubts about Mrs. Luce's prolonged arsenic poisoning through the respiratory and/or digestive tracts. Mrs. Luce felt herself becoming progressively weaker and underwent a battery of tests at the U.S. military hospital in Naples. The diagnosis was quite clear and was confirmed a few days later (it was said) by the examination of samples sent to the navy hospital in Bethesda, Maryland. The intoxication was traced to the excessive coats of paint used in the redecoration of the main bedroom in Villa Taverna. In order to keep a lid on the news the lab samples had been dispatched under the pseudonym of Simon Jones, but when sailor Jones was found to be suffering from arsenic poisoning the CIA had a heart attack and leaks started appearing in the very pages of *Time* magazine. However, the whole matter was dropped when an expert found in an old paper by some professors named Gosio and Spica the description of numerous cases of intoxication due to "arsine," "a derivative of lead arsenate contained in the wallpaper then fashionable, and with increased damage potential when in the presence of blends of color between silver-white and green."

Hence, the Italian and foreign staff members of the embassy were freed from the climate of suspicion which for some months had distressed the small community while everyone ran the gauntlet of stringent controls.

A few years later Mrs. Luce was appointed to represent the United States in Brazil but she failed to receive Senate approval. In a letter written to me around the same time she evoked her years in Italy in rather nostalgic terms and referred to Einaudi's rigid defense of the Italian language. He had refused to sign the decree awarding her the knighthood of the Grand Cross because it was written with the masculine form of the title "ambassador." "Many sacrifices can be requested of a President," he had asserted, "but not the sacrifice of the Italian language." However, referring to a woman as a "knight" is not really a good example of proper use of language either.

Neither then nor later during occasional encounters in Italy or in the United States did she ever mention the harsh criticisms lodged against her by the communists which had even caused protests on Capitol Hill from Senator Homer Ferguson. These protests met with a firm response from our minister, Attilio Piccioni, who declared Mrs. Luce not only a "persona grata" for the Italian government, but a "persona gratissima." Rather farfetched, however, was the attribution to Togliatti's party of an unpleasant episode when the magazine *L'Europeo* published the summary account of a very obtrusive speech delivered by Ambassador Luce at the Mayflower Hotel in Washington.

Henry Luce in person vented his rage with the correspondent in New York, Gianni Granzotto, and the banquet organizer Roscoe Drummond curtly dismissed the matter with a blanket denial: "Malicious deformations seeking to slander the Ambassador and twist the truth."

In fact, the left-wing press was on the warpath against Mrs. Luce over her full support for the Scelba government after having favored Pella's in vain. I remember a cartoon drawn by Camerini for *Il Paese* with Scelba on Mrs. Luce's lap and with the following caption: "The Ambassador's new secretary."

And yet the lowest blows against Mrs. Luce came not from Italian politicians or journalists but from her own fellow citizens. Perhaps the most pungent of all was on the part of a well-known journalist, Cyrus Sulzberger. The publication of his diary revealed the contents of a blockbuster interview with her on 5 March 1954. No one emerged unscathed. Chaos reigned supreme in the Vatican with a pontiff who also wanted to be secretary of state and had two permanent aides: Montini who was leftist and pro-American, and Tardini who was rightist and pro-Spanish. Italy needed a Nasser or a Mobutu since it was totally incapable of democracy and bent upon becoming a right-wing dictatorship. No one in Italy paid taxes and her reaction to such a situation made her sound like a Communist! There was just no end to her string of pleasantries.

I'm sure it would in no way be offensive to her memory if I add that no career ambassador (except for a few cases) would ever utter or write such things even if he or she thought them. Quite perceptive on the other hand were the closing considerations of an article she wrote for *Foreign Affairs* on the centennial of Italian unity.

The three conditions which would most assuredly threaten the existence of the Italian state in its present form and its centrist government are the following: a world war, a worldwide economic crisis, the incapacity of the European forces to remain in the West. The seeds which could generate these conditions are not to be found, most assuredly in Italy—even were it to be admitted that they are to be found elsewhere—but their emergence would rapidly impress upon the Italian kaleidoscope a physiognomy rather difficult to predict, arising from the more than probable appearance of a right-wing or left-wing dictator among the ruins of the free republic.

Despite the persistent and even chronic ambivalence of the Italian political scene, one thing is quite clear: the progress now being achieved by the Italian people after one hundred years of trials and sacrifices is, to a great extent, the result of its heroic and extraordinary effort.

5 | *Four Encounters as Minister of Finance*

After the seven years as undersecretary to the Prime Minister's Office and two weeks as minister for internal affairs in 1953, I resumed government responsibilities as minister of finance in 1955 under Prime Minister Antonio Segni, the man of the agrarian reform and a person with deep empathy for farmers and their world.

Ambassador Luce promptly came to see me with an urgent request to resolve a matter which had been dragging on for more than three years. The Americans had asked our government for an exemption from paying customs duties or other taxes on shipments and consignments assigned to them for common defense purposes. On 5 March 1952, my predecessor, Ezio Vanoni, had signed an agreement with Ambassador Clement Dunn which seemed able to settle the matter from an administrative viewpoint. However, when the United States sought to register the Dunn-Vanoni agreement with the United Nations (perhaps to obtain similar waivers from other countries) some people began to raise doubts about the need for ratification by Parliament. In the meantime, between one opinion and another, the established practice continued. Even though the measure adopted was quite acceptable, people were afraid a parliamentary debate would fan the embers of controversy over the Atlantic Alliance. So, Italy's position was . . . the matter is being examined; but why did I have to be the one to do what Vanoni and Tremelloni had avoided?

In fact, the whole affair limped along for a long time. The Preti bill of 1966 expired two years later due to the end of the legislature and its exclusion of local taxes generated heated American protests; two companies went to court over those taxes and actually won their respective cases.

As part of the internal revenue reform and the introduction of value-added tax (VAT) in 1972–73, an article was approved with a blanket pardon extended to the effects of the Dunn-Vanoni agreement, but still hanging (and so far unresolved as far as I know) was a question relative to registration taxes alone.

Much more entertaining was Mrs. Luce's request in 1956 to do something special for the U.S. team at the Winter Olympics in Cortina. I organized a small reception for them and was given a beautiful woolen fur hat, but the red color made it impossible for me to wear it.

Mrs. Luce's successor was James D. Zellerbach, a businessman from California who had already worked for the administration in Italy at the head of the ERP delegation. The European Recovery Program, similar to the Marshall Plan, had brought aid to Italy and other European nations after World War II. Zellerbach was a powerful individual but had the defect of repeating all too often that as an ambassador he was neglecting his paper mills and giving up I don't know how many millions every month. The third time I heard him say it I replied with most courteous firmness that his presence was not really indispensable and how pleased we would be to have even career diplomats. He must not have been used to such a degree of frankness, and from then on he was always very respectful and even nice to me. In addition, on two occasions he gave me a helping hand.

People were becoming increasingly convinced that the so-called seven sisters of the oil multinationals were very upset over the boldness of Enrico Mattei and the National Oil Agency (ENI), which under his thrust had assumed an undoubtedly important position but, in my opinion, not one to cause the world giants to lose sleep at night. By depicting this presumed cosmic aversion in very dark colors, perhaps the image-makers were trying to crown Mattei with a superman's halo. Since there were still no separate Ministry of State holdings, ENI came under the State Property Office and therefore under the Ministry of Finance. Until Mattei's arrival on the scene, the Ministry officials handled the paperwork relative to ENI as if it were no more than a tedious exercise in accounting procedures. A sample of how such a mentality operated dates back to before the war when an AGIP executive (Renzo Piga) recommended contracting the drilling of exploratory oil wells in Libya to specialized foreign firms and was reprimanded for "nauseating distrust in the nation's mechanical industry." Strongly supported by Ezio Vanoni and "understood" by De Gasperi (quite moving are my memories of the latter's trip to Cortemaggiore for the ceremony inaugurating the development of Italy's natural gas fields), Mattei for the first time shaped a national energy policy which perhaps involved a few rather ambitious nuances, but was certainly innovative and farsighted.

At times he trespassed into the exclusive realm of really big interests, such as when he supported Mossadeq in Iran. This element, together with his excellent relations with the USSR, fed the fires of disagreement and allegations with the giant companies. Acting on my belief in the constant need in life to seek grounds for agreement, I spoke with Mr. Zellerbach about this and saw the possibility of bringing ENI and the foreign companies closer together around a specific issue. At that time we were the victims of a colossal tax evasion scam due to the disheartening spread of smuggling in petroleum products. We knew the extent of what was happening but could do nothing about it. When you think that the price of gasoline then was 135 lira a liter, of which 110 lira were taxes, it isn't difficult to imagine the gigantic temptation to sidestep those taxes.

Mr. Zellerbach suggested we bring in the American companies to join forces with ENI in the antievasion campaign because those perpetrating the scam were practicing unfair competition against the large groups. I called in Mattei and the president of Esso Italy, Vincenzo Cazzaniga, one of the "Americans" trying to work out a peace treaty with ENI, and together we set up a small team to investigate this criminal phenomenon. The team was led by a young officer of the Tributary Police, Capt. Giuliano Oliva, and after a few months everything was crystal clear. In addition to the all-too-easy decoloration of subsidized fuel for agricultural use, the controls on products leaving refineries were totally inefficient. Many companies were using the external water piping installed for firefighting purposes to pump out covert rivers of gasoline, diesel oil, and kerosene.

Moreover, there were foreign countries which issued import certificates for refined petroleum products and actually received tankers full of water.

A decree was issued making waybills compulsory and stipulating imprisonment as the only punishment for violations. Already during the first year the decree was enforced, the state collected tens of billions in additional revenue from production taxes.

Neither ENI nor the distribution networks of the foreign companies were involved in fraudulent practices and the joint success met with full sastisfaction on both sides. Overall relations, however, did not really improve. Cazzaniga's suggestions to bolster ENI's presence on the international market were not heeded.

Certainly, Mattei had a rather difficult personality. For example, when he discovered that protocol arrangements did not include him from the very beginning of a visit to Morocco by Fanfani, he ordered his pilot to simulate an act of sabotage on his plane at the airport so he could cancel his departure the next day and skip the whole trip. His crew ate at the same restaurant as my secretary in downtown Rome and they made no mystery of the whole show.

However, I do not agree with those who attributed Fr. Luigi Sturzo's adamant opposition to Mattei to pressure from America, and I feel it would be insulting to even think so. Sturzo didn't know anything about technical problems and was perhaps quite willing to disregard them. He reproached Mattei for financing a group of Christian Democrats called "The Base" and it was on account of this infiltration into politics that Sturzo, from the Senate and from the columns of the newspaper *Il Giornale d'Italia*, thundered against ENI. He even criticized the installation of service stations along the national highways which had been planned with an intelligent eye on foreseeable traffic developments.

Mattei's tragic death when his plane crashed on his return flight from Sicily at the height of a late evening storm released a host of devious suppositions. The official enquiry excluded even the faintest possibility of sabotage, and yet people continued to believe in the legendary rumor of responsibility on the part of hostile parties (a movie was even made out of it) anxious to get rid of this "lone ranger" who fought fearlessly for redemption from the large monopolies.

The fourth occasion for relations with the United States during those three years as minister of finance assumed the tones of tragic comedy. For sanitary and hygienic reasons the Americans had blocked the importing of certain agricultural products which, for Italy, included a type of Sardinian cheese made of sheep's milk. Recourse to nontariff barriers to slow down or even prohibit the arrival of foreign goods is rather frequent. Later on we were going to have the equally absurd case of Parma ham which was resolved only through laborious negotiations and high fees for expert analyses after years of diplomatic and technical ping-pong. While all this was under way I enjoyed offering my American guests appetizers with the disputed ham and was always careful to warn them of the . . . risk potential. A movie starring Sophia Loren was even made on the subject and the main prop was a huge Bologna salami confiscated by the American immigration authorities.

The insults to the Sardinian cheese was taken as a personal affront by Prime Minister Segni who just couldn't get over it. Drawing upon the wealth of his legal acumen, he had experts study possible retaliation measures involving the customs officers under the control of my ministry. More than once I had to call in Ambassador Zellerbach to appeal that the measure in question be rescinded. It was absurd to even think Sardinian sheep's cheese was dangerous for people's health. I even had to study all the statistics on brucellosis (the scientific title for Malta fever named after the scientist Bruce who was the first to study it) and learned there was absolutely no correlation between that disease and the areas with the highest consumption rate of our cheese. Conversely, the embargo could have very well turned one of the most pro-Atlantic Italian politicians into an anti-American.

The whole matter was partially resolved but, if I'm not mistaken, Segni ran up against it anew when he was president of Italy.

6 | *McNamara and Rusk*

When I first went to the States in August 1954 as a tourist, a New York agency had circulated a brief biographical profile with the usual information on my family, degrees, election results, and former government positions. Nothing strange about that. However, there was an additional item which made me grin with mirth: I was apparently on the short list, who knows why, to become minister of Defense.

I recalled this episode some five years later when Segni left the Defense Ministry to become prime minister and offered me his former post, smiling over my objections of never having served in the armed forces due to the physical I had flunked when applying to Officers Candidate School.

The Italian defense system has long been an integral part of the NATO Alliance in which the Americans constitute the principal component. What began for me, therefore, was a period of intense contacts with the Americans which I had no way of knowing would last for seven years and where the main link was Vernon Walters, then a colonel and the U.S. military attaché in Rome.

Walters was an authentic polyglot and already known worldwide as the interpreter at the side of American presidents during official visits and receptions. He had a very special knowledge of Italy because during the war of liberation he had served as a liaison officer between the U.S. command and the Brazilian expedition troops. Walters was my guide during visits to the Pentagon and on reserved tours to American bases arranged for the ministers of defense on a rotation basis. He was also very helpful in arranging the NATO ministerial meetings which took place every December in Paris (the Alliance had yet to be evicted from Porte Dauphine and transferred to Brussels).

We had some very difficult moments over one of these interministerial meetings (they were attended by the ministers of foreign affairs, defense, and treasury-finance from each country). According to NATO rules, access to the meetings and official documents of the Alliance requires a security clearance with numerous levels, all the way to the top which is called cosmic clearance or something like that. Ministers are also subject to this clearance requirement and they receive it from the head of national security who is the prime minister or, in his stead, from the head of the national intelligence services. As declared adversaries of the Alliance along with the Communists at that time, the Socialists could not obtain the necessary clearance credentials.

For a long time this created no problems at all. While I was fostering the gradual establishment of a center-left coalition, by having it develop from the bottom upwards and not the other way around, I was also focusing (now I can say this) on the needs for a "soft" resolution of differences. However, quite the contrary actually transpired. On the eve of one December meeting it was pointed out that the new finance minister, the Socialist Antonio Giolitti (with a political past as a Communist active in anti-Atlantic protests), did not have clearance and would not be admitted to the meeting room.

Now what? I suggested the following course of action to Prime Minister Fanfani: since the government had only recently been formed, just send the minister of foreign affairs to the meeting. My absence as minister of defense eliminated any suspicion of discrimination, and in the meantime we would have the security regulations updated immediately. I didn't know whether Giolitti had been briefed on this or not, but we very astutely avoided what would have been a critical incident.

I used a similar expedient a year later to help the Moro government avoid a rather embarrassing situation. We were supposed to submit to Parliament an economic program bill named the Pieraccini bill after its author who was the national budget minister. It was a sort of tribute to the cooperation of the Socialists who were making it a "test case," and Moro wanted the bill to be signed in a most solemn form by all the ministers in his cabinet. Fanfani reacted with some timely observations, called the document a fairy tale, and refused to participate in its inception. I advised Moro to explain that, considering the bill dealt exclusively with economic matters, it didn't call for signature by the ministers of foreign affairs and defense; in brief, my signature wasn't necessary either.

The ministers' Parisian week followed a set ritual: briefings by the chiefs of staff on troop deployment; a political assessment of the situation delivered with customary brilliance by the secretary-general, Paul-Henri Spaak, Catherine's uncle; a general exchange of views on each major topic for discussion (foreign affairs, defense, financial policy); a splendid banquet at the Defense Ministry (with the magnificent Sèvres dinner service); and a variable element dependent upon current affairs. Very often the American representatives were the center of attention in the discussions in a sort of comparison of positions between the two shores of the Atlantic. We immediately established intense and frank relations with Robert McNamara who was head of the Pentagon from 1961 to 1968. I liked his realistic and well-informed way of tackling problems, without vaunting the superiority of America's contribution to the Alliance. We became good friends. Such was the praise he showered upon me in an interview with Ruggero Orlando that it was cut by RAI-TV, since I had no saints on my side in TV paradise.

A graduate from the University of California, Robert McNamara had an excellent curriculum vitae, both practical and academic. Among other things, he had been on the faculty at Harvard. Upon his return to the States after the war with medals, ribbons, and the rank of colonel, he placed an ad in the papers offering his services, along with a team of three associates, to conduct corporate salvage operations. They didn't ask for a salary and all they expected was a share of the restored profits. In Italy it would have been considered a joke, but Ford took the offer quite seriously and put the four veterans to the test. At that time, in 1946, Robert was thirty years old. Fourteen years later he had become president of the Ford Motor Company and, in 1961, left that position to become secretary of defense (with a cut in salary, as Indro Montanelli wrote with deep admiration, from $500,000 to $25,000).

When he left the Department of Defense after seven years he moved on with the same energy into a prestigious position in civil affairs as president of the World Bank, where he demonstrated an ever-increasing social awareness. One of his aides, William Clark, has written: "When McNamara took over as president he was concerned only about the return on investments; today he is obsessed only by the poverty of certain populations." During a visit to Rome to explain a global program for the rationalization of agriculture, he spoke to me at length about the firm belief he had developed during visits to more than one hundred poor countries: growth was not a synonym for development, and in many cases it was beneficial to the rich alone. As a result, resilient and even more intense misery in some countries went hand in hand with moderate Third World growth. Laughing to himself, he told me he had converted the more than two thousand bank experts into "priests of development," but true development.

During my years in the Defense Ministry I was a guest on various occasions at his home in Washington, where I was able to admire the simplicity of his family life with the ever-cheerful presence of his wife Margaret, an extraordinary woman to whom he had been happily married since the age of 24. At the end of especially demanding days, Robert and Margaret used to restore peacefulness to their lives by playing chess. I had the Val Gardena craftsmen carve them a chessboard and pieces, and they were overjoyed with the gift, not least because they are the descendants of a family of "whittlers."

McNamara's undersecretaries were open, affable, and businesslike men. There was Paul Nitze, responsible for army-related affairs, who interpreted very well the orders to keep the army ever aware of its central position, despite the decisive role people attributed to atomic weapons. He worked in particular on boosting the morale of the troops stationed abroad, seeking to make sure they struck a proper balance between an understanding of the local psychology and a firm sense of their own identity. A man of Nitze's value was not bound to any one political party and the Reagan administration was very wise in asking him to assume the key position of ambassador-at-large for the disarmament negotiations with the USSR. As a result, all of us in the Atlantic Alliance have been able to renew contacts with him over the last few years (he has often been our guest in Rome), and appreciate the importance of his essential contributions to Reagan's achievements.

He has now left the administration, but his "eighty-odd" years do not weigh heavily upon him. On April 7 this year he wrote me: "I have been the victim of a spooked horse who sat on me and caused quite a bit of damage. . . . I have returned home from the hospital and can't wait for the day in the not too distant future when I will be able to resume my activity in full." This activity how unfolds at the School of Advanced International Studies and in that guise Paul Nitze intends to continue his dialogue with his many Italian friends. He says he is "proud of the role [he] played in fortifying the strong friendship between Italy and the United States. That friendship has been and is ever more a milestone of the Atlantic Alliance."

Quite a different type of person is John Connally who was secretary of the navy and whose Pentagon office was bereft of seafaring symbols and full of saddles and other things extolling Texas (however, he had commanded a corvette during the war). His curriculum vitae is very long and, among others things, includes one term as governor of Texas. As governor he was at John F. Kennedy's side on that tragic day in Dallas and was seriously wounded in the attack which cost the president's life. He later switched to the Republican party and attained excellent results in the campaign against inflation as secretary of the treasury under Nixon.

In June 1976, a full-page (paid) advertisement in the *New York Times* announced the establishment of a Citizens' Alliance for the Freedom of the Mediterranean. John Connally was its founder and deep was the concern he voiced over the growing presence of communism in Italy. Connally loved Italy and during the war he had taken part in the Allied plans for our liberation from his duty station in Algiers. In any case, this relief committee was very strange indeed.

It is nonetheless important to recall what happened that same summer at the Summit Meeting of the Seven Most Industrialized Countries held in Puerto Rico. With Moro and Rumor completely in the dark, Italy was issued a firm warning to avert the entry of the communists into the majority coalition. Such a general climate helps to explain why Connally's initiative met with the approval of people who were ordinarily more prudent in their assessments; for example, Senators John Pastore and Pete Domenici, the former NATO commander in chief, General Andrew Goodpaster, and the movie executive Jack Valenti. At the same time the *Wall Street Journal* was launching harsh attacks against the Italian government's economic policy, attributing a bloated bureaucracy and the disastrous management of the national budget to favoritism on the part of the Christian Democrats. The director of the Washington office of the Citizens' Alliance was Bill Gile, who had left a top position as a

MCNAMARA AND RUSK 37

TV reporter to take that job, and he claimed the Russians wanted to take over Italy by using the Communist party.

The year before this, Connally had been brought to trial in his own state, and had been fully acquitted by what was for him a difficult jury: two whites and the rest of the members black. He had been accused of pocketing ten thousand dollars in order to convince Nixon to give one hundred times as much to an association of dairy farmers.

According to a persistent rumor in Texas where Connally had a law office with more than 200 lawyers, the trap for the former governor was attributed to his declared intention to run for president. The jury members, eight women and four men, were very much of their own mind and Connally walked out of court holding his head high and free to devote his energies to the salvation of the Mediterranean and democracy in Italy. The weekly magazine *Espresso* ran an article on him with a title asking why he wanted "to save Andreotti." In addition, this relief operation was supposedly to take place through the buyout of certain state-held companies, including the Società Condotte d'Acqua which IRI had recently purchased from the Sindona group.

In fact, I was the one who put a stop to the operation, while IRI and the Ministry of State Holdings had given it their warm approval in writing although leaving the last word up to the prime minister. And I decided no. I considered it absurd to accept $10 million in exchange for the controlling share of a civil engineering firm with, if I'm not mistaken, an annual turnover of more than 10 billion dollars. Moreover, the American group made no secret of wanting to buy the Condotte company so they could bid for contracts in countries where people really didn't like the initials "U.S.A." Therefore, they should have offered and paid much more.

Quite naturally, *Espresso* talked about Andreotti's "about-turn," but I have no idea who could have thought I would have approved such a sale. My sole concern was to brief Connally on the objective reasons behind my negative decision so no one would make-believe it was dictated by anti-American feelings generated, perchance, by the parliamentary support extended to the government at that time by the Communists.

I retain a very amusing recollection of a third person on McNamara's team: Undersecretary Roswell Gilpatric. He accompanied me on a visit to San Francisco and it was his last official duty, since he was compelled to return to his professional life: his government salary didn't suffice to cover the monthly alimony payments to his three ex-wives. Either he was an unbeatable fifty-year-old with a definite allure or, for his own misfortune, none of his ex-wives had remarried and he had to support them. He seemed very eager to take me on a visit to the Food Machinery, a plant which produces agricultural machines, but also tanks, and it made me miss a delightful weekend I had planned at Disneyland. A few years later the papers published some very friendly correspondence between Gilpatric and Jacqueline Kennedy.

In the many years spent at the political summit of NATO I have been able to ascertain its exclusively defensive nature; in the numerous simulations and exercises, we have never been asked to consider a plan to attack a potential enemy. When people became convinced of the need to dispose of a broad range of means to respond with due proportion to the thoughtlessness of a possible enemy attack, we moved from the *global* response theory to the *flexible* response theory. This was a very delicate period for the Germans who felt the threat of occupation hard on the heels of any border crossing by the Warsaw Pact troops. Then there was the earlier attempt to weaken the Alliance psychologically with the insinuation that the Americans would have never endangered— by using the atomic bomb—the survival of Chicago or Detroit in order to save Berlin or any other German city. President Kennedy also created a bit of confusion in this regard when he reprimanded McNamara for telling Adenauer an atomic weapon would be the response to a conventional attack.

The Alliance has always withstood doubts and provocative problems, adapting in various ways to change in the political situation. For example, the partial separation by the French in no way affected the actual integration of their armed forces; the recurrent disputes between Greece and Turkey have never induced either country to question membership in NATO (in one case I was entrusted with a mission to Athens through the good offices of Minister Evangelos Averoff). McNamara, who had solved the Ford crisis, considered the frequently resurfacing and unresolved issue of Cyprus to be nothing short of an impossibility. And yet even the United Nations is still working on it, but with no success despite the dedicated efforts of such eminent personalities as Galo Plaza from

Ecuador (who came to give us an excellent briefing) and recently the secretary-general, Pérez de Cuéllar.

The 1960s brought about a rather interesting turn of events in the area of missiles. In Turkey and Italy the Alliance had deployed some batteries of Jupiter missiles which were so long that any semblance of military secrecy was out of the question. The batteries in Italy were based at Gioia del Colle but were easily visible from the civilian airport of Bari-Palese. By way of one of those intelligent and praiseworthy compromises, the Communists kept on asking the government for confirmation of the reported deployment and the answer was always given in interlocutory terms. There was even the adventure on that site of the Bulgarian pilot-photographer, but everything was resolved without stirring up a hornet's nest.

In the fall of 1962 it was rumored that the removal of the Jupiter missiles was part of the arrangements agreed with Moscow to resolve the Cuban crisis. At that time, I must say, the Alliance did not operate in the same collegial way it does today and not a word was said about the matter at the December session in Paris. I raised it with McNamara in private and, while ruling out the removal hypothesis, he did refer to the need in the distant future to modernize the missile system. Exactly twenty-four days later (I remember it very well because it was the feast of the Epiphany and I was at home with my children) I received a call from Ambassador Reinhardt informing me of the arrival of a top secret and very urgent letter from the Pentagon which was delivered right after the call. Under the previous day's date McNamara had written: "You will recall that in Paris on December 13 I had expressed the opinion that the Jupiters need to be replaced with now more effective missiles." He went on into detailed operational clarifications which I will skip even though they are no longer secret, and concluded by referring to the tripartite working group (Italy, the United States, and NATO Command) which would be set up to handle the necessary details if the plan met with the agreement of the Italian government.

When I saw Robert McNamara I asked him what had happened during those three weeks straddling the old year and the new one. I realized he felt somewhat embarrassed because he shifted the emphasis to technical details. However, I did learn about the visit to Washington on the part of the trusted envoy of someone very high up in the Italian government with a warning that the missiles could no longer be based in

Gioia del Colle. He asked me to forget what he had said and all I forgot was the name of that "free agent."

In addition to the Paris meeting in 1962, I had been to the United States in September for a thorough exchange of views at the Pentagon on all the various defense issues and at the State Department on the world situation. Dean Rusk was worried about Berlin (he had already spoken to me about it the year before), Somalia, the theories of an independent European nuclear defense system while there was lagging support for a NATO multilateral force, and about the limited degree of understanding in many countries with regard to the American concern over Cuba.

Against the background of the discussions with McNamara, Rusk, and Rostow, what was quite evident at that time was America's psychosis, with undivided attention focused on a falling currency and the federal debt. Everyone was afraid Congress would make sharp cuts in the armed forces' budgets, thereby weakening the common defense. A few days earlier in Rome, Vice President Johnson had voiced a similar concern in very much the same terms. I had invited Rusk to Rome in June and he had been quite explicit. There was little or no room for surprise if the Americans thought about reducing, for financing reasons, their 300,000 troops stationed in Europe, while the Europeans deemed they could not financially support an increase in their troops. In my diary I wrote down his exact words: "It is very important to avoid giving Americans the impression that their troops are mercenaries for the defense of Europe."

Due to this general climate my visit received quite a bit of coverage in the press. The renowned journalist Drew Pearson issued me a certificate of good conduct when he wrote: "Secretary of Defense McNamara and other federal officials have had an excellent impression of the Italian Defense Minister Giulio Andreotti during the talks of recent days. Andreotti was friendly and did not get lost in futile chatter."

I had organized the spectacular assistance drive to Italy of "the Friendship Train" with Pearson in 1947 and he asked me if the Socialists were loyal to the Atlantic Pact, and in particular if Senator Tolloy was, since he had been the subject of some rather polemical articles on his activities during the war. I reassured him and he reported my remarks, adding words of praise for the Communist members of Parliament who, for the first time, had gone to Africa to pay tribute to the troops who had fallen at El Alamein.

In the talks at the State Department, aside from references to Italian domestic politics to be dealt with in a later chapter, the delicate problem of East-West relations came to the surface every year. In a somewhat paradoxical way, whenever the Americans opened up toward Moscow many Europeans were scandalized by what they considered deceitful behavior. However, when Washington thundered forth in harsh tones, Europe launched appeals for caution and dialogue. It looks like a sort of slalom which has been going on for a long time and doesn't really seem to be over.

More or less the same thing has happened over the value of the dollar. For decades ministers and experts left the Old World on a pilgrimage in order to induce the Americans to devalue their currency; as soon as it happened, however, the same pilgrims returned to lodge complaints, and continue to do so. Now it seems the march has been resumed to offset the overvaluation problem. Rather annoyed by all these sermons, Secretary of the Treasury Regan one day asked me why his European colleagues, if they were so smart in giving advice to the Americans, didn't apply their suggested therapies at home (he was referring in particular to the budget deficit issue).

Rusk, a pragmatic and authentic man of peace from Georgia, suffered immensely over the Vietnam issue and really appreciated any solidarity on that matter. In a speech to Italian Communists in May 1966 I had an opportunity to recall how the Americans certainly could have left their Vietnamese allies all on their own. But, I added, what would we have said if the Americans had succumbed to the pro-isolation temptation in the 1940s and not come to fight and die on our continent?

Dean Rusk delivered a speech shortly after that at Boston University. He quoted me and was quite effusive in his gratitude.

7 | *The Years in the Ministry of Defense*

As minister of defense, in 1960 I was president of the organizing committee for the Rome Olympics. Up until then two distinct villages had been set up for the Olympic Games, with complete separation between athletes from the East and from the West. The war had been over for fifteen years and Giulio Onesti, the president of the Italian Olympic Committee, and I thought it was absurd to continue that separation which had so little to do with a true sporting spirit. We voiced our opinion quite clearly and received the support of ambassadors as well as the agreement, albeit somewhat hesitant at first, of the president of the International Olympic Committee, Averell Brundage (an American billionaire who bought rare antique vases all over the world). As a result, American and Russian youth lived together for a few weeks without the slightest incident, and everyone concerned showered us with praise. It was also the only time since the war that the two Germanys competed with one team, the same anthem, and under a single flag.

Not even two centuries of public life could bestow upon me a degree of notoriety equal to the TV coverage of the games in America. During my next trip to the United States, a few months later, American boys and girls in many cities asked me for my autograph and some of them were even humming the theme song of the Roman games. It was a compulsory topic of conversation when I met with Italian communities, and I was congratulated quite effusively on the successful outcome.

In the preface I described how the defense ministers of NATO (but later on those from the opposite front as well) were invited to Washington for political talks, followed by visits to important military bases. I gained a twofold advantage out of this practice. I was able to acquire a first-hand knowledge of almost all of America in the vast diversity of its landscapes, social contexts, and people. Moreover, even in places far removed from the hubs of activity, I had an opportunity to appreciate in full the enormous contribution made by our immigrants, quite literally backbreaking at first and later on almost never ostentatious, to the greatness of the United States.

During these visits to the bases there were also some rather tiring moments. For example, some generals and admirals didn't realize ministers are more politicians than technical experts, and would linger for hours on a detailed description of the difference between the latest APC and an earlier one or similar "technicalities," as Americans say and Italians now like to say too. And they were really downcast if their request for questions met with silence. I used to have my military adviser give me a full briefing on the subject and always made them happy. Personally speaking, I was more interested in life on the bases, relations between officers and troops, and family housing. Certain details made a very positive impact on me. I once saw a general coming out of the commissary under a load of bags, and the scene brought to mind cartoons about docile husbands. His driver didn't make the slightest move to help him; here it would have been unthinkable.

When there is a shortage of housing on the bases, officers and NCOs often live with their wives and children in large trailers parked in special areas with all the necessary communal facilities. When they are transferred they just take the "house" along, usually by rail, without the complications of packing everything up or the drawbacks of moving. The trailers were rather comfortable inside, and the people living in them didn't seem to be displeased in any way with their quarters.

The reception on the bases was planned in every detail and wherever there were troops of Italian descent or the Italian wives (Venetians or Neapolitans) of men who had done NATO service in Italy, part of the visit was set aside for a special meeting. With some of these families we still exchange greetings at Christmas and sometimes, when in Rome as tourists, they come to see me.

I'll just glide over two drawbacks. The official dinner in my honor was always in tuxedo and often began a few minutes after my arrival. In such cases I always hoped someone would finally invent a truly wrinkle-free cloth, just like a remarkably funny movie with Alec Guinness. In their dedication to precision the American armed forces leave nothing to chance. Even the menu is standard for guest defense ministers: shrimp cocktail, grilled steak, salad with Roquefort dressing, and pistachio sherbet. This ritual at the table is repeated for an entire week, and you subconsciously start to envy vegetarians and to dream about the good ice cream made by Italians all over the world (I would mention the ones from Belluno, in particular) who certainly refrain from using even the most refined powdered mixtures.

However, these are insignificant details. All the rest was perfect and there was even plenty of time to visit cities and tourist sites if they weren't too far away. I recall the trip along the canals of San Antonio in Texas; the reception in the beautiful vineyards of Louis Rossi in California; the stud farm in Kentucky and Louisville's tribute to the first bourbon bottling plant; the pleasant break in Las Vegas (where the battles are fought against the slot machines and the croupiers); the brief cruise in Newport with the head of the Naval Academy; a trip into the countryside after admiring the army's light aviation center; the climb up the Colorado mountains as a side trip on the visit to the Air Force Academy; and the fascinating underground USA-Canada command center.

My memories of two occasions are especially distinct. After a guided visit to the unbelievable launching pads in Cape Canaveral, we had the standard lunch and at the end the commanding officer invited us to have coffee on the terrace. It sounded like a rather irrelevant detail, but with perfect synchrony it coincided with a missile launch and it would be an understatement to describe that as a moving experience.

The other memorable experience occurred in Connecticut at the atomic submarine base of New London as the *Nautilus* returned after a long cruise. The crew members disembarked and looked like they were filing out of a movie theater: cheerful, well shaven, and by no means worn out. When I visited the inside of the sub the captain, Jeffrey Metzel, Jr., explained to me what it means to be able to set aside for crew comfort the enormous space reserved for fuel on conventional submarines. Nevertheless, I wasn't disappointed over the fact that we didn't have the time to go out and "run silent and run deep." I once took part in such an exercise and it really wasn't the most exciting half a day in my life. However, on the *Nautilus*, where I left an excellent Italian copy of the prophetic book by Jules Verne, I would have been spared the added and disturbing attraction of the sharp smell of diesel oil.

Wherever possible the military authorities or our consuls organized something with the "colonies" of longstanding or recent immigrants from Italy. While Italians in New York or San Francisco were used to these contacts, in the smaller towns where such occasions almost never occurred it turned into an event, and at times was even moving for all of us.

Two years ago, during the formal celebration of the centennial of the Statue of Liberty, when President Reagan held a solemn award ceremony for ten illustrious citizens with an immigrant background, I was surprised to notice the unfair absence of someone of Italian descent. I was told that, since our Lee Iacocca had performed so well as the person in charge of fund raising, he could not receive the honor of such an award nor could anyone else be honored in his stead. The explanation didn't really convince me. Most probably, on the eve of the presidential nominations there were fears of shining the spotlight on Iacocca, whom many people would have liked to see as a possible successor to Reagan. Even where they don't have political parties like ours, the party system exists and how! For this reason as well, on 2 June 1989, Italy honored Lee Iacocca by bestowing the knighthood of labor upon him (only the second non-Italian citizen after Charles Forte).

The first time I was invited to a "Lodge" of the Sons of Italy, the Masonic title puzzled me somewhat and my sense of uneasiness was all the more heightened by the terminology and the language specific to the rites of the triangle and the apron, which are quite public in the United States (there is a large Masonic temple just down the street from our embassy's chancellery in Washington). However, this is merely a question of formal identity. The banquet offered by the Lodge of the Sons of Italy starts with a prayer said by a Catholic priest and everything else is just like any other social club.

Equally touching are the invitations to regional clubs (the ones of Friulani, near the Austrian border, are exceptional) and to clubs of veterans and former draftees where those who have served in the Alpine troops stand out tall. Every year they send a delegation to the national gathering in Italy.

Giannini, with the Bank of America, is not the only one to keep our flag flying high in California. Someone with the same name who came over with Enrico Fermi now has a flourishing components industry and does business with NASA. In the universities I met several professors, including the Nobel laureate Segrè, and many students on scholarships. There was a team of technical experts preparing a unique microfilm file of everything contained in the Vatican Library, the result of a rather bizarre legacy in the will of a local rich man. I would become familiar with other features of California on later trips. At that time, I was struck by the harshness of the tones used in the electoral campaign under way for the office of governor. In order to support the Democratic candidate Edmund Brown against the Republican Nixon, President Kennedy sent a message to voters inviting them to "bury Nixon because he had already killed him" (in the presidential elections). Edmund Brown became governor.

During one of these "tours" for ministers we had a slight problem on an airplane which General Vernon Walters, my escort, narrated in his memoirs. We had just left an airfield when wisps of smoke started floating around the inside of the Jetstar executive jet. Walters rushed into the pilots' cabin and then returned with a reassured look about him, while I kept on reading the briefing paper on the next base. However, the smoke increased and so did Vernon's nervousness. With somewhat strained aplomb, I asked him if we were going to fall out of the sky or not. Ever respectful of the hierarchy, the pilot asked me for instructions and I told him to just act as if I wasn't there. So he dumped almost all the fuel into the ocean and we returned to our point of departure where we landed with faulty landing gear (the cause of the problem). The general in command came to receive us saying that, while he had said good-bye with a "see you again soon," he hadn't meant that soon.

8 | *The Kennedy Star*

John Kennedy made it to the White House by a very narrow margin, and for a few hours rumors were circulating about a Republican request for a recount of the votes. However, as soon as he was sworn into office and despite his traditionalist vice president Lyndon Johnson (whom he had invited on the ticket to attract votes, quite sure that he wouldn't accept), he immediately projected the image of a strong-willed and innovative presidency with the choice of youthful and professionally skilled aides, including his brother Robert as attorney general. There was something prophetic in his main policy lines. The "New Frontier" evoked the new heavens and the new lands of the Bible and kindled boundless hopes among the black population and among the poor, almost all over the world. For Latin America he created the Alliance for Progress, but it didn't really have any long-lasting effects. As a symbol of openness and dialogue he offered Africa the establishment of the Peace Corps, dedicated to providing humanitarian and technical assistance to poor Third World countries.

His entourage's activism knew no bounds and struck me as being all too prone to meddle in Italian domestic affairs. Shortly after the president's tragic death, his most trusted aide, Arthur Schlesinger, Jr., wrote a book *(The Thousand Days of John F. Kennedy)* where he described at length the role played by the White House in accelerating the advent of the center-left coalition in Italy. Among other things, the book tells about a meeting at the home of Tullia Zevi, in February 1962, attended by Schlesinger (in June of 1961 he had had Kennedy initial a policy paper to this end), Nenni, Ugo La Malfa, Ignazio Silone, and others; a meeting "repeatedly interrupted by telephone calls from Prime Minister-designate Fanfani who wanted to discuss the composition of the cabinet with Nenni and La Malfa."

Schlesinger reports that Nenni spoke with him at length about his disagreement with the Communists and his "de facto" acceptance of NATO, adding that, if the embassy in Rome and the State Department had assumed a less conservative stance, the United States would have reaped direct merits for the change of course in Italy. The seven printed pages of this diary helped me to gain a better grasp of the reasons behind some of the questions I was asked on my trips to America around that time. Both Rusk and McNamara asked me why, at the Christian Democratic convention and elsewhere, I wasn't in favor of speeding up the center-left coalition process, while their experts viewed the change of mind on the part of 50 percent of the Italian political forces hostile to NATO to be a positive development.

Even though I didn't like to speak about such matters when abroad, I did explain my point of view. I had never considered the left wing to be an indivisible bloc, and so much so that in my magazine *Concretezza* no one ever used what was then the fashionable adjective of "Social-Communists." Nor was I unaware of the fact that the failure to reach an agreement between the Catholic Democrats and Socialists had paved the way for the Fascists. However, I didn't feel such an alliance could be imposed from on high or be the outcome of agreements on the uppermost levels. Nor did I think the Italian front would be more reliable, as regards the Alliance's military obligations, in a climate of more evident anticommunism as predicted by these "experts." Developing a democratic policy step by step would have brought even the Communists to support a common defense platform with a degree of security otherwise most unlikely.

Quite naturally, I refrained from countering Rusk's satisfaction over Nenni's new stance in favor of the Atlantic Alliance and the end of his anti-Americanism by reminding him of what Nenni had said in 1953 when he told De Gasperi the Pact was no problem because all pacts are just pieces of paper. Having expressed my viewpoint, I reverted to the official government line. In fact, I had agreed to remain at the Defense Ministry precisely because people wanted to underscore continuity in Italy's Atlantic policy. I was also convinced that whoever really wanted to work toward the definitive consolidation of democracy in Italy had to operate with the utmost patience in order to overcome the communist schism of 1921, striving toward the concrete reunification of all the socialist forces.

I met Kennedy in person when he came to Italy on 1 July 1963, and had a better perception of the important role played by some of his aides, besides Dean Rusk: the special assistant Theodore Sorensen and William Tyler, the "European" adviser to the secretary of state.

I accompanied Kennedy to lay a wreath at the Tomb of the Unknown Soldier and the next day on a visit to the Southern European NATO Command in Naples. However, more so than at any other time, I had an opportunity to discuss a number of subjects in depth during a luncheon he hosted for a very small group of people in Villa Taverna, the official residence of the U.S. ambassador in Rome, on July 2 (one hour and forty-five minutes of enlightening conversation).

I very much appreciated his personal discretion in avoiding reference to Italian domestic politics. He only mentioned his surprise over the fall of the Fanfani government, whose very long life had been predicted by his advisers. He had met Fanfani a number of times and had even read one of his books on the history of economics. However, he hastened to add that for an American politician, accustomed to a four-year administration time frame and a majority electoral system, it wasn't easy to understand Italian politics (at this point McGeorge Bundy broke in with a quip about my being "eternal"). Quite interesting was his comment on the need to send European students to America and Americans to Europe in order "to contribute over the long term to better mutual understanding and to help respective growth with less distinct models." He expressed particular praise for MIT, even if its positions were not always pro-administration. He hoped his fellow Americans would not consider it superfluous to learn a second language; for example, his wife's knowledge of French gave her greater opportunities for establishing direct contact. Jacqueline had spent a weekend in Rome in March 1962 and had left everyone with an excellent impression. I still have a very kind letter she wrote to me on that occasion.

During the luncheon at the ambassador's residence I asked the president if he didn't consider it strange, aside from the fact of his being a Catholic, that while countries with all kinds of political, religious, and cultural connotations had an ambassador to the Holy See, absent from that diplomatic corps were the governments of Washington and Moscow (the pairing was to stimulate a response). In reply, he referred to the hard work he had done after his election to avoid the explosion of the "Catholic issue" after the lengthy and quite opposite tradition on the part of his White House predecessors. He was even criticized for the mere fact of receiving his old family friend Cardinal Cushing more often than evangelical dignitaries or renowned rabbis. Even for Roosevelt it hadn't been an easy matter to send Myron Tylor to the Vatican as his "personal" representative. For him even this was out of the question. He did agree with me, however, that it was an anomalous situation and intended to resolve it during his second term of office, when he no longer had to fear adverse electoral effects. His reply seemed to herald good prospects for the future, even though it sounded somewhat utilitarian. Yet, we know he never had a second term nor was he able to finish the first one. Another one of Kennedy's young eggheads broke into our conversation at one point, and I noted what he said but considered any reaction inappropriate: when Kennedy mentioned receiving the cardinal, this aide said with a grin that those weren't the visits to the White House that created problems. The president just smiled and continued talking about the Holy See in terms of great admiration for its international prestige and esteem for Pope Paul VI. He told us that John XXIII's death had not only filled him with dismay, but had also created problems for his schedule of visits in Europe. If the conclave had lasted longer, it would have been impossible for him to come to Rome while the See of Peter was vacant, and he expressed the fear that intransigent circles would have insinuated he had come to interfere in the choice of the new pontiff. That seemed somewhat exaggerated to me, and much more reasonable was the motive voiced by his "team"; if the world's mass media were concentrating on the Vatican his presidential tour would have received much less coverage.

Over coffee one of the "youngsters" returned to the topic of diplomatic relations with the Holy See and filled me in on some of the background. There was a general chorus of praise for Kennedy during the Democratic convention and the only reservations expressed were on his belonging to the Church of Rome. The last speaker was President Truman and he literally froze the crowd when he stated that to be feared was not the influence exercised on Kennedy by the "Holy" Father, but by the "father." This man was very influential and was a rather . . .

intricate person. The head of the Kennedy clan, continued my companion at table, had an open channel with Catholic Rome in the person of Count Enrico Galeazzi, who was very well known in the United States through the Knights of Columbus. I didn't even mention the fact that Galeazzi had been on very familiar terms with Pius XII, but not with John XXIII, and I didn't think he had gone out of his way to be deferential to Montini before he became Pope Paul VI and was archbishop of Milan.

Returning to the conversation with Kennedy, I recall his keen interest in the development policy for southern Italy, and what he said about the social progress achieved in the United States by the families of early immigrants whose children and grandchildren were now legion among judges, university professors, and executives of very important corporations. Italians had also excelled in the arena of politics and were quite numerous in Congress, both in Washington and in the various state capitals. He mentioned John Pastore from Rhode Island, the top authority on nuclear control, and referred to two mayors of New York, Fiorello La Guardia and Vincent Impellitteri. Then, almost out of revenge for what I had said on the issue of the ambassador to the Holy See, he remarked that the offspring of Italians were only absent among the Catholic hierarchy (I corrected him by injecting the name of Msgr. Pernicone, the auxiliary bishop of New York, but he was right).

He was very grateful to the Italians of America for their practically unanimous electoral support, clergy included. That offered me an opportunity to plead the cause of someone (I didn't mention any names) of Italian descent for a seat on the Supreme Court. However, the Italian Americans had to wait for Reagan's second term of office to make that heartily desired quantum leap, and Antonin Scalia is now performing his lofty task with consummate skill.

Kennedy was moderately optimistic about the overall international political picture, but it was evident that the Cuban issue had left behind much more than superficial traces.

On the topical subject of the Multinational Nuclear Force (MNF) so warmly supported by the NATO Council at its meeting on January 24, he didn't strike me as being overly enthusiastic even though he did endorse the underlying reasoning behind it. Perhaps de Gaulle's opposition and Macmillan's limited inclination were signals for him of the remote possibilities of getting the plan off the ground. However, I do know he spoke about it during talks at the Quirinale Palace, asking for study to continue on the dossier and offering the services of Admiral Ricketts for technical counsel as necessary.

Two missions had already visited Rome in March to discuss the MNF to be set up within NATO, and they were headed by Ambassadors Livingstone Merchant and Thomas Finletter. According to the American design of this "revolutionary innovation," the Force was supposed to consist of twenty-five surface vessels (mixed crews with no more than 40 percent from the same country), each one armed with eight Polaris missiles and at least 80 percent of them always at sea. These ships were to be operated according to decisions made by the majority of the participating nations, while their actual use had to be decided by unanimity.

The expected expenditure (one-third borne by the United States) was $500–$600 million over eight to ten years, plus a reimbursement of $600 million to the United States to cover capital already invested in R&D.

Fanfani refrained from giving even a preliminary response, while acknowledging due consideration for the initiative and recalling that Minister of Foreign Affairs Piccioni had spoken about it before the Senate.

I asked if the ships could be nuclear-powered, but Admiral Lee excluded the possibility, somewhat hastily, for reasons of costs and complicated systems. I also asked, and this time it wasn't ruled out, if it was possible to review the MacMahon law which practically cut us out of the whole sector of propulsion.

President Kennedy told us in quite resolute terms that he considered the close Euro-American defense solidarity to be permanent. In his reply to the speech delivered by Admiral James Russell in Naples, he repeated that the commitment to respond with all necessary force to an attack against the Allies ("which was an attack against everyone") "is just as solid and firm today as it was the day it was undertaken."

On the same occasion he spoke about the European Economic Community in these terms: "The European Common Market was not conceived by its founders and encouraged by the United States in order to raise walls against the other Western countries or to build other walls against the ferment and the hopes of the developing countries." And he added: "The nations which are united in freedom are able to strengthen their economies unlike those which are oppressed by tyrannies. We work better than the party dictatorships of the East."

Both in Rome and Naples Kennedy received an enthusiastic welcome. Some reporters highlighted the difference between the two cities, but, except for the character differences between the populations, it is practically old hat for the city of Rome to receive the visits of presidents and emperors. Certainly, the Neapolitans were overwhelming, as they formed two solid walls all along the one-hour itinerary between the NATO Command Base and the Capodichino airport.

During meticulous and almost petulant meetings in the months prior to Kennedy's visit to Rome, the American planning team, in their requests for security measures, reached the point of asking for Piazza Venezia to be emptied completely when the president went up the steps to the Tomb of the Unknown Soldier. And this is when a rather amusing episode took place. A small crowd managed to gather near St. Mark's Church, on the outskirts of the *piazza,* and gave the president a rousing round of applause. Kennedy was very pleased and, shedding any pretense of protocol, he walked over to shake people's hands and thank them. His bodyguards looked terrified and, without thinking twice, started pushing and shoving in an attempt to shield the president. One of our policemen pulled a questionable yet most effective prank by lifting the revolver off one of those bustling and totally unaware bodyguards; the man got his gun back that evening with the kindest regards of his Italian colleagues.

Maybe because of this unplanned event, someone invented the story that the Italian police had mistreated a member of President Kennedy's party. In November, however, when I heard about the assassination, I immediately recalled what had happened that day in Rome, and pondered the futility of so much operational fuss over security and the confusion wrought by a minor change in original plans.

Upon his return to the United States, Kennedy wrote to Segni not only to extend the customary words of thanks but also to inform him that he was taking a very close look at Khrushchev's major speech in Berlin on an agreement covering nuclear experiments. The Allies were faced with a choice of whether or not to continue discarding the hypothesis of a nonaggression pact between NATO and the Warsaw Pact. Recalling that the Italian positions were always close to the American ones and were also in favor of banning experiments, Kennedy asked us for a rapid comment before Ambassador Averell Harriman went to Moscow to discuss the matter.

News of the tragic assassination attempt against John F. Kennedy reached me at the Defense Ministry along with a sliver of hope for his survival, which was quickly doused by the official announcement of his death. So goes the glory of the world. I immediately informed the American cardinals who were in Rome for the Vatican Council. Cardinal Cushing departed immediately, while the others accepted the invitation to gather in the Basilica of St. John Lateran for a solemn memorial service presided over by Cardinal Spellman.

9 | *Johnson the Dancer*

Kennedy's death had a very profound effect on Ambassador Reinhardt, not least because, like any good American, he was well aware of the turmoil generated by the fact that for the fifth time a president of the United States had been assassinated. Reinhardt's arrival in Rome hadn't been a simple affair. At the beginning of 1961, as always happens, more or less well-founded rumors were circulating on Zellerbach's successor. The candidate with the best chances seemed to be a former member of Congress with the high-sounding name of Franklin Delano Roosevelt, who would certainly have been most welcome to Italian democrats and certain economic circles since he held the concession for the sale of FIAT cars in ten states. Brosio from Washington was quite satisfied, but the person in question declined Kennedy's offer, since he preferred the prospects of a career in domestic politics (which he never actually achieved). Then people started talking about a rich Texas businessman, Stanley Marcus, who was a friend of Vice President Johnson and highly regarded for his track record on importing Italian goods into that part of the States. However, the person tapped for the position was the ambassador to Cairo, Frederick Reinhardt, despite having been in Egypt for just a year.

At the Ministry of Foreign Affairs they were quite pleased we were being sent a career diplomat since they recalled the excellent work done by Clement Dunn, who had been so considerate and constructive during very difficult times from 1947 to 1952. This is not to say there are no eminently reputable people among the envoys who have not climbed the

State Department ladder, but at times they are hampered by the weight of their personal quirks and do not always get along with the embassy staff.

Reinhardt, born fifty years earlier in Berkeley, California, was preceded by his renown as a well-educated and prudent man. He was conversant in many languages and had received part of his education in schools abroad, including the Cesare Alfieri Institute in Florence. Prior to Cairo he had been ambassador in Vietnam.

Quite evident from the very first steps he took in Rome was his great ability in establishing contacts, and he was well assisted in this by Mrs. Reinhardt. And, except when Washington assigned him somewhat overly active roles in Italian politics (here perhaps career diplomats are subject to a greater degree of obedience), for seven years he generated nothing but good feelings around Villa Taverna and Palazzo Margherita (the U.S. Embassy). And seven years are quite a few years for proper . . . survival in the capital of Italy. Only Max Rabb would have a longer tour of duty.

Five years earlier, when he hadn't even finished his first two years, Reinhardt was rumored to be leaving, since he wanted to take advantage of an American statute on earlier retirement from the administration. In fact, Kennedy was being courted heavily by one of his major supporters, the former governor of Ohio, Mike Disalle, who descended from an Abruzzese family from Vasto which had emigrated at the turn of the century. However, these entreaties did not achieve the expected results and there was no changing of the guard.

Mr. Reinhardt was convinced, just like Dunn, that Italy did not end with Rome, and he visited many cities, cultivating as well his interests in the art and culture of the early duchies. The Rome embassy was engulfed in a growing wave of amiability and, if we exclude the compulsory activism to "recoup" the Socialists, even though it meant sacrificing the Liberals, everyone spoke highly of the man in charge at Palazzo Margherita. His two immediate successors, Gardner Ackley and Graham Martin (especially the latter) were to give people cause to regret his absence.

Reinhardt was very well plugged into the Pentagon and was an excellent channel to McNamara. His mission in Rome came to an end more or less at the same time I left the Ministry of Defense.

The news of my substitution as minister of defense reached me when I was at a meeting on nuclear planning with McNamara, in 1966. Aldo

Moro informed me by telegram that he had had to surrender the minister's portfolio to a Social Democrat. After seven years it certainly wasn't a clamorous decision. Moreover, as an expert in crisis management I fully realized that certain changes had to take place immediately. In addition, my successor Roberto Tremelloni was a sure guarantee of continuity (exactly as I had been when I took over from him at the Finance Ministry in 1955; just an historical curiosity).

The only apprehension concerned stable relations between the people recently appointed to top commands in the army. Had I known I was leaving, I would have left in office the chief of staff of defense, the elderly General Aldo Rossi, an officer and a gentleman with a timely sense of humor. He was replaced by General Giuseppe Aloia, the former chief of staff of the army. The choice of his successor, however, was a most laborious process. One aspirant to the position was General Giovanni De Lorenzo, excellent commanding general of the Carabinieri and of the intelligence services before that. I had gone to President Saragat to propose the appointment of General Vedovato but he did not concur, since he considered it inappropriate for the brother of a member of parliament to be head of the army. The reasoning was rather shaky, especially because he did get the job later on. However, since he wasn't the only possible candidate, I suggested a second name in the person of General Carlo Ciglieri, who had become famous over the prompt way his division had coped with the consequences of the Vajont tragedy, when thousands of people died due to the collapse of a storm-weakened dam. Not even Ciglieri met with the approval of Saragat who was evidently receiving countersuggestions from his aides. But for whose benefit? In both cases he had practically warned me not to submit De Lorenzo's name to him. To my great surprise he summoned me a few days later and told me the ideal chief of staff was precisely De Lorenzo, and went on to stress his engineering background (actually he was a naval engineer). Since De Lorenzo was highly regarded by Moro and I only had objective grounds for dissent, considering it would be better for him to stay at the head of the Carabinieri, I refrained from any opposition. Unfortunately it was a mistake, because relations between Aloia and De Lorenzo turned out to be miserable and led to a series of inquiries, disputes, and diatribes which left poor Tremelloni with his hands full and, even worse, sowed discord and confusion among the armed forces.

I returned to Rome and Moro asked me to remain in the cabinet, offering me the ministry of industry or education. I opted for the economic ministry since I felt no vocation for the complexities of the world of schooling. Here I encountered anew an issue I had worked on with such fervor while minister of defense: the project for a nuclear-powered ship. The original idea was for a submarine, but then it became clear that the use of the atom for civilian purposes was more readily acceptable and more feasible. Therefore, an agreement was signed by the two ministries and I was now managing that agreement on the other side.

Two rocks, or even better a rock and a boulder, tripped up the whole initiative. On one hand there were the exhausting negotiations with the Americans to obtain the necessary amount of uranium. In terms of mere courtesy there was no end to their readiness to comply and at every high-level meeting they always reiterated their *almost* definitive assurances. Somewhat upset over this hemming and hawing, I took the bull by the horns and went to speak with the influential senator from Rhode Island, John Pastore, who, for a long time and with absolute command, had been supervising United States nuclear matters. He finally gave me a frank reply. If I wanted a real answer and not just diplomatic-speak, it was "forget it buddy." At this point it was easy to switch to the alternative solution offered to us by the French government (our friendship with Pierre Messmer was very solid and, besides that, Paris did not suffer the nuclear jealousy of the other side of the Atlantic). However, the long interval of time proved fatal because, in the meantime, the dismaying and unfair Ippolito case (in which the head of the Italian Nuclear Authority was found guilty, perhaps unjustly, of embezzlement) had exploded and almost all the National Committee's programs went into hibernation. This hitch, together with the legitimate desire not to burden the public budget and the less praiseworthy conviction of some people who felt the Americans would have developed this form of propulsion if it were useful for the merchant marine, while they were lukewarm on the applications already developed, produced a second-class funeral with very few expressions of condolences. When the psychosis over the shortage and high price of oil spread, it would have been easy to point a finger at the project's courteous saboteurs. But what was the use of that? Unfortunately, it was necessary to adopt costly measures to offset the additional costs caused by the blocking of the Suez Canal when Italy

was aligned with the United States against a certain anti-Egyptian adven-
turism on the part of some European countries.

Kennedy was succeeded by Lyndon Johnson who, according to the
firsthand memoirs of Arthur Schlesinger, had been offered the position
of vice president on the slate only to curry favor with voters and out of
diplomacy, but had actually accepted the offer. The youthful Kennedy
clan couldn't bear his "old age," and yet the true age of every man is
unknown since it should refer to the years left to live. And unfortunately,
illness and old age are not the only causes of death.

During his visit to Italy in September 1962 as "the number two man,"
I had been surprised by his Texan exuberance. He listened absentmindedly to the toast at the official luncheon in Villa Madama (a site of
frequent ceremonial events), and mechanically read through the response
notes prepared for him by someone else. He made a valiant attempt to
dispel the boredom of protocol by trying to dance, instead of standing
there pretending he was interested in being introduced to people he
would never see again in his life; as a symbolic way of starting the dance,
he lifted the Rome mayor's young wife, Linda Della Porta, right up off
the floor. No way. Ironclad are the rules of protocol rituals. For more
than an hour, while coffee and liqueurs were served, Johnson had to put
up with the procession of guests.

General Vernon Walters had informed him I was about to leave for
the United States on a visit to military bases and he seemed very interested by the mention of San Antonio and my planned itinerary. He
advised me to join a club if I wanted to drink anything with alcohol in
it. When he said it I really didn't grasp what he meant, but the light
dawned when I arrived in that pleasant Texas city with its one hundred
Venetian-type canals. Down there alcohol can only be sold and served in
clubs, and so every bar has its own roster of members, and anyone can
join by just paying the membership fee of a few dollars and nothing else.
They told me the city had more than one thousand of these "clubs."

What really heightened my stature in Johnson's eyes was my reference
to the Space Research Center in Houston of which he was so very proud.
He even wrote me a letter of thanks for my fleeting positive appraisal
and renewed his best wishes for my trip to his country.

I have no distinct personal memories of Johnson's four-year term of office after his interim presidency, both periods unmarked by any out-standing political achievements, since during those years I devoted my attention mostly to activities in Parliament, and hence had fewer occa-sions for official relations abroad.

However, I was able to go and admire the United States from an entirely different viewpoint.

Johnson's visit toward the end of 1967 apparently did not meet with the president's complete satisfaction, and perhaps this was also due to rather inopportune comparisons with the welcome received by Kennedy four years earlier. As a matter of fact, a request was advanced for the acceptance, possibly by the end of the day, of a new ambassador, Dr. Gardner Ackley, who was the coordinator of the economic advisers to the White House. Why the rush? Rumor had it that Johnson had been forced to adopt measures not shared by Ackley who had therefore resigned. The new position in Rome would have avoided polemical interpretations and possible unfavorable comments about the man him-self.

During Ackley's twenty months in Rome I was kept busy at the Chamber of Deputies and had no particular occasion to meet with him.

10 | *Vacation in the U.S.A.*

Relations with America during the years of my interval in government service (1968–72) did not rotate around official commitments but were nonetheless marked by moments of no lesser interest.

The French statesman Antoine Pinay invited me to join a small and entirely informal group of Europeans and Americans set up to discuss current world affairs. We used to meet once or twice a year, ordinarily in Washington at the home of Nelson Rockefeller, but at times also in Europe (I recall one session in Bavaria as the guests of Franz Josef Strauss). Some of the participants varied according to the subject for discussion (highly regarded was Henry Kissinger), while the others, according to their respective schedules, were always the same.

A scholarly Dominican, Fr. Dubois, who was on the Holy See's Permanent Mission to the United Nations, gave a religious touch to the sessions by celebrating Mass for those who wished to attend and offering brief meditations for all. Another participant from Italy was Pinay's good friend, the engineer Carlo Pesenti. Assiduous among the Americans was David Rockefeller. With his travels and personal contacts at the highest possible level in almost all nations he was always a source of the latest inside information.

Pinay also traveled extensively and was always up-to-date on everything. What I most admired in him were his pragmatic outlook and refusal to espouse the pessimism which was quite widespread at that time and not without a certain justification. His prestige at home and abroad was not linked so much to his length of service in government (minister of finance and for a long time prime minister) as it was to the successful campaign to strengthen the French currency and to the fact he was consulted during difficult economic situations and his advice was much appreciated. His many commitments did not prevent him from holding the office of mayor in his small hometown of Saint Chamond until not long ago; this conforms to a traditional French practice for important politicians.

Over the last few years Pinay has been active but has had to heed the precautionary measures dictated by age. Other friends of the group have departed from this world and so those annual appointments no longer take place. We occasionally meet, one on one, when someone happens to come through Italy or when I visit their respective nations.

In a certain sense the heir of that group formula is the Inter Action Council, a club of former prime ministers founded by Takeo Fukuda from Japan and Helmut Schmidt. In addition to the in-depth discussion work, it also prepares an annual report on the eve of the Summit Meeting of the Seven Industrialized Countries. I have joined their initiative but have so far been able to attend only a meeting on religious liberty held in Rome.

Every time our paths crossed, Cardinal Spellman used to tell me I had to give my children a chance to visit America and offered me his hospitality. I thought it would be better to wait until they were old enough to make the most out of the experience, and his immediate rebuttal had to do with his not being eternal and the hope that the Lord would grant him a lot more time to acquire the minimum worth necessary to make it into paradise.

One day during a get-together in Rome some friends and I gave him a field altar as a way of highlighting the work he did as military ordinary with such sacrifice and exemplary intensity. He told me then that he might not make it in time to welcome my family in person but that we had to make the trip anyway. Only later on did I understand the meaning of those words along with his thanks for never having asked him for anything, unlike so many other people. I replied jokingly that it wasn't true because I had once asked him to help a cause founded in the memory of a common departed friend, Fr. Giuseppe Canovai.

Cardinal Spellman passed away a short time later and I deeply regretted not being able to be at his solemn funeral attended by the president of the United States. On the same day, however, I had an important ministerial meeting in Brussels and was duty bound to attend it. I was saddened by the absence of anyone from Rome at the funeral. Yet, in mournful circumstances like that, Cardinal Spellman was always present; even at the cost of embarking upon a marathon adventure as in the case of the funeral of Cardinal Borgongini Duca, when he landed in Rome at eight in the morning and departed at noon.

As a way of compensating for my absence at the farewell in New York, in his memory I published a book with the text of St. Paul's First Letter to the Romans and brief commentaries by ten international personalities. The two editions, in English and Italian, were prepared with admirable skill in Verona by Giovanni Mardesteig with the further embellishment of an original drawing by Renato Guttuso.

In the meantime, the engineer Galeazzi had to come to deliver me an envelope given to him for me by the cardinal. It contained thirty thousand dollars "for the delayed trip."

I organized the vacation trip with Livia and our four children during the summer of 1971 and respected in full the advice of my friend the archbishop: New York, but not only the city, and short visits to New Jersey, Washington, and the Pacific Coast. To make it up to the children for not enjoying a seaside holiday, I decided to start off with the Bahamas. For me, as well, it was a unique occasion to travel as a tourist and visit America at my leisure, instead of just squeezing things into the rare free moments of an official journey. Very helpful indeed were the enterprising Della Grattan and her sisters.

We reached New York on August 2, had lunch at a Greek restaurant, and went on to Nassau for a week, and from there headed for California.

In Los Angeles we stayed at the Century Plaza and were immediately somewhat astonished by the numerous options offered to us on how to spend our stay in the best way. We decided on a rather intensive program, beginning with a visit to Universal Studios where the magic of Hollywood spun its web on everyone. I ran into Anthony Quinn, an old acquaintance from Cinecittà, and was overjoyed to spend a few hours in the company of the great scenographer Novarese, the winner of numerous Oscars and then involved in important research on the history of America for the new Disneyland in Florida. That marked the beginning of a friendship which helped me to discover the greatness of that man's inner fiber in a progressive way, up to the moment when he wrote a letter telling me he had an inoperable heart disease ("It's like having a bomb in my chest which could explode at any time and I don't know when"). And unfortunately it exploded. I went with Novarese to see the theater of the celebrated Academy Awards and then visited the bizarre and cheerful Forest Lawn Cemetery. There, Novarese spoke with feeling about his friends who had recently passed away: Spencer Tracy, Vivien Leigh, Judy Holliday, Ed Begley, and Paul Muni. Only the last one had reached seventy years of age, he observed with a tone of sadness in his voice, and Judy was only forty-three.

This cemetery is based on the rather unique philosophy of offering a sense of joyfulness to "residents," relatives, and visitors. On the grounds you can see the most famous works of art in the world, massive amounts of flowers, and even tombs which open automatically at set times so the coffins can get some fresh air. Not by chance, festive weddings are celebrated almost every day in one of the chapels on the hill.

The guide thoughtfully informed us that there were still a few lots available, and most of them were on the sunny side of the cemetery; we weren't supposed to miss such an opportunity. We missed it most willingly and left for Disneyland, a real paradise and not only for children.

Rich Californians, prompted by tax-cut legislation as well, are extraordinary in the way they purchase works of art and donate them to museums. Some even give an entire museum to the community. In the city of San Marino we were very pleased to admire the site created by Mr. Henry E. Huntington (1850–1927) with manicured gardens, an impressive library with important medieval manuscripts, and a well-endowed art gallery.

From there we went to Pasadena where we spent a few hours at NASA; to the children's great joy and interest, they were about to launch a satellite which in five years, if I'm not mistaken, was supposed to tour the stars and return with a vast store of precious information. The technicians talked about it as if it were a matter of ordinary administration, and maybe it was for them. On our way back to the hotel we stopped at Long Beach to visit that glorious ocean liner, the *Queen Mary*. Four years earlier it had made its one hundredth ocean crossing and was tied up permanently for use as a museum and amusement park. If you ever happen to see a picture of me dressed up as a Confederate soldier, it was just part of the fun and games on that delightful afternoon.

But the day was by no means over. In the large open-air Los Angeles Arena people dine and listen to outstanding symphony concerts, as they sit in the boxes furnished according to personal taste. Our host was Vittorio Sanguineti from ICE (the Italian Foreign Trade Institute) and he did not fail to point out some of our neighbors with very distinguished names. Their picnic was served by white-gloved waiters on tables set with the best china and heavy silver candlesticks.

The next day, attracted by the large Mormon temple dominating one of the Los Angeles hills with the golden statue of an angel glittering in such a suggestive way, I went up the hill all by myself to learn something about this Church of the Latter Day Saints. I met a very kind pastor, Dr. Valentine, who for an hour told me about the life of Joseph Smith, the first president of their church in 1835, and explained the human side of their understanding of existence: from birth to education, love to marriage, labor and service, the unity of the family, adversity, the growth of children, and death which is followed by the hope of an eternal happiness with the final recomposition of the body and the soul.

I told Dr. Valentine I would be glad to see him if he came to Rome. He took my invitation quite literally and, with his wife, called on me the following month. He returned again last year. He is now retired and, like many Americans, he delights in occasional trips paid for by the small monthly installments he made throughout the decades of his working life.

So far I have said nothing about the port of Los Angeles which is the most important one on the West Coast. It was discovered by Juan Rodríquez Cabrillo in the sixteenth century, and completely rebuilt in 1899 at a cost of 200 billion dollars. The port facilities could handle eighty-five ships and at that time there were another one hundred anchored off shore and motionless. The stevedores had been on strike for forty days(!) and not a single hold had been touched. The strike had been unbelievably long, with grueling negotiations, but up to the day before without a single incident. The port authorities explained that strikes can be very tough at times, but once an agreement has been signed there is no further danger of work interruption for a few years.

Unfortunately an unexpected and disturbing event had taken place. One day earlier, President Nixon had announced the immediate application of a 10 percent surtax on all imports. The shipping companies were up in arms because they maintained that ships already docked or anchored offshore shouldn't have to pay the high federal levy which, in that case, would be retroactive. Washington had immediately issued a negative response to their request and was looking for a way to circulate the decision without making the situation explode. I shortened my visit in order to avoid being involved in something unpleasant.

I had listened to Nixon's announcement on TV: "I intend to protect the dollar, improve our balance of payments and increase jobs in the U.S.A. The measure is a temporary one and is intended to rebalance the disproportions created by unjust exchange rates. When this unjust treatment ends, the surtax on imports will also be lifted."

I was at the home of a Stanford University economics professor and his comments were by no means positive, and quite contrary to the postulates of protectionism. He estimated that one-third of European imports would have been blocked by the measure. The fact of the matter is that something new in the history of world trade came to life during those days in mid-August. Frenzied discussions took place between countries and their respective groupings around the globe.

When interviewed by the *New York Times,* I spoke out in favor of easing the surtax and made no mystery of being opposed to the quotas on the imports of textiles and footwear. I sidestepped the issue of the lira exchange rate, both because of the delicate nature of the matter and because I harbored hopes for a concerted move on the part of Europe. However, to make sure my silence would not be misinterpreted, I said I did not expect oscillations greater than those of the yen.

In Italy the Communists launched tough attacks against the "U.S. blackmail." Criticisms within GATT were just as harsh and, in addition, the president's decisions were proclaimed to be ineffective for the American economy.

In any case, returning to my California vacation, I will always remember the forest with the immense sequoias and the visit to the city of Bakersfield where I met Ben Sacco, a man from Basilicata who had emigrated right after the war and had achieved a top economic and social position. In San Francisco the children experienced seventh heaven over a fishing trip, a raid along famous Lombard Street, a visit to the port where the dominant feature is the Joe Di Maggio restaurant, and the folklore of Chinatown.

Particularly instructive for me were my contacts at the university, especially as in Italy we were in the middle of discussions on the reform of higher education. These professors quite openly criticized the tenured status of our teachers which, in their opinion, stymied any stimulus to intellectual progress and any control over the professional dedication of faculty members. On the other hand, they made many an ironic comment about "full-time" teaching. Once they had conscientiously done their research, delivered their lectures, and assisted their students, they had to be left free to add something to their not too extravagant salaries. "Otherwise," they said with a smile, "who would pay our wives' bills?" The keenest one on this subject was an economist whose name had been proposed for a Nobel Prize. He had used his sabbatical year to travel around Europe selling equipment for bowling alleys and was pleased about the money he had made.

The length of the trip from San Francisco to New York helps to recall that America is a vast continent. We arrived late in the evening and immediately went to the top of the Empire State Building where the sweeping panorama is breathtaking, even for someone who has already been there.

The next morning, after saying a prayer at Cardinal Spellman's tomb in St. Patrick's Cathedral, we visited the United Nations. Through the good offices of Ambassador Vinci, I received a coveted invitation from his colleague George Bush to return that same afternoon and, at the side of the Secretary-General U Thant, attend the ceremony in honor of the astronauts who had returned from their trip to the moon. It was a truly fortunate coincidence and a very kind gesture on the part of George Bush.

When you travel with the family and want to follow a single itinerary it is necessary to shape plans in order to satisfy all members of the family equally. As a result, Livia and out daughters enjoyed the visits to Saks, Bonwit Teller, Bloomingdales, and Macy's. The youngsters were excited over the musicals, and I was able to delight in the flat races at Belmont Park and the trotters at Roosevelt Raceway.

On the printed program at Roosevelt Raceway we found the words "Saluto all'Italia" at the top of the fourth race, a personal touch provided by one of the top men in the world of New York horse racing and an alumnus of the Catholic University of Milan (something Fr. Gemelli would never have imagined).

The classical sights in New York and the surroundings, including the ferry ride toward the Verrazano Bridge, the George Washington Bridge, and the Statue of Liberty (guests of our friends, the Forbeses) captivated everyone, and the same applied to the attentive visits to the Metropolitan Museum, the Guggenheim, and the Museum of Modern Art. Then there were the logistical arrangements so well handled by the Grattan sisters: from the Steak Joint in Greenwich Village to Quo Vadis and a Chinese restaurant run by a general from Formosa who had been military attaché in Rome; from the Grotte di Bacco and the Iperbole, two adjacent places owned by a recent immigrant who had been a member of a Christian Democratic youth group in Rome, to "21" where they show you the hidden cellars dating back to the years of prohibition. No less entertaining and pleasingly swift were the meals eaten in the self-service cafeterias.

We also took a trip to Niagara Falls. Informed in advance of our arrival by my friend John Marchi, a senator from the State of New York (still in office), our hosts and guides were the mayor of Buffalo and the temporary president of the Senate, Earl W. Bridges.

Upon our return to New York and along Fifth Avenue we ran into a crowded protest march. According to the marchers, two days earlier the police had brutally attacked a protest march of gays in Hauppauge, Long Island. Delegations of feminists had joined the march, but I don't know if it was out of solidarity or to share the organizational expenses. They were calling for peace and equality. When asked for a comment, I enquired about the absence of black girls and received a scowl in reply. Overall, the march, taking place amidst so much indifference and the scornful chuckles of some passers-by, was rather disconcerting.

Quite different in nature was the noisy hustle and bustle on the floor of the New York Stock Exchange. I have never seen the Italian stock markets and can draw no comparisons, but over there the daily movement of stocks and bonds is impressive to say the least. They also perform a well-planned ceremony for guests, and it includes the sudden appearance of personal greetings on the electronic display of stock listings and the festive launching of notes (unnegotiable for the occasion) toward the gallery from where you watch the frenzied trading.

They told me few Italian companies were listed, since they found it difficult to live with the openness to public scrutiny which is the *sine qua non* condition guaranteed by the Securities and Exchange Commission.

My wife and children, however, did go to Washington, even if only for a few hours. I wanted to savor the completely apolitical nature of the trip and also wished to dedicate a bit of time to Cardinal Spellman's friends and his successor. The visit to Capitol Hill, the White House, the Smithsonian Institution, and the National Gallery were commented upon as the stereotype of a capital city so different from the rest of the country. Capitals, however, are always at least a little bit different.

We boarded the plane for Rome full of affectionate gratitude for the memory of our friend the cardinal and overjoyed with this exceptional month of vacation.

11 | *Nixon's Turn*

Nineteen hundred seventy-two was a very important year for me. Since the center-left coalition governments (Moro-Rumor-Colombo) had entered a momentary period of irreversible crisis at the beginning of that year, the head of state had appointed me—I was then the chairman of the Christian Democratic caucus at the Chamber of Deputies—to form a cabinet in preparation for early elections which everyone, more or less peacefully, deemed indispensable. Two years earlier Leone's predecessor, Giuseppe Saragat, had asked me to resolve the crisis, but I had been blocked precisely by Mario Tanassi, the secretary of the Social Democrats, who looked on my good working relationship with the Socialist leader at Montecitorio, Luigi Bertoldi, as a propensity toward the Socialists on my part. I had returned to the ranks of Parliament, continuing my work in an office of great political interest.

As always, the elections did not bring about any major changes and I was duty-bound to try and bring the Liberals onto the four-party platform which had floundered. But the Socialists (who talked about a special relationship!) refused to reach a compromise with the Liberals for a preliminary examination of their respective positions. It became essential to bring the willing parties together, while waiting for less inflammatory times to come along. The government was called "Andreotti-Malagodi" and, with its very slim majority in Parliament, was the daily target of all kinds of plots launched by the hyperactive parliamentary snipers. Unfortunately, the left-wing Christian Democrats wanted to stay out of the cabinet and Moro himself said he was sorry he had to comply with their wishes, even though it meant I had regretfully to leave the Ministry of Foreign Affairs, which I entrusted to Giuseppe Medici, a former Liberal converted to the Christian Democrats by Dossetti.

Even though I had to cope day-in and day-out with the opposition forces and the "infidels," I devoted time and attention, together with Moro, to the Soviet idea planned with the Americans and Canadians of a policy of cooperation and common security for all of Europe. The world of official diplomacy had given very little weight to this proposal, which was considered little more than an expedient for consolidating the borders established during the postwar period. However, it could represent a real turning point, and I shared Aldo's hopes in that sense. That was why I accepted a visit to Moscow in the fall (much to the distaste of the opposition and the snipers), while declining an analogous invitation to Washington. I first wanted to ascertain the real possibilities of realizing what would come to be known as the Helsinki Accords. I therefore intended to go to the States the next year if there were substantive issues for discussion, including ensuring concurrence between the grand plan for cooperation and security in Europe and Nixon's program for "1973, the Year of Europe."

I readily admit that I wanted to wait and see if the government would hold up under the constant broadsides, since I deemed it most imprudent for a president of the Council of Ministers to be "on parade" at the White House while he was about to be shot down. We had already experienced two analogous cases (Scelba and Fanfani), and I didn't want to follow in those footsteps. Last of all, I didn't think it wise to expose myself to possible one-sided manipulations of my visit just before presidential elections in America.

Early in 1973, the Americans renewed the invitation and, by not accepting it, we ran the risk of endorsing inaccurate political interpretations; all the more so since they left the date up to us. In a report to Minister Medici, Ambassador Ortona advised that the president, triumphantly reelected (he took all states except Massachusetts), wanted to discuss directly "what may be considered in the near future Italy's validity as an important element in an alliance to which the American administration, despite the new emphases in its foreign policy, considers itself totally bound as a top priority."

In addition, Nixon let me know through a friend of the "Pinay Meetings" that after Washington it would be most useful if I made a brief working trip to Tokyo, as a way of beginning to bridge the gap in European-Japanese relations which caused him some concern.

Accompanied by Rinaldo Ossola, then the director general of the Bank of Italy, Medici and I went to the White House on April 17 after a night in Williamsburg, Virginia to catch up on jet lag. We received the protocol welcome with anthems, flags, speeches, greetings, smiles, TV cameras, and photographers. Just as for ministers of defense, the liturgy for prime ministers during a two-day stay in the capital is very rigid and in this way no one feels slighted: talks with the president; meetings and lunch at the State Department (a post then held by William Rogers, but under the heavy shadow of Henry Kissinger cast from his seat on the National Security Council); the wreath to be laid at Arlington National Cemetery; the reception at Capitol Hill offered by Congressman John Sparkman (Foreign Affairs); lunch hosted by Italian-American senators and representatives; talks with Treasury Secretary Shultz, Defense Secretary Elliot Richardson, and Undersecretary Paul Volcker; and the return cocktail party at the Italian Embassy. The crowning touch was the formal dinner offered to my wife and me by President and Mrs. Nixon, with entertainment in the form of the Marine musicians and a show by Frank Sinatra who had been readmitted to high society after two years of quarantine over allegations of Mafia connections.

In addition to the scheduled appointments, I willingly accepted a visit from that most powerful trade union leader, George Meany. He went right to the heart of the matter (in his opinion) and in harsh terms censured what he considered to be our conceivably open attitude on communism, toward which his intransigence was proverbial. In particular, he had it in for Bruno Storti over his running of the free International which, once again in his opinion, had led the American Federation of Labor to withdraw. He listened quite calmly to my rejoinders on Storti's undoubted fidelity to democratic principles and on the need to help workers free themselves from communism by convincing them and not by cutting off all communication with communism. I still had vivid memories of the Dantesque sight of the Los Angeles harbor blocked by strikes and tried to point out that, basically speaking, strikes in Italy were less severe. However, he rebutted my comments with the other side's explanation, in the sense that the entire struggle concentrated around the period of contract renewal. I also referred to the change in American policy toward the major Communist countries, but he sidestepped the issue. However, he did tell me he would have liked to meet Italian trade union leaders and considered a visit by the minister of labor, Dionigi Coppo, would be most useful, not least because of the signing of an agreement on social security. While bidding one another farewell, I jokingly turned the tables on his accusation that the Italian labor confederations interfered too much in politics by observing that his influence over American politics and even over elections was much greater. He liked my frankness and we departed on very cordial terms.

Naturally, the highlight of my whole visit was my direct contact with Nixon, and especially the first round of talks lasting far beyond the scheduled two hours. Also present were Henry Kissinger and, on our side, my diplomatic adviser Andrea Cagiati. I have no idea if Nixon had his tape recorder on or not. Except for some notes I later jotted down in my diary, I rely on my memory alone. For the rest of the talks I was helped by Ambassador Egidio Ortona's book, *The Years in America 1967–1975.*

Nixon was mostly interested in the international scene because, as he said, a nation's domestic problems have a very different dimension and degree of resolution according to whether or not there is good anchorage abroad. He considered NATO a firm point, which had enabled the United States to develop an articulated policy with Eastern Europe (here I interjected Kosygin's preelectoral forecast in his favor) and said it was necessary to strengthen understanding among top Western leaders in order to continue in the same direction without any ambiguity or leap-frogging. In the case of China he had been able to overcome Congress's traditional tabus which, in this case, were more than ever before the expression of a hostile state of mind on the part of the population (I recalled the word "never" used by Mrs. Luce). Was it the result of lobbying by Chiang Kai-shek? I didn't believe it to be that decisive, and to a great extent it was past history.

The fundamental elements in a sagacious international structure were cohesiveness among members of the Alliance, a more "habitual" rela-tionship between America and Europe (he was respectful towards the EEC and in any case not alarmed), and mutual understanding with Japan.

I reassured him on Italy's attitude. The difficult situation in relations among the democratic parties, further heightened by inflation and by the arduous management of the national budget, in no way affected the major lines of foreign policy; on the contrary, even the opposition was converging in that same direction. I described the now complete and enthusiastic commitment of Communists in Strasburg and Brussels, once upon a time singled out as hotbeds of classist reactionism. Among the Socialists the fringe groups hostile to the Atlantic policy seemed to be dying out. The effort on my part had been aimed toward bringing the Socialists back into the sphere of active cooperation with the Liberals as well. No matter what our domestic developments might be—I really stressed this point—there was no question about Italian loyalty. If the preceding administration (Kennedy) hadn't pushed so much to hasten the center-left coalition in Italy, perhaps the formula wouldn't have run aground so soon.

Nixon took note with evident satisfaction of my reassuring statements, which must have been in contrast with the memos of some distant "desk jockey." I spoke to him about the need to give greater momentum to preventive American cooperation with Europeans; also to avoid situations of disinformation which had created uneasiness in the past when, at times, we had found out about things first from the Soviets and then from Washington.

The same principle applied to intelligence matters. Objective and psychological information on the planet's hot spots from someone closer to the crisis areas could benefit the United States which, having to deal with the entire world, does not always have the time to screen all the data. I referred in particular to the Middle East, where it was useless to expect spontaneous solutions or improvements in the situation due to the passage of time alone. In his contacts with the Egyptians, Medici had become convinced that an economic support program would perhaps defuse tension and foster contacts with Israel. (Had a plan already been prepared? No. These were just ideas presented as food for thought and for possible consideration with other parties.)

We discussed energy, and since Italy is dependent on foreign supplies for four-fifths of its energy requirements we stressed the need for a broader concerted energy policy. And this could constitute a point of agreement and not necessarily a collision with Arab oil. Nixon mentioned the alternative research program, and Secretary of the Treasury Shultz touched on the same issue with me the next day in saying that, if the United States had been able to invent the atomic bomb and send men to the moon, it would not give up in the face of any type of energy blackmail.

President Nixon praised De Gasperi a number of times and was most appreciative of the contribution Italian immigrants had made to the progress of America. He was also very interested in and by no means upset by my theory that we Italians should cultivate relations of equal intensity with the United States in three parallel directions: the president, Congress, and Italian Americans. Moreover, his landslide election had been stupendous, but in three years, because of their system, he would once again become Mr. Nixon. Wasn't it possible to give former presidents some sort of status? Was it logical to hold elections to the House of Representatives every two years? Nixon just smiled and replied that for them the roots of the Constitution were untouchable.

On the morning of the nineteenth, we flew to New York and began work immediately with a visit to the new secretary-general of the United Nations, Kurt Waldheim, who was then a most respected guest in America. We discussed various matters, including the issue of Cyprus on which U Thant had passed on to his successor rather special instructions.

I then went to the *New York Times* to field a barrage of "off the record" questions and afterwards visited the Council on Foreign Relations to answer more questions, this time "on the record." With the strongest Communist party after the USSR and quite evident difficulties in cooperation among the pro-democracy political parties, Italy gave rise to a certain degree of apprehension in people's minds. However, everyone recognized the unswerving Atlantic loyalty and European spirit of its governments, and these elements were most effective in correcting the impression of instability.

David Rockefeller, the president of Chase Manhattan Bank, organized a luncheon on the sixtieth floor of their corporate headquarters building, which provided us with an opportunity to have an exchange of information and opinions with leaders from the worlds of finance and business. David made me promise I wouldn't miss the Pinay appointment in December at his brother's home.

That evening 1,200 guests gathered at the Waldorf Astoria for the ritual banquet. Speeches were delivered by the organizers, Fortune Pope and Howard Molinari, and also by Thomas De Rosa, Mayor John Lindsay, Governor Nelson Rockefeller, John Volpe, and the ambassador to the United Nations John Scali (another American of Italian origin). The whole atmosphere was warm and friendly.

Nixon was very grateful to me for having accepted his advice to travel to Tokyo (he was quite worried over the shakiness of the United States-Europe-Japan triangle) and he invited me to use his airplane for the flight to Hawaii, a ten-hour trip with a fueling stop at the California base of El Toro Marine. Everyone in the Kahala Hilton of Honolulu seemed very excited and yet the red carpet had been laid not for us, but for Liza Minnelli who arrived at the same time. However, we were treated to the welcome dances and many garlands of flowers, including the ones sent by Clare Luce.

To my greatest surprise, I learned that the man who had been mayor of the capital city of Hawaii for the last five years, Frank Fasi, was of Italian origin. He had recently been reelected, but had the governor and all the state lawmakers fiercely against him. Out of spite they had all deserted the inaugural ceremony for his second term of office. He was a very strong-willed man, who had lived through the years of the Depression in Connecticut working in the fields and running errands in an ice factory. He moved to Hawaii after seeing action in the war as a marine and had set up a medium-sized construction company. I was very pleased to make his acquaintance.

The next morning, we went for a short cruise on a fleet cutter and made a chilling stop at Pearl Harbor where the sunken ships are a constant reminder of one of the most tragic moments of modern history.

After Easter Sunday Mass at a church in Honolulu, we boarded a JAL flight for Tokyo. Thus ended a visit to the United States full of food for further thought and consideration. But was I going to have the time?

I had been pleased to hear Nixon praise me in public ("After having spoken with him, I can say he is continuing the work of De Gasperi; a strong man like the ones the country, the people, and the free world need"), but I knew very well that such praise meant little or nothing at home in the struggle among parties and even within the Christian Democratic party. On the next day the socialist newspaper *L'Avanti* ran the following headline across four columns in its coverage of my trip: "Andreotti's Arrogance in the Quest for Investiture by Nixon."

12 | *Costantino Brumidi*

During my stay in the United States for talks with President Nixon, neither he nor anyone else spoke to me about the "case" that had been churning up a lot of public controversy for ten months. On Capitol Hill we also met with Senator Sam Ervin, who chaired the congressional enquiry into the presidential reelection campaign (the Watergate Commission), but he referred in no way to his delicate task. On the other hand, Nixon seemed quite sure about his future and during those days had no inkling of the intensity of the brewing storm. He most likely thought he would not be personally involved in the excessive zeal of those Republican militants who had gone all the way to illegal spying on the Democratic party offices and who had been sentenced to jail by Judge John Sirica in March. In fact, the accusation which brought him down as president concerned not what the "plumbers" did but his reiterated official defense of the act and his obstinate refusal to hand over to the investigators some tapes of telephone conversations with his secretary, Haldeman. In the end, however, he had to give them up following a unanimous court order by the Supreme Court. In the meantime, his prestige had suffered a blow delivered by Vice President Spiro Agnew, forced to resign over charges of tax evasion. He was replaced by Gerald Ford, a highly regarded member of Congress.

Congress initiated impeachment procedures against Nixon and everything was placed in the able hands of the influential chairman of the Legal Affairs Committee of the House, my old friend Peter Rodino. Only one other time (against President Andrew Johnson) had there been recourse to such a clamorous "iter" to seek the removal of a president. Completely off the beaten track, however, are all those who read nationality elements (the Italian origin of Rodino and Judge Sirica) into the episode, and equally evident was the fact that Vice President Spiro Agnew's position in the Greek community was of no relevance whatsoever to his problems with the IRS. However, I do feel it pertinent at this point to mention what Cardinal Spellman had confided to me in 1962, when Nixon lost the governor's race in California two years after his narrow defeat by Kennedy in the presidential election (a difference of 113,000 votes out of 69 million voters).

In Spellman's opinion, Nixon had a twofold original sin: his middle-class family background, and his ability to mobilize a personal following without any strong linkage with the party structure. In addition, he added, he didn't have any "important backers." He didn't tell me who they were, but his words came to mind later on, when I happened to come across a fancy booklet with pictures and captions for each president of the United States, published by an important American Masonic organization after the Watergate affair. According to the booklet, almost all the American presidents had been Masons and Nixon was one of the few exceptions.

On 8 August 1974, Nixon announced his resignation and on the next day Gerald Ford took the oath of office as president. Because of his personal prestige no one ascribed any importance to the fact that neither he nor the vice president had been elected by the people.

Ford's first official act was to grant Nixon a presidential pardon, thereby eliminating any risk of having to appear in court to share the destiny of his aides.

The following summer, I went to Mexico to visit my daughter and passed through California on my return trip. I met Vernon Walters who was there to deliver a speech to a conference of veterans and had visited Nixon in his San Clemente home. I too wanted to go by and say hello, because I just can't stand people who pay homage to the powerful when they are in office and then, when they fall into disgrace, ignore and often despise them.

I was surprised by Nixon's isolation with no visible security screen. He wasn't in very good health and apologized for having to keep one leg in an upright position because of phlebitis. I wouldn't say he was in a good mood, but I was struck by his apparent peace of mind. He referred to his experience in rather bitter tones, but without any personal animosity. All he seemed worried about was how easily, in his opinion, a hostile campaign could be mounted to make someone plummet in the polls. I asked him if representatives and senators might have resented, as I had read, his landslide reelection (except for the District of Columbia, he had failed to carry only Massachusetts, the Kennedys' homeground), which did not match the results achieved by Republican candidates who felt they had received little support from the president. He discarded that hypothesis, but even if he had believed it he never would have admitted it. He reminisced about his moments of glory during his two terms of office—Moscow, Beijing, and Europe—and the times when he had had to shoulder grave responsibilities.

Over Christmas in 1972, for example, in order to force the North Vietnamese back to the negotiation table with Kissinger in Paris, he had had to issue and reiterate the order for the B52s to bomb Hanoi and Haiphong as well. Major newspapers and numerous circles disapproved of his decision, and yet negotiations did resume and the terrible war came to an end. The longest war in their history, "a war not started by a Republican administration."

I still maintain polite relations with Nixon, and a few months ago he invited me to lunch at Le Cirque restaurant in New York to explain why he could not attend a meeting sponsored by the Italian Christian Democratic party to celebrate the fortieth anniversary of the Marshall Plan. The local organizers had been zealous supporters of his impeachment and he would have felt somewhat ill at ease. By being seen together with me in public he wanted to prove that there were no other reasons for not attending (in fact, the whole thing was cancelled). Also present at lunch was former Secretary of State Haig, an old acquaintance as NATO commander, who had been dismissed by Reagan, whom he treated with rather sophisticated malice in his recent memoirs. He began by saying that he had met Reagan on a very sad day in that man's life, the day he had gone to the funeral of a ventriloquist, a fellow artist. Nixon has aged somewhat (he is 76 years old), but his mind never stops and his memory is perfect. He has undertaken very important journeys, has been very well received everywhere, and has written successful books and diaries.

In June 1973, I left the office of prime minister to clear the way for renewed relations between the Christian Democrats and the Socialists. For me this implied keeping the Liberal party in the government, a condition which was not acceptable to the Socialist party. I returned to my activity as a member of Parliament with heightened intensity. In particular, I began to devote special attention to the Interparliamentary Union, the club which has been bringing together the elected representatives of assemblies from all over the world for exactly one hundred years.

This Union discusses current affairs in one or two annual conferences, held in different countries on a rotation basis, and does so with much greater freedom of expression that could be found in intergovernmental talks, which are conditioned by formal records and the like. However, besides the conferences, it sets the stage for continuing relations between representatives and senators from member nations, both collectively, with mutual bilateral visits, and individually, during their trips to Rome or our journeys to their capitals. There are also friendship groups: I have headed the Italy-U.S. group since that time, despite my government duties, and I am also chairman of the Italian Delegation to the Union, where for four years I was in charge of the International Commission on Policy and Disarmament.

In 1975, we were invited to visit Capitol Hill (in the meantime, I had been appointed minister of the budget, but went to the United States as a member of parliament), yet we had a problem: Washington did not want Communists, and we could not accept the veto. The somewhat Byzantine negotiations were settled on two conditions: I had to tender my personal guarantee that my colleagues would indulge in no unscheduled meetings, and Secretary of State Kissinger was to receive me as minister, and not the entire delegation. Despite everything, I was very pleased to make this trip in return for a Union meeting in Rome seven years earlier.

The group, led by a Christian Democrat, Giuseppe Vedovato, left in November, and was made up of the following: Pietro Lezzi (Socialist); Giuseppe Amadei (Social Democrat); Sergio Segre and Franco Calamandrei (Communists); and Sam Quilleri (Liberal) and Luigi Turchi (Social Movement-National Right Wing). At the last moment, Michele Cifarelli (Republican) dropped out and we understood why when we read a political commentary in *La Voce* which called the inclusion of Communists and right-wingers "an Italian-style hodgepodge." However, it turned out to be anything but a hodgepodge.

Beginning with the speaker of the House, Carl Albert, we received a very warm welcome, and on numerous occasions were able to embark upon fact-finding talks most useful to us and to them. I took note of the satisfied reactions on the part of Senators Mike Mansfield and Hubert Humphrey, and Representatives Claude Pepper and dela Garza when they asked pointed questions on the fundamental stability of democracy in Italy. Everyone was impressed by the unanimous support of the Italian delegation for the European Community, in the general context of friendship with the United States. Our U.S. colleagues were also struck by the atmosphere of cordial relations among all members of our delegation.

The representatives of Italian descent (Lagomarsino, Annunzio, Mazzoli, Conte, Rinaldo, Biaggi, Zeferetti, and many others) escorted us on a tour of the building, and even showed us some of their committees in session. I absentmindedly listened to the oft-repeated praise of the patriotism of Costantino Brumidi, the artist who painted the large fresco in the dome of the plenary hall during the last century. Guidebooks boldly refer to him as the Michelangelo of Capitol Hill and a *political* exile from Italy.

In fact, as a minor scholar of nineteenth-century Roman history, I had read somewhere that Brumidi had had to take to his heels after Pius IX's return to Rome from Gaeta, because, during the Republic, he had devoted his efforts to sacking cardinals' residences and keeping quite a few souvenirs for himself.

In the United States, each of the 435 congressmen has his own office and a number of aides; the 100 senators, who have broader responsibilities, have even more staff members. There is no point in considering that there are twice as many parliamentarians in Italy. The states of the Union, however, have a very complex structure and rights much broader than those of our regions. In addition, each state has its own Senate and its own House of Representatives.

Accompanied by Ambassador Roberto Gaja I had a very open exchange of ideas at the State Department with Kissinger, who explained the domestic reasons why party-related objections had been raised to the visit of the Italian delegation. The Nixon crisis and the Communist

victory in Vietnam had troubled public opinion; and the election campaign, which had already begun, left no room for anything that could
lead to misunderstandings. Moreover, Vice President Rockefeller's decision not to run for office and Secretary Schlesinger's resignation, although not to be taken as serious drawbacks, were still the sign of
somewhat turbulent times.

We discussed the Italian situation and the major problem then on the
table: the foreign debt which had reached an emergency level. Kissinger
expressed his pleasure over my return to government, and kindly referred to my long-standing theory on the need for the gradual evolution
of democracy in Italy without the pressure which, in my opinion, had
been applied so improperly by the Kennedy administration. In that sense
the secretary of state appreciated the political significance of our fully
representative parliamentary delegation, and observed that we would
have interesting contacts outside of Washington as well. He was referring, in particular, to Colorado Springs, where we received a very warm
welcome at NORAD (the U.S./Canada Joint Air Defense Headquarters),
located under Mount Cheyenne, and to the Air Force Academy. I had
already experienced the charm of such visits as minister of defense, but
my colleagues were quite favorably impressed.

In Colorado something funny happened. One day, by 6:00 P.M. we
had already finished our schedule of events, including dinner with the
base commander, timed to suit the off-base activities of the troops.
Something had to be planned for the rest of the evening, in order to keep
everyone together and . . . under control. And, since there was nothing
better to do, we ended up having a good time at the dog track, even
making some money off our small bets. I thought back to the way my
mother had scolded me light years ago for having gone to the Rondinella
dog track in Rome, then considered "a place of ill repute."

The next morning, we traveled to the Nevada/Arizona border to visit
the giant dam built in the thirties by President Hoover. After thirty
minutes of a highly technical briefing, we slipped in the opportunity to
go to Las Vegas for lunch as the invited guests of the wife of Senator
Vance Hartke (Indiana). Even though this fantastic strip of desert is less
spectacular in the daytime, it was still a most enjoyable break. Las Vegas
is certainly not all of America, but it is one feature of America well
worth seeing (besides the entertainment, to be sure).

From there, we moved on to Phoenix, Arizona, where we made the most of the enjoyable climate and witnessed a gathering of female university students in religious garb, who were trying to belie an advertisement describing the area as the best place for those suffering respiratory diseases and for the elderly. The young women we met were called "the Daughters of Job," since that is the only book of the Bible they read. They didn't seem displeased by our presence at their annual reunion.

We then continued on to Houston, Texas, where we attended a briefing at the space center on Russian-American cooperation in the field of remote sensing analysis. With utmost interest and a touch of emotion, we visited the hospital where Professor Cooley operates and where a few hundred Italians go every year for valve operations in an attempt to save both heart and life. Our guide was Dr. Francesco Sandiford, the son of the professor of maritime law who in 1939 had asked me to do a study on the pontifical navy which led to my encounter with De Gasperi in the Vatican Library. Sandiford, Jr., introduced us to his wife, an American as well, and they looked like an engaged couple right out of Peynet. Shortly after that, the lass started taking shooting lessons and used a .44 Magnum to send her husband off to meet his Creator. I read somewhere that she had avoided jail by putting up a $10,000-bond and got off with a pittance of a sentence.

At the Houston airport people were handing out a mail-order catalogue of Christmas gifts, which covered the entire range from a bag of pistachio nuts at $9.00 to a diamond-studded bathtub for $118 million (83 billion lira in 1975).

In addition to the receptions given by our diplomats, in New York we were fortunate to be able to attend the debate at the United Nations, promoted by the Arab states, on equating Zionism with racism. No matter what may have been the motivation and even the provocations, this opened a rift destined to weigh quite heavily on coexistence in the State of Israel and on a political solution to the Palestinian cause. We could well understand why a crowd of Jews, Protestants, and Catholics were giving voice to their dissent in front of the UN building.

Together with our colleagues Robert McClory and Edward Derwinski, we drew positive conclusions from our trip and promised to maintain closer contacts. Governments and administrations pass away, even though every four years as a rule in America, but parliaments remain.

We boarded our return flight to Rome in quite a satisfied frame of mind, after reading an interesting statement to the Italian press by Ambassador Volpe: "Détente is one thing and Communism is another. Certainly, we cannot say to Italy: do not put the Communists in government. That would be outright interference. We hope Italy will remain a free and democratic country, and will work hard to help it stay so."

13 | *A Tribute to Ford*

Before the end of 1975 I returned to the United States for the third time that year. I didn't want to miss the Pinay-Rockefeller appointment, especially after I found out the latter had announced his intention not to stand for reelection as vice president.

Without delving into strictly American matters, I had the impression Nelson didn't want to be caught up in Ford's possible defeat. He did not consider him a winning candidate and, if Ford received only lukewarm support during the primaries, he did not discard the likelihood of becoming the Republican candidate in his own right.

In the course of our annual meeting in Washington the year before, I had willingly accepted an invitation to lunch from the chairman of the Franklin Bank of Chicago, Michele Sindona, who had been elected "Man of the Year" by the Americans in Rome.

During my tenure as finance minister I had met Sindona in Milan. A most esteemed and widely heeded expert in tax matters, he was praised by men like Franco Marinotti in such a way as to make even Adam Smith pale in comparison. At meetings held in the Chamber of Commerce and the Industrial Union I had heard Sindona deliver down-to-earth speeches with ideas which seemed both sound and original, and not only to me. At the time when nobody was speaking about a world crisis over black gold, Sindona launched the proposal of pooling Western silver as a way to create a worldwide financial counterweight to such an event. Gold would have been much better, but for a number of reasons a cartel including the USSR and South Africa, the world's largest producers of this precious metal, was not feasible. Let me add that, in the same year, 1973, I received letters from friends at the Graduate School of Industrial Administration (Carnegie-Mellon University) expressing their admiration for a seminar held there by Dr. Sindona, and which had been sponsored, if I'm not mistaken, by the former secretary of the treasury, David Kennedy.

This luncheon with Sindona reemerges every so often whenever someone feels like taking shots at me. In fact, Sindona's fortunes began to decline shortly thereafter, and many of his partial and impartial proclaimers and partners began to smear his name as much as they could. Ugo La Malfa, my deputy prime minister in 1979, kept repeating that half of Italy had supported an increase in the registered capital of Sindona's holding company: as La Malfa knew so well, I belonged to the other half. It is both senseless and unfair to harp on 1975 in the light of the later events: financial crack, prison sentence, Mafia connections, extradition, disappearance, obscure death. I have no direct information, nor is this the right place to dwell on these matters. Ever present in my mind, however, is the unanswered question of how a person could attain such heights so quickly and then plummet just as quickly in a country like America, where transparency on the stock market and in financial dealings seems so deeply rooted and unquestioned. What happened recently in the Georgia branch office of the Banca Nazionale del Lavoro raises similar doubts.

I hastened back to Rome from Washington because there was considerable unrest on the political-parliamentary scene over the Christmas period of 1975. Inflation had climbed to alarming levels and the government had been obliged to put up its gold reserves as collateral for last-resort loans from German banks. The progress made by the Communists during the local elections in the fall hung over the situation like a nightmare.

Things did not improve in the following months as Italy prepared for national elections in June 1976 in an atmosphere of widespread disorientation.

On 20 June, 1976, the Christian Democratic party gained three percentage points over the previous year's regional election results, and won 262 seats in the Chamber of Deputies and 135 in the Senate, losing only 4 seats in the Chamber. However, quite impressive were the Communist gains: from 179 to 228 deputies and from 94 to 116 senators. The

Socialist party lost 4 seats in the Chamber and 4 in the Senate, and the Social movement dropped from 56 to 35 in the Chamber and from 26 to 15 in the Senate. The Liberal party literally collapsed: from 20 to 5 deputies and from 8 to 2 senators. The Social Democrats suffered considerable losses (from 29 to 15 and from 11 to 6), while the Republican party and the Sudtirol party held their positions. Newcomers, but only to the Chamber of Deputies, were the 6 deputies representing the People's Democratic party and the 4 Radicals.

It was anything but an easy situation for governing the country, particularly in view of the tremendous economic and financial problems Italy had to face.

Moro and Rumor went to the United States for the annual Summit Meeting of the Seven Most Industrialized Countries but they were hardly in the mood to dwell on world problems, so entrapped was *Italian* politics in an ever-meandering maze. And then there was the mystery of the admonition to Italy against the possible entry of the Communist party into the government coalition, announced by Chancellor Schmidt also on behalf of the United States, France, and Great Britain following a four-party consultation convened under the pretense of a separate meeting of the powers occupying Berlin, and held on the fringes of the Puerto Rico summit meeting. The Italian delegation was not informed, or so they told us on their return. Years later, however, Ambassador Roberto Ducci's memoirs revealed that Moro had been invited but had elected to remain with his aides to study the briefing papers for the full summit meeting, which he hadn't had time to read in Rome.

In a nutshell, the four so-called "major powers" warned Italy against opening the way to the Communist party, forecasting that any such opening would lead to our separation from the Western community or something just short of that.

What was the reason behind such a spectacular step so contrary to customary diplomatic practice? No matter how alarmed they might have been over Italy's future, if anything the major allies should have come up with an effective plan to support our prostrated finances instead of preaching to us in public the same way neighbors do to a penniless mother who would know very well how to do more for her children if she only had the money. In my opinion, this "warning" was the idea of some American adviser, not Ford in person, for U.S. electoral purposes. Only a few months before the presidential election perhaps someone wanted to focus on the Communist threat in Italy, thus highlighting the responsibility of Kennedy's Democratic administration in encouraging an opening to the Left. It should not be forgotten that in the heat of the psychological uproar over the debacle in Vietnam (the TV coverage showing Ambassador Graham Martin folding the American flag as he left Saigon had been a stinging blow to American feelings), the word communism evoked in public opinion Saigon's final capitulation to Marxist North Vietnam.

I recall what Cardinal Spellman said to me upon his return from South Vietnam where he had celebrated Christmas Mass for American troops stationed there. A war like that would never be won; and this would bring about a traumatic letdown for the American people because it belied their historical belief in being the conquering arm of God in the world for the defense of liberty at any price. He foresaw devastating reactions, worsened by the countless forms of corruption which had spread as a consequence of American involvement in Vietnam. As we shall see, this was the mood which brought Jimmy Carter to the White House.

Coming back to Italy, even the Communist opposition and the trade unions were aware that the impending economic bankruptcy would not only hurt the Christian Democrats and the other government coalition parties, but would engulf everyone, opening the way to adventures whose political hue could not be predicted. Under such circumstances the need for a political truce became clear, and President Leone asked me to form a cabinet. In particular, this was Aldo Moro's idea because he believed I was the right man to appease the . . . Puerto Rican concerns at a time when we had to attain a promise of non-belligerance from the Communists (the Christian Democratic party refused to deal with the Italian Communist party but it allowed me to do so, almost on a personal basis, in order to save face). Craxi had been elected leader of the Socialist party only a few days before, and lent me a hand by declaring that at least for one year their position toward a government made up of Christian Democrats alone would be identical to the one assumed by the Communists (pro, abstention, or against).

Thus was formed the government which Luigi Cappugi, then my economic adviser, quite brilliantly called the "no no-confidence" government. The cabinet included Rinaldo Ossola as minister of foreign trade, and he provided sound input in both substance and prestige. Communists, Socialists, and other parties abstained on the vote of confidence which virtually amounted to positive support.

I was greatly encouraged a few days later when I met in Rome with the German undersecretary of foreign affairs who brought me the following message from Schmidt: "Draw up a bold program and the United States, France, Great Britain and Germany will support you." Had Moro been right?

The Americans went to the polls in early November and found relief from their collective guilt complex over Watergate and Vietnam by following the Baptist preaching of the governor of Georgia, Jimmy Carter. His Messianism was no affectation. He had the habit of reading a passage from the Bible in Spanish every evening before retiring and he came across as the right man for the catharsis. On the other hand, his membership on the Trilateral Commission had ensured the support of a considerable share of the business community which no longer identified its interests with the Republican party as was the case in the past. As a matter of fact, the year before in Washington, the director of the Electoral Research Center, Richard M. Scammon, had told us: "The political system in the United States is substantially bereft of parties." In any case, for what it was worth, most congressmen and senators of Italian origin were Democrats and could perhaps give us a hand. But how could we make it until the new administration had settled in? We needed immediate support, more psychologically than financially, and received wholehearted backing from Ambassador John Volpe, who was not deterred by the tradition barring visits from foreign leaders during the transition period. Ford invited me to Washington, thereby disproving that passive Communist support in Parliament might have placed us on the blacklist.

As if the problems of government did not suffice, I had to be on my guard against the callous intrigues of my opponents. At the height of the heated controversy over the scandal centering around the illegal commissions paid by Lockheed for the sale of aircraft to the Italian air force, Eugenio Scalfari's weekly magazine L'Espresso hit me from the blind side with a clamorous cover story: the Antelope Cobbler (the bribed person's code name) was none other than me! I turned the matter over to the Investigating Commission which had no trouble in dispelling such a slanderous absurdity, but in my mind lingered a doubt as to whether behind that despicable plot there wasn't some foreign agency or circle with an axe to grind over the formation of the government. As I traveled toward America on December 5, a reporter by the name of Giancesare Flesca filled me in on all the details. Also present was Senator Calamandrei who was on a follow-up trip to our earlier visit as members of Parliament. No CIA or other complicated "strings": it had been a fraudulent hoax perpetrated by a money-hungry American named Hauser. He had just picked out my name since I was the only Italian politician he knew about, and had concocted false documents which had been purchased and then published by *L'Espresso* at the lightning speed dictated by the fear of someone else making the scoop. They hadn't even waited for Flesca to return from New York where he had been sent on purpose to check over the source. Once they realized they had been "taken for a ride" they hastily retracted and sent Mr. Hauser before the Commission to make a full confession.

For the third time (after the Giuffrè affair of 1956–57, when a banker with strong links to the Vatican went bankrupt, and the delirious statements made by Ambassador Martin) *L'Espresso* had tried in vain to destroy me. However, while the first case over the dealings of a partially demented and minor bank official from Emilia Romagna was a domestic matter, the Martin affair brought Italo-American relations into the picture.

Martin had come to the embassy in Rome from Saigon after the flag had been lowered and when he was still in very deep grief over the death of his son. He lived a very retired life, and I recall learning that he still hadn't made a courtesy call on the speaker of the Chamber of Deputies despite having been the U.S. ambassador in Rome for over a year. That, however, was his concern. But after he had already left Italy, there was a real outcry over his statement to the effect that substantial funds (CIA or thereabouts) had been given to Italian parties and politicians in 1972 to support the democratic system. The news, mentioned in the record of a thorough congressional enquiry in America, was first published in Italy by the newspaper *Stampa Sera*, with a reference to reliable sources, and then picked up by *L'Espresso* with a cover story calling for the ousting of the ministers supposedly implicated (myself, Donat Cattin, and others). We reacted in a most resolute way, and also had the Executive Committee of the Christian Democratic party approve a resolution asking the U.S. administration to refrain from classifying, and to shed full light on, this loathesome affair. As a matter of fact, we had read that the president was planning to veto or in any case prevent the publication of documents on CIA activities in Italy and in Angola (!).

I also wrote a formal letter to Ambassador Volpe ("Precisely those who have always been, and feel honored to be, friends of the United States without having ever received or requested any personal or group benefit have the right not to see shadows of any type cast on such sensitive matters of scrupulosity and independence"), and served notice on former Ambassador Martin to remain silent. While Volpe, however, hastened to reply and say that nothing like that had ever happened under him, Martin did not respond at all, despite several reminders. I was sorry he did not contact me, all the more so because I would have liked to advise him to deny or clarify the information provided from the intelligence services on their role in helping him to purchase a house in Tuscany in the 1970s.

Upon our arrival in Washington we were escorted to meet with Ford by Ambassador Shirley Temple, a superstar as a child, who had become the White House chief of protocol (she is now ambassador in Prague).

We went through the customary liturgy with the picture on the balcony and talks for an hour and forty minutes in the Oval Office. I gave an overview of the situation, making it quite clear our difficulties derived not from foreign policy problems but from the economic and financial situation. Parliament was in the phase of being a responsible onlooker, even if the brunt of responsibility lay on the shoulders of the Christian Democratic party. The forecasted increase in the price of oil made prospects for us all the more grim. We needed an expression of confidence and not . . . a Puerto Rican–type excommunication.

Ford posed the question about the Communists' position on the legislation to strengthen the three branches of the armed forces, and I felt I was being put to the litmus test. In reply, I said they hadn't voted against the navy bill and would do the same for the other two. The smiles were so obliging that I felt he was most understanding about Italian current affairs (maybe he had the feeling he had been too understanding because later on, under someone's urging, he asked me if he had been clear about being opposed to Communists *in* the government).

Most of the time was dedicated to the oil issue. Ford briefed us on the steps taken, even personally, with the producer countries to persuade them to be moderate. However, the results were modest, with the possible exception of Manuel Pérez of Venezuela. A hypothetical 10 percent price increase meant the United States would reach a total bill of $35 billion for oil imports, with serious effects on the balance of payments and on economic recovery. The inability of the European Community to agree on a common position was rather inconvenient for the American government.

Ford inquired about our negotiations with the International Monetary Fund and instructed Treasury Secretary William Simon to sit down with us and see if and what they could do to help, even though, as he stressed, he had one foot out of the White House door.

We lunched with Kissinger, to whom I had brought the Italian decoration of the Grand Cross because he had seemed somewhat disappointed when Ambassador Gaja had conferred it upon Nelson Rockefeller. He ruled out the possibility that the Communists had decided to "donate blood for a good cause" and therefore "either I had erred in accepting, or else they had miscalculated their own returns."

He made no mystery of his personal belief in the first hypothesis. The state of need (an abacus was enough to figure that out) would have more than sufficed as an answer, but I went on to develop my long-standing conviction about the convertibility—without undue haste—of political sinners.

In our private talks after lunch, I was pleased to note that without his staff around (e.g., Sonnenfeld, Hartman, Robinson) Kissinger showed a greater degree of understanding. However, even in the toast at table he praised my democratic dedication, wished the government well, and confirmed anew "full support and solidarity on the part of America to the president of the Council and to Italy."

Even though we were on a working visit, Gerald Ford held a formal banquet in our honor and it took place in an atmosphere of both affection and feeling showered by the guests upon the defeated president who maintained an air of exemplary detachment. I saw his eyes become misty only when the master of ceremonies, Tony Orlando, referred to the regrets over the voters' choice. However, in order to help them dispel any melancholy and since I have never espoused the arts of Terpsichore or felt at home on a dance floor, I returned rather early to Blair House while they danced the night away. The Marine musicians took to the strings. This is the form of combat to be preferred.

The next morning I received a visit from Senator Walter Mondale, the incoming vice president on the Carter ticket. He enquired about general matters, voiced feelings of courtesy, promised to report back to the president-elect in Plains that same day, and advised me of a forthcoming encounter with Cyrus Vance who would become secretary of state after the inauguration.

Mondale also stayed for breakfast with eight other senators (Roman Hruska of Nebraska, Charles Percy of Illinois, Claiborne Pell of Rhode Island, Robert Griffin of Michigan, Charles Matthias of Michigan, Richard Schweiker of Pennsylvania, Pete Domenici of New Mexico, and John Pastore of Rhode Island), as well as the hyperactive founder of the National Italian American Foundation, Jeno Paolucci, a man of Italian origin who was a very influential industrialist from Michigan and one of Mondale's top backers. John Pastore and Claiborne Pell helped us out by steering the questions and answers.

William Simon arrived at Blair House at 11:00 A.M. together with the president of the Federal Reserve Board, Arthur Burns, Alan Greenspan, who was Ford's number one economic adviser, and Undersecretary Edwin Yeo. For more than an hour there was a rather courteous exchange of converging appraisals on the IMF's independence with respect to the American administration and on the need for the negotiations with the Fund to come to an end, and in the right way, in order to be able to have swaps with the Americans. It is true: the Italian trade unions were showing signs of great understanding; new investments were flowing in (for once Libya turned out to be an asset with its purchase of stocks in FIAT); and we had the approval of Parliament, but the American Treasury did not have the appropriate instruments for funneling direct assistance to Italy.

John Volpe was the one who gave a different and decisive turn to the meeting. Almost with a tone of incitement in his voice, he spoke about Italy's difficult situation and the courage I had shown in accepting the responsibility of government at the risk of annihilating an entire lifetime (how good of him) of prestige and political merits. Our failure would not have been *ours* alone. Where there is a will, there is always a way. And then, no one could forget how the assistance given to Italy at the time of De Gasperi had been repaid by remarkable steadfastness in the defense of Western democracy. Therefore, a show of solidarity had to be decided upon at all costs.

Simon and Burns eased up on their positions and the treasury secretary told us Ford had made a point of telling him he *had* to satisfy us.

I once again made it clear we were not asking for money, nor did we want to circumvent the International Monetary Fund. All we needed was an American pledge to come to our aid in case we had a new foreign currency crisis like the one two months earlier.

And so it was. Simon issued a statement in public expressing *positive views* on the effectiveness of our stabilization program, *confidence* as regards the Fund's conclusions, and *plans* for an immediate study on ways for tangible support from the United States "in order to assist Italy during the implementation of its economic program."

With raised spirits, I went to a luncheon hosted by Nelson Rockefeller where I heard words of well-grounded confidence in Italy, always able to overcome obstacles, from him, from the influential and delightful Mrs. Katherine Graham, Richardson and his wife, the secretary of housing and urban development, and others. In the toast, Nelson recalled our December meetings, and especially the time when he had not been able to come and had sent one of his young aides, Henry Kissinger.

As part of my very busy schedule of engagements, I granted interviews to *Newsweek* and the *Washington Post;* with delegations from the Brookings Institute and Council on Foreign Relations I discussed the opportuneness of revoking restrictions on visas for Italian Communists, but to do so always through our government; I spoke with Meany, the powerful trade union leader, who grasped the psychological sensitivity of automatic wage increases indexed to the cost of living for our workers, and promised to explain it to the IMF experts (he told me the AFL-CIO had been a determining factor in Carter's victory, but Ford had done everything he could to prevent them from helping him).

On December 8, after attending Mass at Holy Rosary Church, I headed home. At the step to my plane Nelson Rockefeller said to me in French: "Everyone was positively impressed."

The trip had been most useful, not only for slowing down the slipping lira, but also for dissipating domestic hostility toward the government fanned by the firm belief we had been excommunicated by America. The lack of a contrary vote by the Communists also troubled several Christian Democrats who said they were sure unemployment would soon reach the two million mark and the dollar would be worth 1,000 lira. During my three-year tenure as prime minister, thanks be to God, exactly the opposite occurred. The balance of payments went into the black by 5,000 billion from being in the red by 2,300; the foreign currency reserves rose in value from 1,000 to 15,549 billion lira; savings jumped from 55 to 95 billion lira; inflation dropped from 23 to 11.6 percent. Quite clearly, this was not to be ascribed to the efforts of Gerald Ford and John Volpe alone, but I will always be extremely grateful to them.

14 | *Carter*

Shortly after taking office, Carter sent Vice President Mondale to Italy for a thorough examination of the international situation. He was accompanied by top-flight aides: Mainard Glitman, David Aaron, Richard Cooper, Fred Bergsten, and David Glift.

I was sorry to see the way John Volpe was slighted by the new administration on that occasion. He received instructions to depart in a hurry without waiting for Mondale's arrival, as would have been logical even if he was not necessarily included in Mondale's party at the political talks. Perhaps there was an old grudge between Volpe, former secretary of transportation, and Carter, former governor of Georgia. I can think of no other explanation.

At the end of his round of talks, Mondale released statements very favorable for the situation in Italy, and five days later wrote a letter informing me he had reported to Carter both the substance and the spirit of our talks which had provided new opportunities for "developing increasing cooperation between the two governments from now on."

The first European government leader to visit Carter was James Callaghan who reported to us at the NATO Council meeting on March 25 in the following terms: "He will not be an easy travelling companion, but we will make progress together." We met him all together in London in the month of May for the Summit Meeting of the Seven Most Industrialized Countries and the NATO Council. During the four days we spent working together, I was particularly struck by two features he displayed: the will to take control of economic interests by pledging to reduce oil imports drastically by 1984 (two terms of office?), and a marked degree of caution on the use of nuclear energy, a caution which turned into hostility for projects involving self-breeder reactors. He had served under Admiral Hyman Rickover and his apprehension over the military use of that technology almost touched on anguish. Since it was all too easy to object that countries without uranium were at a disadvantage, he referred to a possible pooling of this precious element in order to obviate speculative profit taking. In addition, he urged people to step up studies on alternative sources, for oil as well as nuclear energy, announcing special allocations in the U.S. budget with what seemed to me somewhat unrealistic forecasts, at least as far as solar energy was concerned which I knew a bit about because of studies conducted by one of my sons at MIT in Boston.

In the course of bilateral talks at the American Embassy in London, Carter insisted on my coming to Washington before the summer holidays. I went at the end of July and a rather fortuitous circumstance made the welcome extended to me a rather special one. When leaving the French presidential palace after talks a week earlier, I had fielded a few questions from French reporters, and denied that Carter's stress on the defense of human rights could create difficulties between East and West in Europe. It was true that Brezhnev had objected to Giscard that Carter was "breaking the code of détente." However, equally true was the fact that all the European nations, together with the United States and Canada, had underwritten the Final Helsinki Accord, an essential part of which is the acknowledgment of human rights. In the White House they had appreciated my casual remarks and Carter expressed this to me in public, whereupon I restated my position and did so by quoting his speech in London on the value of détente and on the possibilities of extending concrete negotiations to the USSR.

During the two lengthy rounds of talks at the White House the "energy" issue was rehashed, from a military viewpoint as well. A friend of mine at the Pentagon had told me the new president was not at all enthusiastic over the neutron bomb project which his predecessors had supported so warmly that we Europeans had even been asked to assume a common front in response to a litigious letter we had received from Brezhnev on the matter. The fact that there could be a change of opinion on such complex policy issues every four years seemed to me rather disquieting, and I asked Carter to share his thoughts with us.

He replied that he had yet to decide on the matter, but there was truth in his opposition to this type of weapon out of fear that its lesser degree of destructive potential might induce people to use it, thereby triggering a fatal nuclear escalation process.

Were his final decision different, I remarked, he would have to worry about the way Washington had approached the problem. A leak in the newspapers, in my opinion planted to probe reactions, had exalted this innovative weapon because, in the final analysis, it only killed human beings and didn't destroy the environment. If the contrary had been reported, perhaps we would have had pro-neutron bomb manifestations in the name of human lives. In any case, President Carter had to avoid undermining the widespread trust he enjoyed as a man of peace and détente. The United Nations had convened a Special Session on Disarmament for the following year, and it was necessary for the United States to assume the leadership of this world movement. All too often the United States had unjustifiably adopted a defensive game plan, leaving others to play the psychological role as partisans of peace.

Carter asked me to outline our position on the Middle East, inviting me to work on the PLO so they would drop their bias against Israel's right to exist. I replied that if it were possible to get them seated at the same table with the Israelis, even if only for a preliminary consideration of procedural matters, mutual recognition would have already taken place in fact. However, this was not the real problem. Up until this time the Israeli government had never spoken about a willingness to return the occupied territories. Therefore, the obstacle lay in the very substance of the problem, and not in a few paragraphs in the PLO statute. If Tel Aviv were to accept the idea of political satisfaction for the Palestinian people's fundamental needs, the way would be paved for all the rest.

Carter's optimism seemed to me rather unrealistic. He had his own plan and, in this regard, felt he had obtained understanding on the part of Hassan, King Hussein, and Begin; but even Sadat had given him a good welcome. He considered it possible to have a PLO delegation attend the Geneva Conference without Israeli vetoes, in the spirit of that homeland to which they have a right. As for returning the territories, that was *overdue* and the United States would ensure compliance with the UN resolutions. At that time the American administration was in no way thinking about excluding the Soviets from coresponsibility for the Middle East negotiations.

We discussed the matter anew with Cyrus Vance both during and after the luncheon at the State Department; also present were Philip Habib and Richard Cooper. They didn't attach too much importance to my pessimistic forecasts about an agreement on Jerusalem. However, they did give us some useful information on developments in Rhodesia and I was able to provide them with some elements from our side, because I had spoken with the president of Zambia, Kenneth Kaunda, shortly beforehand.

We then had substantive talks with John Moore and the vice president of EXIMBANK, Vito Gianturco; with James Schlesinger and George Vest on energy issues (still against nuclear propulsion for the merchant marine); with Secretary Joseph Califano on health care and relations between school systems; and with the treasury secretary, Werner Blumenthal, who confirmed the pledges made by Simon.

The star attraction at the official banquet was Shirley Verrett, a former member of a choir in the Church of the Latter Day Saints in Los Angeles and now applauded everywhere she performed, even at La Scala. She sang pieces by Pergolesi and Rossini.

I began my "toast" with the Latin motto on the American emblem *(E pluribus unum)* and evoked the Italian-American victims of the war, quoting the names I had read on the monument to those who had perished in Hawaii during the surprise attack on Pearl Harbor (Bonfiglio, Restivo, Brignole, Puzio, Giovenazzo, Pedrotti, Valente, Criscuolo, Riganti). I did not neglect to speak about the recovery effort being made by Italy "helped along by a very broad parliamentary consensus." "We are proud," I added, "to show early emigrants and their descendants that Italy is modernizing its daily life, is strengthening its spiritual heritage, and is able to follow paths of concord and peace making."

The next day there was another round of talks with Carter at the While House. Speaking about energy, he returned to the point raised at the London summit about a study on the fuel cycle in order to avert the temptation of military use to the utmost. We then discussed cultural and training programs, and considered how American business concerns could take part in sound development projects in southern Italy (there were already seventy-three plants with forty thousand workers). I resumed this subject at a working breakfast with numerous businessmen, some of whom had traveled quite a distance to be there. I also asked Carter to reconsider America's negative position on the International

Labour Organization, but he told me that to do so *immediately* was impossible.

We moved on to Capitol Hill for a working luncheon with the House Foreign Affairs Committee. Chaired by Clement J. Zablocki (Democrat, Wisconsin), we were joined by the following Italian Americans: Matthew J. Rinaldo, Robert J. Lagomarsino, Silvio O. Conte, Bruce F. Caputo, Leon E. Panetta, Teno Roncalio, Martin A. Russo, James D. Santini, Joseph P. Addabbo, Mario Biaggi, Bruce F. Vento, Leo C. Zeferetti, Robert N. Giaimo, Peter W. Rodino, Frank Annunzio, Joseph A. Le Fante, James J. La Falce, Robert L. Legget, Romano L. Mazzoli, and Joseph J. Minish; the senators came in for coffee. We saw John Sparkman, Edward Kennedy, Hubert Humphrey, Howard Baker, Jr., Frank Church, Claiborne Pell, John Glenn, Jacob Javits, Abraham Ribicoff, Edward Brooke, Adlai Stevenson, Pete Domenici, and Daniel Moynihan. I also paid a visit to the speaker of the House, Thomas "Tip" O'Neill.

The afternoon was spent with officials of the Brookings Institute: Philip Trerise, Robert Solomon, Joseph Jäger, and William Cline. With them we spoke once again about entry visas to the United States. I stated my position in favor of the greatest possible degree of liberality, and recalled what was said in Italy thirty-seven years earlier, and it was not a mere stroke of wit: if Mussolini had visited and known America, he would never have declared war.

Frankness in the relations established with Carter, together with some attestations to our seriousness (quite significant was the one by Burns, the *dominus* of the Federal Reserve, who the year before had perhaps harbored doubts on the programs I had announced), seemed to me positive contributions to Italian foreign policy. This is why I was so rudely taken aback by a statement made on the following January 12 by the State Department spokesman on "the changeless attitude of the American administration toward Communist parties, *including the Italian one.*" Why such a useless and interfering declaration, when everyone was so well aware of the sensitive nature of political-parliamentary relations in Italy? I regretted Volpe's wisdom and had him call Ambassador Gardner who was then in Washington. The latter professed he had nothing to do with the statement which, as a matter of fact, he had tried to soften down by reiterating to the press the Carter administration's full support for our government. The dynamics of the two countries' domestic situations, he added, do not always coincide. And more or less the same concept ("domestic policy requirements impose certain attitudes on the U.S.A.") was voiced that same evening to the head of my press office by an influential American journalist.

I was very disheartened by the whole episode and let people know it; also because in it I could detect awkward moves of Italian origin linked to the ever-difficult situation of dialogue among the political parties. The domestic needs of the United States, my foot!

On May 30, still under the shock of the assassination of Aldo Moro (during Moro's captivity Carter had written me a message of full support —and prayers as well—for the defense of democratic principles being demonstrated by the government, and had sent Secretary Califano to express their solidarity), I went to Washington for the Atlantic Council. In talks with the president I received nothing but praise for our government, which at that time even had the supporting vote of the Communists and no longer just their abstention. When people talk to one another face to face and don't leave things up to spokesmen, many errors are avoided and misunderstandings dissipated.

Carter told me he wanted to visit Italy after the Bonn summit meeting, but Leone's resignation and the subsequent vacancy in the Office of President caused the visit to be canceled. I do not believe it was true, as *Newsweek* reported, that the American intelligence services had discouraged the visit because of terrorism in Italy; in fact, they were convinced the terrorists could also operate abroad, and during my stay in Washington our embassy was guarded by forty agents with the help of tanks and helicopters. The same was true in New York. I went there on June 2 to address the Special Session on Disarmament at the United Nations and the security forces were out in full: all the more so since someone had used a wall (such literature is not that customary over there) to send the following message "Moro = Andreotti."

I had gone in person to the Special Session on Disarmament in order to highlight the importance attributed to it by Italy, which linked together the themes of peace, international solidarity, and the fight against terrorism (it was also the right forum for thanking all the countries which had been so close to us during the grievous Moro episode) and also to reiterate that Italy was not going to surrender in the face of the attack by the Red Brigades.

The Summit Meeting of the Seven Most Industrialized Countries took place in Bonn on 15–16 July. Carter said he was sure the Soviets intended to conclude the SALT II negotiations just as he did, and in order to avoid raising hurdles he would not adopt a rigid position in the linkage with the USSR's political trials, even while continuing to place the utmost stress on human rights. At the luncheon hosted by President Walter Scheel I was seated next to Carter and asked him for a firsthand interpretation of his statements in Berlin on potential openness to Euro-communism. He fielded my question by asking me what I thought about it, and I said a gradual Communist evolution would benefit the Warsaw Pact countries and also the Communist parties of Western Europe. He concurred but hastened to say he certainly didn't intend to encourage communism in Italy or in France. We then spoke about the European Monetary System toward which Carter had seemed rather chilly at an earlier meeting, perhaps because he had been briefed by someone who saw it as a maneuver against the dollar and therefore anti-American. He was very interested in my quite different interpretation, and immediately gave Treasury Secretary Blumenthal instructions to maintain close con-tacts with Minister Pandolfi. Upon his return to America he sent me a note of thanks for the work done together in Bonn. In the meantime, since he was not coming to Rome for the moment, he was going to send his mother in the hopes she would be received by the Pope and by Pertini.

Behind the scenes Carter forged ahead in the attempt to sort out the Arab-Israeli crisis; no longer, however, on the hypothesis of a Geneva conference, as he had initially told us, but rather on the basis of a Sadat-Begin agreement guaranteed by the United States.

It is still too soon to express a final judgment on the matter, but I was all too aware of the risk inherent in such a bold undertaking. In a letter the president asked for understanding and support, from the EEC as well, saying he was certain the other Arab countries would only protest a bit and do nothing more. I saw Brzezinski shortly after that, and he explained it was the only possible road, and that Sadat would now be able to promote the pro-Palestinian process in a truly effective way. Both Carter and Sadat were asking us to visit the Arab capitals—where the reaction was quite different from what American intelligence had fore-cast to the White House—in order to convince people to place trust in the Camp David solution.

Forlani and I set out for Cairo and together laid out before Sadat the theory of "the first chapter" of a book of peace for the Middle East whose other chapters would follow immediately. From there we traveled to Tripoli, Amman, and Baghdad and were received everywhere with personal respect, but with words of deep hostility for what they called the Egyptian act of betrayal. Sadat had regained the Sinai and had weakened the common front: this was what the three governments thought.

I sent this information to Carter and also suggested the resumption of relations with Iraq which seemed to me quite willing to do so. Unfortunately, the Americans delayed doing it for years. The concerns expressed over Camp David didn't seem to have an impact on Carter. He confirmed to me in writing that Camp David had given the Palestinians the right to choose freely their own political destiny.

In another letter informing me about the normalization of relations with China, he recalled my idea about tripolarity with Russia, and pointed out he was "in contact with Chairman Brezhnev to reassure him that such normalization has no other purpose than to promote peace in the world." And he even added: "I will make quite clear to Brezhnev my continuing determination to strengthen the relationship between the United States and the Soviet Union."

In my reply to him I extended my compliments over this position and urged that there be a direct Carter-Brezhnev meeting, and that the SALT II negotiations be concluded as soon as possible.

In January 1979 a four-sided get-together between Carter, Giscard, Schmidt, and Callaghan gave rise to a certain amount of discontented grumbling. The nightmare of an unacceptable "directorate" returned to muddy the waters, even though it had been nothing other than the casual use of New Year's holidays in the Caribbean by two of the heads of government. Nor had the encounter been preceded by well-thought-out considerations because the subsequent forecasts were rosy and more makeshift than political (in fact, a few days later the shah fled Iran and anything but a calm year began).

Carter wrote to me on March 3 predicting the conclusion of SALT II, which was useful as well for correcting the *international turbulence* which was threatening world peace, and he concluded as follows: "I share your viewpoint on the importance of an encounter between President Brezhnev and myself; the *sooner* such an encounter takes place, all the better will it be for American-Soviet relations."

Cyrus Vance came to Rome on May 29 and informed us that for the first time Begin had declared that the Camp David agreements had been a *first step* toward global peace in the area. He also told us that the SALT II Treaty was about to be signed. It was signed on June 18 and we all congratulated Carter at the Summit Meeting of the Seven Most Industrialized Countries held in Tokyo nine days later and once again dedicated almost exclusively to energy problems and the high price of oil.

Back in Washington, Carter wrote to the six other participants at the Tokyo summit—at least I believe he did, since there was no reason for writing to me alone—reiterating the intentions expressed in Japan and even expanding them: absolute commitment *never again* to import more oil than in 1977, and then gradually to reduce imports all the way to the 50 percent mark by 1990; strong promotion of public transportation to reduce automobile addiction; and lavish budget allocations for research on oil substitutes. "If these policies meet with your approval," he asked me, "I hope you will be able to find an occasion in the near future to say so in public."

I had a press release issued by the government press office at Palazzo Chigi in order to comply with Jimmy Carter's well-founded desire for solidarity, even though the technical data worked up by his experts appeared farfetched. In addition to receiving a visit on July 19 from Carter's security adviser David Aaron, this was one of my last acts in my three years as prime minister.

On 4 August 1979 I left the office of president of the Council of Ministers and I received a very kind letter from Carter:

At the moment when, after three difficult years of service, you cease being head of government, I wish to express my appreciation for your solid friendship and wise counsel. From our first meeting in Washington, immediately after my inauguration, to the recent Tokyo summit, we have worked closely together in a spirit of cooperation and mutual respect. I deeply appreciated your contribution to the development of closer relations between our two countries. I also valued the support given by you and your government to the effort deployed, within the Alliance and in other international fora, to improve security and the quality of life of our peoples. Rosalynn joins me in extending to you and to Mrs. Andreotti our best wishes for the future.

A few days later, when meeting Rosalynn in Quito for the inauguration of the president of Ecuadór, Jaime Roldós, I received new demonstrations of a nonperfunctory friendship on the part of the Carter family. Besides, Jimmy Carter was perfect in personal relations. The first time I met him, it was easy for us to speak in a mutually frank and perhaps useful way. And I was surprised, shortly after returning to my hotel, to receive a handwritten note from him: "I was pleased to have been with you. Thank you for having been so helpful to me. Yours, Jimmy."

Once I left the government, I had no further occasion to meet Jimmy Carter, except at the state dinner hosted by Pertini during his brief visit to Rome. However, the day he lost his bid for reelection I was one of the first to arrive at the gathering which Ambassador Gardner had organized —deep down, I believe—to celebrate the Democratic victory in the presidential election. At the moment when Ambassador Gardner made his comments many of the invited guests were not there.

This marked the beginning of revised appraisals on Carter voiced by the countless legions of opportunists and turncoats. And during these years, except for a journey to China and a recent unofficial peace mission to Ethiopia (in which he also asked us to share), international headlines have no longer had occasion to focus on Jimmy Carter.

15 | *Reagan Arrives*

It is difficult to say in precise terms how much the issue of the American hostages held prisoner for over a year in the U.S. embassy in Tehran contributed to Carter's defeat. Yet, there is no doubt that public opinion was so frustrated that, in April, the rash decision was made to mount a rescue mission which failed miserably. A role in this gamble was also played by groundless intelligence on a presumed mass upheaval against Khomeini which would break out as soon as the first American helicopter appeared on the scene (maybe from the same sources who convinced Saddam Hussein, at the outset of the Iran-Iraq conflict, that he could just walk right over his foe. Carter believed he had a reliable channel and declined one made available to him through me).

Through mutual friends, I had made the acquaintance of M. Chéron, a Paris attorney who had handled the ayatollah's affairs during his stay in France. Immediately after the criminal capture of the American hostages, and quite concerned about what was happening, I asked him if there was a way to untangle the situation before traumatic complications arose. Chéron, *after due consultation,* proposed a "plan of operations": (1) an American *court* should process the request for the deposed shah's extradition with a detailed list of charges; (2) court proceedings should receive full coverage in the press and on TV; and (3) most likely, the judge would object there was no extradition treaty between the United States and Iran, and the case would be suspended, or rather, "buried." At this point, having received political satisfaction, the Iranian government would release the hostages.

Naturally, I hastened to inform the Americans (on 26 November 1979) and, much to my surprise, the next day I received the following answer: "Better not to interfere with the initiative undertaken by the UN." I didn't believe this and felt Washington had another ace up its sleeve. And they must have thought they had it since, on the eve of the presidential elections, they sent a plane to Europe with the hostages' ballots; evidently, they were sure they could celebrate the spectacular release before the American people went to the polls. However, the hostages did not return home until the beginning of the new administration. Perhaps Khomeini had not forgotten a New Year's Day Carter had celebrated with the shah in Iran. On that occasion, the president had delivered the speech—the contradictions of life!—expressing support for human rights and reservations on the shah's secret police which had given wings to the insurrection. As a matter of fact, in January I was asked to reactivate my channel through Paris, but I put them in touch directly as I didn't want any further exposure to unsuccessful personal involvement (and Chéron let me know it was too late anyway).

Another moot question is whether the Democrats would have had a greater chance of victory with a candidate other than Carter. During a dinner at the Rockefellers in October of the year before, I had heard people forecast that Ted Kennedy, as a candidate, would beat Reagan (not Connally, they said, but the latter had had too many setbacks to be nominated by the Republican party).

Around Christmas time, however, some senators told me Ford would be the Republican candidate since Reagan, Connally, and Bush would knock each other out. They, too, were almost certain the Democrats would run with Kennedy (who suffered the final blow from the merciless campaign of his opponents: "The American people cannot trust a man who could not be trusted by his own secretary").

Even Vittorio Nino Novarese, who came to see me in June to speak about a big movie he was planning to make on St. Paul's journey in the Mediterranean basin, expressed a negative outlook on Carter's chances.

John Volpe, who was in Rome to attend the beatification of Fr. Orione, thought the contest between Republicans and Democrats in November was still wide open.

In early 1980 I was elected chairman of both the Chamber's Foreign Affairs Committee and the Italian delegation to the Interparliamentary

Union: two offices which offered frequent opportunities for contacts with the American embassy and with visiting dignitaries.

I attended the Union's spring conference in Athens (heading the Policy and Disarmament Committee) and a session on disarmament held in Brussels. On both occasions, I worked closely with members of the U.S. Congress (especially Senator Claiborne Pell), but also had a constructive relationship with the Soviets; in fact, the head of their delegation turned to me for a text presaging the withdrawal of Europe-based missiles. My role in preparing this document, along with the unanimous vote on my election to chair the Committee, when reported back to Washington were the cause for some concern, but not among the policy makers who were well aware of my ideas on the bilateral and verifiable nature of disarmament. On the other hand, despite some hardline objections against alleged weaknesses toward the Italian Communist party, Napoleone Colajanni and Romano Ledda, members of that party, traveled to the United States that same week.

I also had a minor clash over . . . my anti-Communist stand with the *Osservatore Romano* which criticized a speech I had delivered to the Italian Catholic Press Union on the military vulnerability of a divided Italy.

The editor, deputy editor, and even the Secretariat of State of the Holy See disavowed the criticism, and the newspaper quickly found a way to put a lid on the whole matter.

As regards U.S.-Italian Communist party relations, the embassy in Rome entertained none at all prior to Richard Gardner's appointment. Gardner arrived in Rome with a well-publicized reputation as an open-ended *liberal* (among other things, he was described as a sociologist while he actually has a legal background). And when I was received by Carter as a great friend, Scalfari wrote: "Carter accepts the Italian Communist party in the government," hence the necessary clarifications. Members of the Communist party were invited to Villa Taverna, but not Berlinguer. And while there were grounds to praise their position on the Atlantic Alliance, Afghanistan, and on not attending questionable international meetings, differences persisted on other issues: the American presence in the Persian Gulf, the base at La Maddalena, the deployed missiles.

In my opinion, Gardner, ably assisted by his wife, Danielle Luzzatto, adequately dealt with the challenge of a policy of innovation in continuity. They were grateful to me for having gone to the embassy at 7:00 A.M. on November 5, unlike many other invited guests who just turned over and went back to sleep when they heard on the radio that Reagan had carried the election.

Gardner has returned to teach at Columbia University but frequently visits Italy. At times we have discussed the 1980 election. Besides the issue of the hostages, Carter's supposed errors were: the vote on Jerusalem at the United Nations, some of Billy's doings, Andy Young's somewhat exuberant behavior, and the policy toward Cuba. On the other hand, however, remarkable achievements marked his term of office: Camp David, the SALT II treaty, the strengthening of NATO, and the Panama Canal Agreement.

In fact, having gone through catharsis over Watergate and Vietnam, public opinion now needed another uplifting message. And Reagan had identified that message with the return to the great American dream. With his checkmate, Khomeini had humiliated the United States. Resurgence was a must, all across the board.

Shortly after taking office, Reagan repealed the restrictions on grain sales to the USSR imposed by Carter who had counted on the shortage of feed to undermine the program to increase meat supplies in the USSR. Farmers and dealers cheered; the supporters of détente commented favorably on the decision; and the vast majority of the people didn't care.

It opened the way for a very pragmatic and oscillatory policy toward the great opponent: the carrot and the stick. At the same time, the new administration opened up to Europe, announcing plans for more intense and diversified cooperation between the two shores of the Atlantic. The majority in the House, for what it may be worth, was in the hands of the other party. So what? Reagan could count on his enormous media appeal.

16 | *A Disappointed Bishop*

When the president of the United States sends you a message, when you are in Washington, inquiring whether he can ask you a personal favor, it can be a rather emotional experience. And it certainly did not occur to me that he might be asking for "favors" like retaining a person *extra legem,* like in the dark days of the airbase at Sigonella. (See chapter 21 for a discussion of the *Achille Lauro* event.) In fact, it was only an appointment this time—which I granted immediately—with the archbishop of New Orleans, who had come to Washington for that purpose.

Msgr. Philip Matthew Hannan had been assigned to set up the Vatican pavilion at the Louisiana Expo, and heartily desired having on loan Michelangelo's statue of the *Risen Christ* which is kept in the Church of Santa Maria sopra Minerva in Rome. I have no idea if he had a special feeling for Michelangelo, or if he aspired to equal Cardinal Spellman's success in having the *Pietà* from St. Peter's exhibited in New York, but he pleaded his case with such earnest warmth that it was both moving and somewhat embarrassing. I said I would refer the request to the appropriate authorities, but warned him about the difficulties involved due to the Holy See's decision not to grant the temporary loan of its works of art after what had happened to the *Pietà,* which had been gravely damaged by a deranged man, even though that misdeed had been perpetrated on Vatican premises. George Shultz also raised the same subject, telling me that the president had taken it very much to heart.

Enzo Scotti was the minister for cultural assets, and, with some difficulty (contrary to what I believed, there are more risks involved in the shipping of sculptures than of paintings) he was able to obtain the necessary technical and artistic permits. However, there were red-tape delays, and Reagan kept on insisting, and even offered to have the statue transported on board a U.S. naval vessel to eliminate any possible risk factor (Michelangelo would never have imagined that!). We had explained that an insurance policy, no matter how astronomical the amount, was of no importance, because any damage to the statue, let alone its loss, was out of the question.

In the meantime, Scotti had been replaced by Nino Gullotti, and finally everything was quietly worked out, and I was able to inform the White House of this. The packing was done with the utmost care and the faithful curiously eyed the iron crate as it was prepared for shipping. Only prepared—because one of the Dominicans, who was opposed to the loan, called in a reporter and a photographer. The Roman press raised such a clamor that the ministry had to revoke its authorization. In the days after that I asked everyone I met how many times they had gone to admire the *Risen Christ* and none had. As a politician, Reagan understood that there are boundaries that not even ministers or those above can cross. Much less resigned was Msgr. Hannan, and to sweeten the bitter taste of his disappointment I sent him a miniature silver copy of the contested statue. It was my own personal gift to him, for which no permits and authorizations were required; not on loan, it was for him to have and to keep.

This casual reference to the archbishop of New Orleans leads me to relate a few passing impressions on American Catholics, after deciding an in-depth development on this subject would be out of place in this book.

Cardinal Spellman once told me jokingly that if I wanted to form an idea about American bishops, I should think in terms of characteristics totally different from his own. His words were certainly paradoxical, and yet they offered me an opportunity to tell him that for me—a European and a Roman to boot—it was difficult to understand even some mundane aspects of their diocesan offices, with responsibility for such demanding "earthly" tasks as constructing and running schools, hospitals, and the like. Furthermore—and here I may be exaggerating a bit—some of the employees in the Madison Avenue curia offices looked as if they just came off the cover of a fashion magazine. He explained to me that this represented an intelligent way to overcome some of "our" taboos, and made male/female relations healthier and complex-free.

What did not quite convince me in this Catholic *nouvelle cuisine* was the application of the laws on matrimony. At that time I was less removed from my studies of Canon Law: it became apparent to me that recognition of the difficulty encountered by the Anglo-Saxon world in assimilating the Roman-Western code of Canon Law, all too deeply influenced by Justinian models, had led—in my opinion—to a disquieting laxity (the New York Archdiocese had prepared a good study for the reform). And even today I wonder, when I read that in 1987 (latest statistics available) the U.S. Diocesan Rotas granted 58,232 annulments and ruled against 1,305 cases over the twelve-month period; and that, as of 1 January 1988, there were 67,018 cases pending in the entire Church, of which 49,109, that is over 70 percent, were in the United States alone.

Considering that there are 54 million Catholics in the United States and 56 million in Italy (the number of "civil" weddings is very low), and that the number of annulments in Italy during that same year amounted to 950 (126 applications were refused), there is plenty of food for thought. Nor should people maintain that the figures should refer not to citizens but to *residents,* because here we get into the complicated issue of *legal domiciles,* some of which have given rise to heated feelings.

Take no umbrage over these remarks. A few years ago I wrote a short novel (*I Minibigami* [the mini bigamists]) to highlight the absurdity behind one of the reasons for nullifying matrimony, and that is the lack of the necessary delegation of powers to the priest celebrant. I was happy to see the deletion of this condition from the new Code of Canon Law.

On the other hand, American Catholics, and on their behalf the Episcopal Conference, deserve full praise and approval for the publication of documents on outstanding issues in current affairs. Quite laudable, to begin with, is their method. An initial draft is prepared and circulated for feedback in the form of comments, possible additions, or changes. At times, new drafts are prepared and submitted, following the same consultative procedure, before the final document is published.

I found two of these position papers particularly interesting: the analysis on nuclear weapons and the principles of social policy in a nation where long-standing poverty has not disappeared and where new forms of poverty are emerging in a disturbing way.

I know governments do not greatly appreciate these stands on various issues, and, in fact, claim that anything military is their exclusive concern. However, it would be difficult to make *human rights* a government priority in foreign policy, and at the same time deny the oneness and globality of man's problems, even in consideration of his physical survival. Of course, I cannot assess the extent to which the bishops' document may have encouraged the Reagan administration along the road of disarmament and may continue to do so with Bush; no doubt, however, it is a psychological and cultural antidote to those circles in favor of a rigid status quo of nuclear deterrence.

I was deeply impressed by the remarks of President Gerald Ford, a non-Catholic, in Philadelphia at the International Eucharistic Congress, in August 1976: "On this occasion, we pay tribute to the Church's contribution to the edification of a more peaceful world and to the lofty and wise inspiration she gives to the world. For millions of men and women, the Church is the refuge of the soul, the school of the spirit, and the safe depository of moral ideals."

The document on social policy may well serve to dispel the worldwide belief that all Americans are wealthy and happy. It was, in any case, a long-overdue statement delivered in a very responsible way by a Church which cannot remain blind to human suffering.

I know that Joseph Cardinal Bernardin, now the archbishop of Chicago, made a substantial contribution to what could be called the soundly progressive spirit of the document when he was the ordinary of Cincinnati; I am pleased to think that he descends from Trentino stock.

As a foreigner it would be out of place for me to comment upon other issues under discussion in the United States, like the ordination of women and ecclesiastical celibacy: yet social and security themes transcend all boundaries. American Catholics are also to be praised for their great generosity and for their deep religiosity. There are quite a few who attend 12:05 P.M. Mass during their lunch break (the first time I saw this timetable my curiosity was piqued, and when I heard the explanation I had to admit this does not happen "in Rome where Christ is Roman").

In fact, in military academies and on aircraft carriers, I have often seen Catholic, Protestant, and Jewish military personnel regularly attend religious ceremonies in large numbers. At the Air Force Academy in Colorado Springs, a single consecrated building houses a church, a temple, and a synagogue. Francis Cardinal Spellman, the military ordinary, was very proud of it.

I'll stop here. But I cannot help but recall the emotion instilled by De Gasperi at the Chamber when, on his return from the United States, he commented upon the inscription over the Tomb of the Unknown Soldier in Arlington Cemetery: "Unknown to all, but God."

17 | *Arafat*

A number of times I have mentioned the importance of relations with the members of the U.S. Congress. This is not only because many of them have a long, active life in politics, as opposed to people in the U.S. administration whose parabola is almost always very short, but because a good number of congressmen and senators can have little more than a superficial knowledge about the situations and problems of individual countries that demand discussion and decisions on their part. Therefore, it they do not use auspicious opportunities, they run the risk of being guided by emotive states of mind incited by persuasive TV commentators or by the lobbyists who, over there, are a registered and legally operational corporate entity.

To this end, all kinds of contacts, both individual and group-based, are helpful; hence the specific role of the Interparliamentary Union. In January and December of 1982 we received delegations from Capitol Hill as our guests in Rome. As always, alongside the mutual update exercise (How are the Communists doing? Is the pro-peace movement active in Italy too? What do you think about the situation in South America? Anything new in cancer research? etc.), current affairs are also discussed. At that time the major issue was the emergency in Lebanon and I was pleased to note how our colleagues from overseas had understood so well that we had joined our ships to theirs out of Western solidarity, and not because we were convinced that using gunboats was the way to resolve the crisis situation in that tormented nation.

Our guests in January, led by Peter Rodino, were Frank Annunzio,

James La Falce, Joseph Minish, Leon Panetta, Matthew Rinaldo, Leo Zeferetti, George Danichson, Lawrence De Nardis, Bernard Dwyer, Edward Don, Frank Guarini, and Bruce Vento. Besides Rome, they toured the Friuli region and also went to Pisa, Florence, Avellino, and Naples (NATO). In Majano the delegation visited the Senior Citizens' Center named after Marianna Stango Rodino and saw another social assistance center in Villa Santina: two American contributions to the reconstruction effort after the earthquake.

During this parliamentary mission's stay in Rome I had to go through a moment of sheer tragicomedy. After an excellent working luncheon at the Casina Valadier (the chef had outdone himself with a delicious course of fettuccine, a sumptuous saddle of veal, a tempting assortment of cheeses, and a delightfully immense nougat "semifreddo"), four congressmen asked me if they could pay their respects to President Pertini who immediately agreed. Unintentionally, Frank Annunzio started off on the wrong foot when he extended greetings to the president on behalf of the Italian-American members of Congress who, he said, had by now become an influential group. "You people don't amount to a hill of beans," Pertini replied, "because in all American movies the bad guys are always of Italian descent and you take that insult lying down." Taken aback, but not vanquished, the congressman from Chicago rejoined: "It may be like that in the movies back home, but here you have the terrorists walking the streets."

Just the thing he should never have said! The president challenged his statement and said the terrorists were all foreigners anyway. Icy beads of perspiration were dotting my brow while, luckily enough, the three other congressmen, in the throes of . . . postprandial fatigue, seemed to have dozed off. Quite generously, however, Pertini changed his tone and brought the smile back to Frank's face by saying: "You know I belonged to the anti-fascist movement and the Resistance, but if America had not come to our rescue, fascism would still be in power." On that note, and with other wartime recollections, the audience came to an end. On the way out, much to the embarrassment of the presidential honor guard, Annunzio made a few cracks which were meaningless to his colleagues who were just becoming alert once again (now I understand why alcoholic beverages are not served during lunches in America).

During the seven years of Pertini's term of office, I attended countless audiences at the Quirinale Palace, and this was the only time I saw someone leave dissatisfied.

A nasty event took place in December 1981: An American general, Dozier, was kidnapped in the Veneto region; he was later rescued in a spectacular operation conducted by an Italian special forces unit. The American Congress decided to send a delegation to Italy led by Representative Rostenkowski to express gratitude, but we had to decline since we were all in Lagos to attend the Interparliamentary Union's spring session. Senator Stafford and other parliamentarians took that occasion to extol and applaud the Italian law enforcement services. They made it quite clear that public opinion would have been outraged over the captivity of an American general.

In September, the U.S. delegation attending the conference of the Interparliamentary Union in Rome had a special working session with the Italian group. And I was quite pleased to read the statement released by their leader, Representative Claude Pepper (one of the old-timers on Capitol Hill):

> We have just finished a very warm and almost fraternal discussion with our colleagues in the Italian Parliament, and have been able to note that, as legislators, we share many of the same hopes and concerns.
>
> In our opinion, our highly positive meeting constitutes a further sign of the growing bond uniting our two countries, and the increasing strength of relations between Italy and the United States. As we see it, such relations are exceptionally close and most beneficial for numerous reasons. Our governments, our peoples and we ourselves as representatives of our parliaments, hold very close positions on a number of international issues, such as repression in Poland, Soviet aggression in Afghanistan, and support for President Reagan's new peace initiative in the Middle East. We hereby declare specifically that in our opinion, the Italian armed forces, together with American and French troops, did a magnificent job during the evacuation of PLO members from Lebanon.
>
> All these points, together with others, show the value of the ties binding Italy and the United States, equal members of the Atlantic Alliance and the community of nations. We would like to underline this concept. We know there are those who seek to stress the differences of sizes and roles within the Alliance. The truth is, however, that our countries are partners who share common values and are committed to the achievement of common goals. Together, we Parliamentarians address the great problems of our times, knowing that in the final analysis we can count on mutual support.

Such a statement was all the more important from a political standpoint since the climax of the conference had been Yassir Arafat's speech, so enthusiastically applauded. Outside of rigid government discipline (he only met with Foreign Minister Colombo, and not even at the Ministry) everyone felt that it was not by keeping the PLO in a ghetto that the Middle East problem could be unraveled. And the time had come for a bold change of course since, at the recently attended Arab Conference in Fez, Arafat had made moderate statements (that he repeated in Rome), and looming ahead were prospects for a breakthrough that it would have been wise to cultivate. Yet, neither Washington nor London consented to receive the Fez Committee, thus unfortunately postponing the onset of a solution.

The ninety delegations also attended an audience in the Vatican where John Paul II delivered a significant address: "Liberty is a single prism of which religious freedom is but one facet. Without religious freedom there is no liberty, and without global liberty there is no religious freedom."

There were also two Interparliamentary Union sessions in 1983. In January the U.S. delegation included Clement Zablocki (House Foreign Affairs Committee chairman), E. Kika de la Garza, Donald Pease, Bill Nelson, Bruce Vento, William Broonfield, Robert Lagomarsino, Larry Winn, and Mario Castillo. We had a thorough discussion on security problems and economic issues. Our American colleagues, who were tempted every year to curtail U.S. military spending in Europe, openly asked us if we were planning to shoulder a greater share of the burden on account of our fairly good production and growth rates. I recall that at the end of a . . . verbal skirmish full of concrete facts and figures, the head of delegation asked us: "Are the Italian people at least grateful for this American effort?"

Zablocki, of Polish origin, was quite anxious to hear any information we had from Warsaw; and naturally what he most appreciated about his visit to Rome was the opportunity to meet his (and our) Pope. He spoke to me about the development of Polish communities in the United States, especially in Chicago, with a rising birth rate most promising for their future importance. As an adamant anti-Communist, he saw no possible evolution on the horizon and considered unrealistic the hopes Edward Gierek had shared with me a few years earlier, and which I had relayed to him.

Once again our visitors appreciated and praised the climate of cooperation which reigned among Italian parliamentarians, both within the Union and on the Foreign Affairs Committee. It seemed strange to them, accustomed as they were to thinking of Italy as the theater of endless battles between Guelphs and Ghibellines or among conflicting political colors.

When the thirty-two members of the congressional delegation led by Claiborne Pell came in August, I no longer received them at Parliament, but at the Farnesina (Foreign Ministry) since, after the elections, I had become foreign minister in Bettino Craxi's cabinet. Naturally enough, the first question focused on the meaning of this new turn in Italian politics. It would not be fair to consider an American superficial who finds it difficult to understand that there are no grounds for concern over a *Socialist* prime minister when in their terminology, and not theirs alone, *Socialist* countries were the ones in Eastern Europe. Moreover, being unfamiliar with the proportional voting system and coalition governments, they failed to understand how some cabinet members could belong to a party different from that of the prime minister.

Another fact Americans find so amazing is the high percentage of voters who go to the polls in Italy. A curious theory was mentioned to me, quoting a political analyst, whereby half of those with the right to a vote can delegate the other half to vote for them on a regular basis. This sounds to me like an excuse for justifying the high rate of abstention in the United States, further fostered by the system of voter registration for each election, which doubles the required commitment for every voter. Add to this the great mobility of the population: I don't know if it was an overstatement, but they told us, for example, that less than one-third of business executives remain with the same company for over five years; and even that a good share of the population moves from the East Coast to the West Coast.

Some congressmen met managers of American firms operating in Italy who confirmed the politically reassuring picture we had presented.

The Lebanese and Israelis signed a bilateral agreement on May 17, which came as a surprise to practically everyone. The first to take it as a slight was the Syrian president, Assad (he told me so during a visit I made to Damascus upon their invitation), who also felt he had been betrayed by the American ambassador-at-large Philip Habib, who visited him frequently and who had said nothing about it. This is not the proper place for an analysis of the episode, but it is difficult to rule out that the assassination of the Lebanese head of state Bechir Gemayel might have been linked to this agreement (and/or the expulsion of the Palestinians?). The agreement soon fell through, but Amin Gemayel, who took his brother's place, never forgot those days.

In the meantime, Washington had appointed Ambassador Robert MacFarlane, a former Marine officer assigned to the State Department, to coordinate diplomatic activities in the area. I gladly received him on August 25, upon his return from a difficult series of discussions in Damascus, Jedda, Amman, Cairo, and Jerusalem. In some form the United States was guaranteeing that Israeli forces would move back to the Awali river as part of the total withdrawal stipulated in the May 17 agreement which Beirut was unable to ratify. In Lebanon, the Washington envoy had come upon an inflamed situation due to the split between Gemayel, considered a representative of the Falange alone, and the Christian-Druse-Sunni alliance of Franjeh, Walid Jumblatt, and Karame, all pro-Syrian.

I shared my opinion with MacFarlane, and in a nutshell it was: Syria on its own was not able to solve the Lebanese problem, but it was sheer delusion to hope that it could be resolved without or against Syria. And since the Lebanese army as such was very weak, the withdrawal of foreign troops was unthinkable without agreeing on a platform with the Druses and the Moslem left wing. It also seemed hardly possible to me that the men of the Multilateral Force could go into the Chouf mountains to avoid massacres and chaos upon the withdrawal of the Israelis.

MacFarlane's goodwill was unquestionable, but he could hardly be more successful than Philip Habib, who had started off with the considerable advantage of speaking Arabic. The Western powers could certainly count on the use of diplomacy, but not on the persuasive role of the military forces deployed in the area. Quite the contrary!

In this connection, a certain amount of commotion arose over a slight incident during President Mitterrand's visit to Venice, which unfortunately coincided with an attack against French troops stationed in Lebanon, and I was tormented by the thought that our soldiers might also be exposed to this vicious chain reaction of violence and counterviolence. We were most careful to provide General Angioni's troops with constant political protection, and did so successfully. Hence I deemed it necessary to say that when Italians had been murdered in an ambush in the former Belgian Congo, our airmen had not called for retaliation and the misdeed had remained isolated.

Between courteous silence and the safekeeping of our soldiers in Lebanon, I did not hesitate. The French might not have liked this, but in no way did it ruin my relationship with their president. All the more so —the press did not know this—because a few days before I had met in France with the foreign ministers of the countries party to the Multinational Force and Claude Cheysson had been the most resolute in barring retaliation in the case of attacks since that might lead to a most dangerous chain of events.

Early in September I went to Madrid for the Conference on Security and Cooperation in Europe (CSCE) and had an opportunity for two lengthy talks with George Shultz whom I had known before as secretary of the treasury. In talks with Gromyko, Shultz had eased tension over the South Korean airplane downed by the Soviets. We all had to maintain a firm position on the temporary suspension of civil flights both to and from Moscow, but not jeopardize the negotiations under way, nor the one about to be concluded; and not even the effort to cut continental missiles which the United States, quite correctly, wished to decide in full agreement with all the Allies.

On this last point, the firmness shown in deployment (Comiso for Italy) was bearing fruit, even though further concessions had to be requested of Andropov. And here, for the first time, I found myself confronted with the issue of the French and British missiles. Shultz left them out in his talks with Moscow since "the Chinese missiles were not included in the count either." Taking a more pragmatic approach, I more readily accepted the explanation that, for the time being, it was impossible to twin the issues, and that it would be senseless to imperil the principle for secondary considerations.

I then asked him to convene a meeting, even a symbolic one, of the four ministers from countries with troops in Lebanon, to show that, in the absence of military coordination—which wasn't entirely negative— at least there was political coordination. Shultz agreed immediately, and we met a few hours later.

I saw Shultz again later that same month, during the General Assembly of the United Nations in New York.

Our loyal attitude—quite consistent, however, with Italy's foreign policy during Emilio Colombo's tenure—placed us in a good position with the major ally who explicitly appreciated our tireless efforts to foster progress in the Geneva missile negotiations, about which George was rather optimistic. I myself raised the issue of the French and British missiles, predicting (and it did happen) that the two governments would use the UN rostrum to say that at the right time and in the right place they would not refuse to sit at the negotiating table. Before we parted, Shultz touched on three other matters.

First of all were Washington's continuing concerns over Libya, which he raised on account of Italy's relations with its Mediterranean neighbor. I rejoined that we had our ups and downs in that relationship as well, but that at this time we felt Ghaddafi (as he had said a few days before to the Yugoslav minister Lasar Mojsov, who informed me in New York) was leaning toward a somewhat moderate position, with his stated intention to promote political solutions in both Chad and Lebanon.

This meant that new Libyan messages of good intentions toward the United States could be expected. Rather than sending messages, Shultz retorted, Tripoli should come up with concrete signs of its alleged will to improve relations with Washington.

Another subject had to do with difficulties between the United States and Europe in the field of agricultural policy. He felt there were good reasons for these difficulties, but governments should view them in broader political terms so as to keep them under control and prevent them from having too many repercussions.

Lastly, the secretary of state spoke about the great importance the United States attached to increasing cooperation with us in the fight against drug abuse and, in particular, in curbing heroin traffic. This was the purpose of the forthcoming trip to Italy by the attorney general, who expected to establish increasingly productive cooperation with our responsible authorities. I fully reassured him, pleased that intense joint efforts, which so far had been lacking, could now begin in this field.

We would soon meet again, on the occasion of Prime Minister Bettino Craxi's trip to the United States.

18 | *Craxi's Trip*

Prime Minister Craxi's trip to the United States was very carefully prepared, both in planning the schedule and in choosing the subjects for discussion (it is always a good rule to focus talks on a few points and not indulge in "overall discussions" which bring nothing new into the picture for either side).

My commitments at the Farnesina allowed me to attend only the meetings in Washington, while Craxi went to Providence, Rhode Island, to receive an honorary degree from Brown University; paid a courtesy call on the UN secretary-general; attended a luncheon hosted by David Rockefeller at the Council on Foreign Relations; and unveiled a monument to Garibaldi on Staten Island.

Besides other useful meetings (secretary of the treasury, IMF, World Bank, secretary of trade), our stay in Washington included discussions and a working luncheon at the White House, a conference at the State Department, a dinner at the Italian Embassy in honor of Vice President Bush, a visit to Congress, and a press conference.

It didn't take long to confirm our common approach to the missiles issue (never break off negotiations and never deviate from the downwards balance of forces); we saw as a positive sign the caution shown in Sofia by the Eastern European countries after the missile deployment by the Western countries in order to reduce the imbalance of forces. We expressed our congratulations over the new American contacts with Syria and our encouragement to pursue them, without expecting . . . alignment. In an Islamic country, I pointed out, polygamy even applies in family life, and one certainly cannot expect the opposite in foreign policy, all the more so, I added, since other non-Muslim nations are not all that faithful either. The rumors about a preliminary study on a U.S.-Jordanian agreement were true, even though the Americans were annoyed over the leaks in the press; we strongly recommended they not lose a global vision of the region and not make *faux pas* like the short-lived agreement between Lebanon and Israel. Speaking about Lebanon, it would have been wise to check out the conciliatory stance of Walid Jumblatt whom I saw frequently in Rome during his frequent visits to his mother who lives there. Jumblatt has a difficult personality, but fortunately he is not touchy. One day during a press conference Sandro Pertini called the leader of the Druses a drug addict, but he did not submit a note of protest and just laughed it off.

With Reagan we probed the possibilities for a joint United States-Europe-Saudi Arabia plan, open to other countries as well, to assist reconstruction in Lebanon once the fighting and the skirmishes were over. There was respectful attention, but nothing more.

The American positions on the various international problems could be summed up as follows: reiteration of concerns over Libya; declared willingness to sustain the development of Somalia, but with no antagonism toward Ethiopia; respect for the Contadora countries, but continuing distrust of the Sandinistas in Nicaragua; and a cautious tribute to freedom aspirations in Chile because "we can try to hasten the process toward democracy, but it is difficult to ask Pinochet to commit suicide."

On the subject of Chile, we had to iron out the texts of the statements the two leaders would make after their talks. We accepted a toning down because the Americans had greatly revised their position as well, considering that Mrs. Kirkpatrick, who was in Santiago when Alwyn and the opposition leaders were expelled, had publicly complimented "Chilean stability."

This lady is both tough and charming. When representing Washington at the United Nations she lived a secluded life, to the point of staying out of New York society; but when she came to Rome to speak on peace, and to Venice to talk about human rights, she said some very beautiful and heartfelt things. At the dining table Craxi asked Reagan to tell one of his jokes, thereby strengthening a budding personal affinity between them. The president didn't have to be asked twice. He joyfully set aside the itemized file cards he followed most scrupulously and pulled two "good ones" from his repertoire which abounds with stories poking fun at diplomatic activity. Telling them here is not disrespectful; all the more so since at the summit meeting in Venice he publicly dedicated forty-five minutes to this obliging type of performance during a reception with a guest list kept short by the security people.

An ambassador in tails, wearing all his decorations, but without his glasses—easier to make a hit that way—made his entry into the presidential ballroom just as the music began. With a slight bow, he paid his respects to someone in a flowing red gown, offering to lead onto the dance floor. "I cannot dance for three reasons," was the icy reply, in a deep and husky voice. "First, I don't know how to dance. Second, they are playing the national anthem. Third, I am the Apostolic nuncio."

In other Reagan versions, the nuncio turned into the archbishop of Berlin or Paris, variations on the same theme.

The other joke was about the pilot of a hot-air balloon drifting helplessly in the wind. He finally caught a glimpse of someone on the terrace of a stately building and, dropping some ballast, descended a bit and cried out: "Where am I?" The answer was so obvious ("You're flying on a balloon") that he realized he was in the skies above Washington, and was right on top of the State Department.

Apart from rare exceptions—I will refer explicitly to an important one later on—Reagan discussed matters with the help of file cards prepared by his aides. Whenever he was able to do without this rigidity, for example during luncheons and informal dinners, he came across as a very warm and charming person. The jokes were an excellent way to sidestep issues not on the agenda, as was the case in his contacts with the press.

Craxi made a good impression on Capitol Hill and at the National Press Club, answering questions in a direct way with that touch of humor which is compulsory in the United States and helps to create the right atmosphere. Seeing the many congressmen and senators who came to greet me, he jokingly told me I could have run for office there too. At other times I would have read a note of hopeful malignity in his remark, but after months of working together, our relationship had become productively excellent.

I will mention just two of the issues touched upon in the talks with

Shultz and his staff. We urged Washington to work out stable mechanisms for sincere and trustful contacts with the European Community in order to avoid unnecessary controversies and to seek positive joint solutions instead of *feuds;* for example, drawing up a coordinated plan for food aid to poor countries. Shultz did not dissent, and regretted not having been able to implement the agreement he had made with Gaston Thorn the year before.

The other subject was much more explosive because of what happened a few days afterwards. I asked what was the State Department's appraisal of the situation in Grenada after the assassination of the prime minister, Maurice Bishop. And I explained that I was asking this question because, in talks with Fidel Castro in 1981, he had told me it would be necessary to coordinate Cuban military defense with Nicaragua and Grenada if it proved impossible to find a *modus vivendi* with the United States (in the wake of the early preliminaries with the Carter administration). George and his staff seemed surprised: Bishop was a Communist just like his successor, and so nothing could be said to have changed.

A few days later I was dumbfounded when I learned the Americans had landed in force on Grenada in order to avert an "unbearable" situation. I certainly do not claim that an ally has to reveal his strategic plans to us, but it was not right for him to tell us there was no emergency and then turn around and launch a massive military operation which was quite delicate in terms of principles as well. We had every right to an explanation, especially for reasons of Italian prestige.

George asked me to receive the president of the island of Dominica because, together with the head of state of Barbados, she had been the one to sound the alarm and call for the armed intervention. This explanation, I must confess, heightened my uneasiness. With its various and powerful intelligence services and with hundreds of college students on the island, was it possible that the United States found out about a potentially dangerous situation only because two tiny Caribbean countries had taken the initiative?

If George had told me that the wave of emotion in the United States over the destruction of the Marine barracks in Beirut had called for an immediate psychological move to shift attention elsewhere, I would have understood. But not this. Open arms to Madam President from Dominica (she came twice and was very well received), but in the meantime, at the United Nations, we could not approve the military operation which had been decided upon independently and without even attempting lawful international action. That was the position we assumed, raising criticisms and reservations even at home. However, this act of respect for the proper rules had the contrary effect of increasing consideration for us in Washington and elsewhere. We had almost immediate proof of greater attention toward Italy.

The Atlantic Council met in Brussels in December. It was ordinarily attended by foreign ministers, and during the 1983 meeting Shultz dedicated an hour-and-a-half to bilateral talks with me, even though we had seen one another shortly before that.

He spoke about the remarkable effect of Atlantic solidarity, using words I'm so fond of: firmness, patience, reasonableness, dialogue. He accepted the invitation to come to Stockholm—the Conference on Disarmament—in January to have an opportunity to meet with Gromyko. In Italy, there was a good convergence of views in Parliament, and the Communists had sent party delegates to Moscow to work on Andropov, even though without results so far. It was also necessary for colleagues from neutral countries to come to Stockholm, beginning with Yugoslavia. We promised to urge their presence.

I briefed Shultz on the EEC Council Meeting in Athens, stressing the importance, *all across the board,* of what was by now the probable entry of Spain and Portugal into the EEC. The negotiations, which had lasted for seven years, would be concluded, at any cost, during Italy's semester of presiding over the Council meeting.

We then discussed the Middle East. For Lebanon we had made twice the effort agreed upon with Beirut and were there with 2,500 troops on land and 600 aboard ship. But to what end? We certainly would not have planned unilateral withdrawal, but everyone had to consider a gradual reduction, and it was necessary to insist on transferring law and order operations to the United Nations. Reagan had announced a "plan" for the Middle East: in realistic terms, what could we expect?

Shultz gave me a rundown of his recent talks in Washington with Gemayel and Shamir.

Gemayel planned to expand his government to include some of the major leaders like Franjeh, Karame, and Jumblatt who had been opposed to him so far. Syria was keeping a low profile, but pressure could be brought to bear upon Damascus to keep them from succumbing to the temptation to take military steps. Washington had informed Syria again and again that American action after the attacks on the Marines and on the American negotiators was purely defensive.

Regarding the talks with Shamir, Shultz explained that the stories in the press were inexact, especially with respect to a U.S.-Israeli operational unit against Syria. Nonetheless, Shultz was elusive in replying on the problem of the occupied territories and on the specific point of the Israeli settlements.

I understood that the Americans hoped King Hussein would be the first one to declare his readiness to begin negotiations, on behalf of the Palestinians as well, since at that point they felt Israel would no longer have been able to refuse: "In one way or another, Israel will have to get moving, even though the problem of the settlements was anything but easy." I didn't feel Shultz had good grounds for his optimism.

The next day, Shultz, Howe, Dumas, and I got together to discuss Lebanon, but it added nothing new to what had emerged during the bilateral talks with the American secretary of state.

I was quite insistent on the need for the United Nations to take over for the Multinational Force in Lebanon; and also on not letting the Palestinian issue just fester, with the risk of lending wings to those who considered the possibility of negotiations to be wishful thinking. Even with the greatest respect, both past and present, for Israel and its susceptibility, some steps had to be taken to get moving in those very dangerous waters.

Shultz assured us that their trusted envoy of the moment, Ambassador Rumsfeld, would take action.

At the end of every year, people usually try to take stock of their own deeds and omissions. I was rather satisfied with the "running in" period at the Foreign Ministry. And, thinking back to the trip to Washington with Bettino Craxi, it was easy to compare the Italy of 1984 with that of the immediate postwar period when it was not unbecoming—because we neither offered nor were asked for anything humiliating in exchange —to go to America even to beg, so that the Italian people would not die of hunger and to be able to begin their rebirth.

19 | *The Olympic Games*

While thinking highly of the initiative, I had been hesitant about going to the United States at the beginning of the New Year for the presentation of the English version of the comprehensive collection of writings and letters by Filippo Mazzei, the adventurous Tuscan doctor and merchant who was a pioneer of Italian emigration and, in the eighteenth century, became one of Jefferson's advisers and a co-signer of the Declaration of Independence. Mazzei's biographer, Sister Margherita Marchione, and the president of Fairleigh Dickinson University in New Jersey, Peter Sammartino, were most insistent, as were the executives of the Monte dei Paschi Bank who wanted to inaugurate their first branch office in America by having me deliver a conference on Italy's position in the economic and political problem scenario of 1984. However, what swept away all hesitation was the invitation to Washington for talks with the president, Shultz, and with the secretaries of the treasury and defense, Donald Regan and Caspar Weinberger. I confess that I was also satisfied by the implicit rebuff to all those who were grumbling about the Italian position on the Grenada issue.

The two events in New York went very well and the conference on the prospects for Italy in the economy of the 1980s gave eminent Americans an opportunity to express their views and make some interesting suggestions.

I was at the White House on January 13, and the chief of protocol brought to my attention the exceptional nature of an audience in the morning, since the president ordinarily devoted that time to meeting with the National Security Council. He received me in the presence of Bush and Shultz.

Reagan brought the talks around to Lebanon and, since I too had noted some small signs of openness through my recent trips and contacts with Israeli leaders and other countries in the area, I urged them to exercise pressure on Gemayel to ensure progress in all directions in the national reconciliation effort. Reagan concurred, and said that my idea not to overlook Syria had been pursued and that he had just received a very warm message from President Assad. I also recommended that the Multinational Force continue providing protection for the Palestinian camps in order to avert the risk of new massacres at Sabra, Chatila, and anywhere else.

I then expressed my thanks for the importance the United States had agreed to give the upcoming conference in Stockholm by sending the secretary of state; this had raised the level for all thirty-five countries. Reagan briefed me on what he was going to say during a televised speech to the American people three days later. He considered it very important in terms of clarifying the spirit with which America addressed not only the Stockholm conference, but, in a broad sense, the problems of disarmament and security.

I thanked him and recognized that the approach was an excellent one since public opinion throughout the world and young people, in particular, needed to develop a deep understanding of the ideals of peace and defense underlying American democracy. I expressed the hope that this approach would pave the way for another constructive moment in America's determining presence on the international scene, similar to what had been accomplished by Nixon in opening up to China without ever jeopardizing dialogue with the Soviet Union.

The later talks at the State Department were equally substantial in content and took place in a very cordial atmosphere. Shultz expanded on the subject of the Stockholm conference, accepting the idea of maintaining close links as well with the neutral (Austria, Switzerland, and Sweden) and nonaligned (Yugoslavia) countries.

In order to show that the West was not isolated at all and that, in the absence of progress in negotiations, it would have to rearm, Shultz told me once again that the purpose of the president's speech scheduled for the following Monday was precisely to delineate the framework for the resumption of constructive dialogue with the East.

It was quite courteous of Shultz to tell me that my comments to him on Stockholm during the NATO Council's December meeting had made him even more convinced in pursuing the line of *openness in firmness* with the president. In his opinion, therefore, Reagan's talk would be "a straightforward speech focused on the prospects of American-Soviet relations."

On the issue of disarmament, I feel it necessary to draw attention to how sensitive people were in some North African countries, especially Libya, about the deployment of missiles in Sicily. This sensitivity could serve as the basis for a campaign which had to be taken into consideration in order to react in an appropriate manner, if possible, and, in any case, not light fires at such a delicate moment.

We discussed the Middle East once again, stressing the need to urge Gemayel along the road of national reconciliation: despite all the difficulties, it seemed to me that the various Lebanese factions had not abandoned the goal of an independent and unified Lebanon.

On the more general aspects of the Middle East, I offered Shultz a more detailed picture of my impressions after recent trips to that part of the world.

In quite correctly pursuing an improvement in relations with Syria, and if possible revived negotiations on the occupied territories as well, it was important not to lose what had already been achieved, and that was the peaceful relationship between Egypt and Israel. The secretary of state was of the same opinion, and told me Israel was concerned more than ever before about the "ice cold" peace with Egypt. The return of the Sinai in exchange for peace risked turning out to be a sterile exercise for Israel, and could therefore discourage further steps. On the other hand, I remarked, Egypt could not go too far because the Camp David plan had run aground and the Arab world held Cairo responsible for a global weakening of their position. It was necessary to work patiently on reestablishing Egypt's "Islamic communion"; and Shultz was interested in my planned schedule of visits to Cairo, Khartoum, Tripoli, and Saudi Arabia with President Pertini.

I then raised the UNESCO issue. I knew the Americans (and other countries) looked with a critical eye upon the stewardship of the secretary-general, Amadou-Mahtar M'Bow, but their threatened withdrawal would have worsened the institution's crisis, and not only from a budgetary viewpoint. Shultz replied that things had gone too far and the decision had been made. However, he would send their representative in Paris to Rome for an analytical review of the issue (in this way I met Jean Gerard, a very intelligent person in the American diplomatic line-up who later became U.S. ambassador in Luxembourg). In order to avoid erroneous deductions, I did not raise a matter which filled me with deep-felt joy: the normalization of diplomatic relations between the United States and the Holy See. Finally!

I left Washington the next day, which was my sixty-fifth birthday. I thought to myself that were I one of the ambassadors traveling with me, and returning in an equally satisfied frame of mind (Bruno Bottai, Umberto La Rocca, and Bartolomeo Attolico), I should have retired on that same day. Instead, I was on my way to Stockholm for the Conference on Disarmament in Europe, and the Farnesina was in no way alien to its success.

The apparent harshness of the Soviet speech did not lessen this appraisal. Shultz had his meeting with Gromyko and, since he had to leave Sweden in a hurry, he informed me in writing on January 19 with one of those many personal letters which, for the next five years, could provide an exact picture of international development all by themselves. Shultz was disappointed by the tone of Gromyko's public position, so in contrast with his own and with President Reagan's. However, Shultz wrote:

> Despite this prelude, I find that the five-hour meeting was useful. . . . Our substantial differences remain, especially with regard to the reduction of nuclear weapons. Despite this, and in contrast with his public performance, Gromyko was cautiously insistent on discussing the future possibilities of negotiations on chemical weapons, on the resumption of the MBFR talks, and with respect to the Conference on Disarmament itself. . . . I stressed the need for continuing dialogue between us, and Gromyko *agreed*. . . . In a certain sense I was heartened by the serious and in-depth nature of this exchange of ideas.

In February I assisted Pertini at a meeting with Vice President Bush which took place at our embassy in Moscow on the occasion of Andropov's funeral. We spoke about a U.S.-Soviet summit meeting, an idea which by then was taking shape. We also discussed the modalities of the military withdrawal underway in Lebanon, which the Americans had decided all of a sudden, and which we did not criticize due to our never-ending trust in diplomatic and political initiatives. Necessary, however, was an intelligent coordination of those initiatives. I explained there was no contradiction in the opinion that Israel should give up the occupied part of Lebanon, but that it had to do so concurrently with Syria, otherwise everything would have been made all the more difficult. In fact, I knew American circles were pressing Israel also in order to relieve the heavy burdens on the budget.

At the meeting President Pertini and I had with Chernenko during that same "funeral" occasion, we were pleased to note there was a will to negotiate the reduction of armaments and that the U.S. missiles stationed in Italy at Comiso did not represent an obstacle to open and constructive dialogue between the Soviets and ourselves as well.

The apparent cordiality of Chernenko and a glimmer of openness in talks with Gromyko had misled me to believe there might still be room to avoid the Soviet boycott of the Olympic Games in Los Angeles. The new Soviet leader only seemed anxious to put an end to the liturgy of the audiences and take a rest after the morning's tiring burial rites, and had willingly acceded to Pertini's suggestion to let the foreign ministers deal with the problems. Even during a later visit to the Kremlin the door still seemed to be ajar, to the point of admitting that, had Reagan undertaken in writing to protect Soviet athletes, the doubts concerning their safety would be dispelled (they referred to a Ku Klux Klan threat, but what they really feared were defections). Reagan wrote the letter immediately, but just as the International Olympic Committee (IOC) president—former Spanish ambassador to Moscow—was about to leave to deliver it, a blunt communiqué from the USSR announced their final decision against participating in the 1984 Games. In vain did I try to understand this relapse to hostility, even out of legitimate curiosity; Gromyko smiled when I asked him about it and minimized the whole issue. "Glasnost" had yet to arrive; however, after noting that the organizational impact of the Olympics in California had been splendid even without Eastern European participation, the Soviets were among the first to sign up for the Seoul Games of 1988, despite the angry reaction of North Korea, which had rejected a more than honorable sporting compromise (with the possibility of one or more competitions being held in North Korea).

Why had I devoted so much effort and worry to Soviet participation in Los Angeles? Well, I am convinced that the Olympics, with their enormous and ever-increasing appeal to worldwide public opinion, are a factor contributing to international détente. This is why, in 1980, I had been one of those opposed to the American camp asking for the games in Moscow to be boycotted; and since the Italian government at that time was concerned and hesitant, in Parliament we prepared a document worded as follows: "The Chamber, in the conviction that the decision on participation at the Olympic Games pertains exclusively to the competent sporting authorities, will proceed to address the day's agenda." Such a text would have passed with a vast majority, but there was no need to put it to a vote. The government itself handed the hot potato back to the National Olympic Committee; and Franco Carraro ably withstood even a final adverse attempt on the part of some of his influential political friends, afraid the Americans might consider our presence in Moscow as an act of . . . lesser Western loyalty.

Going back to 1984, the main issue in diplomatic circles was not the Olympics, but Moscow's clever proposal for a solemn treaty whereby all countries would pledge to forgo the use of force to settle disputes. Such a protocol might have been naïve and sterile, but we had to be careful we did not hand over to Moscow the banner of international peace, as in the times of Stalin and early Brezhnev. Moscow had also proposed to start negotiations on prohibiting nuclear first strike; but this was impossible to accept as long as the enormous advantage held by the East in conventional weapons was not corrected. Was the linkage of the two treaties surmountable?

When invited to Moscow, I had explicitly declared that insisting on the demand for linking the two meant bringing down the entire plan; and my firm belief after talks with Chernenko was that the two diplomatic endeavors could proceed separately.

I informed Shultz of this when we met in Brussels in May for the spring session of the NATO Council. Shultz showed interest in such a possibility—also because we had to consider the psychological reception of the Soviet proposals by public opinion in the nonaligned countries— but he linked the possibility of a Stockholm round of negotiation on the non-use of force—which he did not rule out—to a serious Soviet willingness also to negotiate Western proposals on confidence-building measures. During this period of harsh polemics, the Soviet Union was putting the Alliance to the test, and more than ever before it was necessary to project strength and unity in order to overcome the moment's difficulties without ever closing the door to dialogue.

We also spoke of Poland that day, and I briefed George on the EEC proposal to assist in a recovery plan for Polish agriculture, separate from the state's initiatives, which the Church had been striving to launch for a long time and which Solidarnosc also looked upon with favor. Shultz confirmed that, along with other prospects for improving the situation in Poland, this issue had come up between the Pope and Reagan when they met in Alaska. I told him the United States should reconsider that trade embargo measures still applied to that country, which also covered the supply of agricultural commodities (animal feed grains) shipped, however, in large quantities to the USSR: in the end, Poland, which had so far tried in vain, would be forced to import such products through Moscow at an increased price, thereby worsening its economic dependence upon the USSR.

In view of the Summit Meeting of the Seven Most Industrialized Countries in London the following week (we joked about this endless series of opportunities to get together) Shultz mentioned an American idea to expand use of the seven-country formula, by having meetings, during the year, of foreign ministers and other ministers, and making the summit a focal point for policy making and verification: all of this was intended to ensure improved harmonization of Euro-American and Japanese policies I observed—and the experiences of later years confirmed my opinion—that the importance of the summit resided more in the event's photo opportunities and media coverage than in the speeches. As far as the rest was concerned, perhaps the substance of the other institutional opportunity for dialogue with Japan (the spring session of OECD in Paris) was more important; but the impact remained confined to the sphere of experts.

As the Olympics approached, once the thread of hope with Moscow had been severed, there was still fear of acts of violence on the part of isolated fanatics. IOC president Samaranch spoke to me about this, and I thought it would be better for him to get in touch directly with Shultz, who was very pleased and received him immediately, and wrote me about the meeting:

Dear Giulio, I wish to inform you about my meeting with the President of IOC, Samaranch, which you made possible. In my opinion, the meeting was positive for all parties concerned. Samaranch was worried about various matters, including the inadequacies of security installations. I couldn't agree with him fully on this point, and pointed out that we have no intelligence about possible incidents in the near future. I nonetheless assured Samaranch that we will be anxious to receive any details that he may come to know. Our efforts have been prevention-directed, and I underlined that we prefer to exceed in this sector rather than be caught unprepared. We have allocated substantial funds and will have over 17,000 security personnel on duty.

He also informed me that he had given Samaranch a statement to forward to the National Olympic Committees in order to reassure them on both security and the sensitive issue of possible requests for asylum by athletes who were minors.

Samaranch had been very insistent upon my accepting his invitation to Los Angeles, but I was uncertain, because those days in August are the only ones devoted to the family and to a brief respite from political-ministerial life. This is why I have always repressed my strong desire to go to Saratoga during its fascinating racing season, precisely in the month of August. What made me decide was a personal note from President Reagan, indicating that he would be happy to meet with me in California during that period. Wife, children, and grandchildren could not object to my absence, and thus—arriving a few days before my appointment with the president—I was able to delight in the superb Olympic performance, enriched by the enchanting Hollywood-style choreography and brought to perfection by masterly management.

Ever faithful to their business philosophy, the Americans had contracted out the entire organization to a private group, set up by a medium-sized tour operator, who even assumed part of the responsibility for construction at the airport, whose importance extended far beyond the Olympics alone. Of course, except for the International Olympic Committee members and a very limited number of IOC guests (including me), everyone had to pay for the entrance ticket, even the mayor of Los Angeles, except for the opening and closing ceremonies, where protocol assigned him a role. Ticket prices were sky-high, but with their tax system, many companies had bought whole sets for their employees and deducted the cost from their taxes as a business expense. Then there was an endless series of items with the Olympic logo: dolls, T-shirts, hats, playing cards, lighters, buttons.

The mandatory royalties on such massive sales supplemented the returns on tickets. In conclusion, the end results were not a cent paid by the taxpayer, a satisfied IRS, and good dividends for the shareholders in the private group.

I was fortunate enough to be present when Italian athletes enthralled the crowd with their performances, and then to see our tricolor flag ripple in the wind and hear the notes of the Italian national anthem fill the air. However, pathetic indeed was the soccer game played by the Italian team against Yugoslavia. I regretted having gone to Pasadena that evening, and felt all the more grateful for men like the weightlifter Alessandro Andrei who won his gold medal without even dreaming about the advantages of the rich sports where competition, I would say, seems far removed from the spirit of the good sportsmanship of Baron de Coubertin.

During the breathtaking closing ceremony I noted some examples of collective absurdity. The foreign teams receiving the loudest applause were the Chinese—I can see that—and the Romanians. Evident was the crowd's approval of their dissent from Moscow, but what struck me as exaggerated were the expressions of warmth for countries with a structure so different from the one propounded by Americans everywhere they went. However, I did appreciate the display of public spirit as the speaker read out the list of past Olympic cities one by one; when he said "Moscow 1980" there was not a single jeer or offensive shout. As good sportsmen, many people like me thought about the bitter disappointment of so many young Soviets, Czechoslovaks, and East Germans who for years had given it everything they had in preparing for the Olympic appointment in California, and had seen all their sacrifices go up in smoke. This was one of the factors I had pointed out to Gromyko and Chernenko, but to no avail.

I spent my evenings—except for one—with Californians of Italian descent, and appreciated more than ever before their liveliness, social importance, and scientific prestige. There is absolutely no difference between the *Nobel laureate* Segrè, the *Oscar*-winner Rambaldi, and Joe DiMaggio, and each one of them, along with everyone else, adds something distinctive to the true picture of our presence there.

On August 12, I was a guest at a grand banquet held by the Italian Heritage Center Foundation in the Bonaventura Hotel, but I must confess that equally interesting was an invitation to the home of James Stewart who was celebrating his thirty-fifth wedding anniversary (rare indeed are wedding jubilees in that orbit). The cream of the movie industry was there, from Gregory Peck to Audrey Hepburn. The dinner served in the garden was enlivened by music, intervals with well-known TV announcers, and repeated anniversary wishes. Upon my return to Rome, my family was much more interested in my description of that evening than in my talks with the president of the United States.

Together with Ambassador Petrignani I also lunched with the kitchen cabinet of Ronald Reagan, who had a very solid base in California. They took his reelection as president in November for granted and were already drawing up plans for *Ron's* return to California early in 1989.

In addition, I went to a luncheon hosted by Franklin Murphy, the director of *Times Mirror,* and took part in a round-table discussion on U.S.-European-Soviet relations at the Rand Corporation in Santa Monica with the director, Arnold Horelick, and several scholars in that important political think-tank (Abe Becker, Andrzey Korbonski, Don Rice, Jim Thomson, Jon van Oudanaren, and Charlie Wolf).

Likewise, I was able to fit in a rapid visit to J. Paul Getty's museum, and was quite envious about its practically unlimited financial resources.

Before going to Los Angeles, I had made the already-planned second visit to Tripoli, after the one for the Joint Committee. The Libyans were still very upset over the missiles located in Comiso, since they considered themselves to be a potential target, all the more so since the Americans never missed an opportunity to speak out against Ghaddafi's republic, even though people said that behind its origins were the backing and understanding of American oil interests adversely affected by certain forms of . . . open-mindedness during the final stages of the monarchy (however, the distinction between the American *administration* and Americans' *interests* applied for Libya more so than for other countries, and continues to apply).

The Soviet propaganda campaign after the deployment of the Western European missiles was very active in the smaller countries throughout the Mediterranean, inviting them to become allies with the Warsaw Pact in order to confront the "American arrogance" which had shunted aside the role of the UN and its Security Council; and the propaganda added that it was "all the more perfidious since America was far away and, in the case of conflict, the first damaging impact would have been on the European theaters or the adjacent shores."

My line of reasoning with the Libyans went like this. The fact of being allied with the United States didn't mean we considered them error-proof; Grenada had been an error and we had condemned it. However, to divide the world into good guys and bad guys and bestow upon Moscow the certificate of goodness was already an arbitrary decision before the invasion of Afghanistan, but after it they could really no longer claim any respect for the nonaligned countries. Besides, who had been Moscow's ally in defeating Hitler, if not the Americans?

As far as missiles were concerned, if there had only been the U.S.-Soviet intercontinental ballistic ones, it would have been possible to address matters in a different way. However, the Soviet Union had been the one to deploy a large number of shorter-range missiles over the last few years. As long as they were SS4s and 5s we had not reacted; but the SS20s had quite a different range and we couldn't remain defenseless. The USSR knew very well that if they declared a willingness to dismantle those missiles, we would have done away with ours. All we sought was deterrent parity. If the nonaligned countries were to side with Moscow, the political imbalance would get even worse, and that would mean a sharp increase in tension. The true *nonalignment* of a group of countries represented an element of collective security. Moreover, Italy maintained sincere and above-board relations with Moscow; and we were working confidently on all levels for the U.S.-Soviet meeting, aiming for general disarmament which could only be gradual and verifiable.

As regards Comiso, and using a map for support, I showed them how the range of those missiles was such that their deployment around Bolzano could have the same alarming effect. Therefore, the choice of a site on the Sicilian coast involved no underlying anti-Libyan intentions.

My counterparts in these talks (first Jalloud and then Ghaddafi) did not seem willing to have their minds changed. The Americans, they said, hated the Libyans; the missiles in question were American ones; hence, quite natural was their reaction. And they gave very little importance to the remark that no U.S. military equipment in Italy could be used without our government's consent. They kept on saying: "We want to be the most nonaligned country of all, but people are making it impossible." They quoted what General Haig had said—when at the State Department—on a possible war fought only on European territory (and, they added, he was a former NATO commmander-in-chief).

When speaking about Lebanon, they regretted the Italian and English presence supporting an old (France) and new (United States) policy of interfering colonialism. The Lebanese are Arabs, and the quest for ways to bring about internal reconciliation had to be left up to the Arabs. Instead, it was necessary to study global plans for general economic development based on criteria of justice. The many hotbeds of rebellion in the world had not been instigated by the Libyans or anyone else; they were a sign that hunger and oppression were intolerable.

I omit my reactions to the general topics and the dialogue on Libyan-Italian bilateral problems. On Lebanon, I said we were there with the government's consent and upon the request of Arafat after the massacre of Palestinians at Sabra and Chatila. The doors of our hospital in Lebanon were open to everyone. The withdrawal of the troops without the Palestinians having the protection of the UN (or even an Arab buffer force) would have been an enormous risk for them. Besides, I did not believe—and I said so—that Reagan wanted to go to the election in November with his armed forces still in the Lebanese area.

I found occasional points of understanding with Ghaddafi by quoting him excerpts from his Green Book which I had studied most attentively. It was accurate to say that no one is free if the house (or the tent) where he abides or his means of locomotion are not his own; however, each country has an economy different from others, raw materials or not, surplus or limited population. Therefore, an intertwining of relations, bilateral ones as well, was necessary, in a context of peace negotiated among everyone. Urgently required for the consolidation of peace were disarmament agreements, surmounting the present grave disparities.

In his replies and frequent interruptions, Ghaddafi interjected comments on the demonic nature of the missiles in Comiso which, as he interpreted it, the Israelis had wanted to see deployed there as an anti-Libyan plot. Nonetheless, he quite clearly said they were also concerned about the Soviet SS20s.

In addition to Ghaddafi's critical comment on the SS20s, I did not miss something he said about how it was impossible for *atheistic* countries to be truly the friends of a country when the religious element was the central feature. And I asked him to be so kind as to elaborate on that, pointing out that I was not there as an advocate for the Americans and against the Russians. My purpose was to reassure Libya after Comiso, and also to counsel the colonel against provoking (with some of his fiery speeches) reactions and fears, which certainly did not serve his country's best interests.

The final part of our discussion took place just between the two of us, the interpreter being the only other person present. Ghaddafi felt he was the victim of a hostile propaganda campaign which had even reached the point of inventing the story of a Libyan commando force which had broken across the U.S. border to go and kill Reagan (and another one in Italy to assassinate Pertini!). Such propaganda might have also been spread by those exiles who had departed Libya, not for political reasons, but with their pockets full of the people's money. America was a great power and it was absurd to think Libya might want to attack it. The risk of a possible clash between its soldiers and the Americans depended not on its expeditions, but on the interfering and "useless" U.S. presence in Lebanon. Libya wanted to construct its own strong and blissful nation, not threatening anyone, and wanting to remain strictly nonaligned.

In truth, I said, some of his recurrent speeches on the intention to *liberate* half of the world gave rise to fears, and were quite different from these eminently wise and moderate considerations. Both we and the Americans sought nothing else than to bring our troops home, but the Arab countries also needed greater dialogue and greater sincerity among themselves, beginning with relations between Libya and its neighbors. We had always worked to soothe relations between Arab countries and the United States, in order either to get them going, or to start them up again from where they had been interrupted. And I felt that a few positive steps forward were being made with Syria and Iraq.

Ghaddafi told me he had extended an open hand to the United States through more than one emissary, but to no avail. Since I would be seeing Reagan the following week (the embassy grapevine at work), he asked me to try my hand at it. And, for the president, he gave me two of his Green Books in the English version, with an impromptu dedication.

The oral message had to do with the Gulf of Sidra. Ghaddafi offered to submit the dispute to a panel of impartial arbitrators chosen by Reagan himself. In Libya, he remarked, they had no jurists of international renown.

At the end of my talks with President Reagan, held in the large suite where he resided in Los Angeles, the spokesman made the following announcement: "Foreign Minister Andreotti was not the bearer of a message in the formal sense of the word, but he did relate Ghaddafi's interest in having better relations with the United States. The president replied that he *welcomes the Libyan affirmations* but that he awaits concrete facts." We agreed that no reference would be made to the Green Book, but Reagan willingly took it and told me he would read it.

Away from the White House, Reagan seemed more at ease, and did not rely on file cards alone. After congratulations on the fourteen gold medals won by Italian athletes, he made very positive comments on the serious nature of our international commitment in support of the common peace policy. "If there were doubts in the Alliance—and in some countries," he said, "doubts have emerged, but not in Italy—we could not talk with the Soviets with so much certainty."

He stated his firm conviction that the United States and the Soviet Union had to find some grounds for agreement on reducing the threat represented by nuclear weapons and their ceaseless stockpiling. And he asked me what I thought personally about the Soviet intentions, inquiring whether Shultz had provided me with detailed information on Moscow's proposal (not only had he done so that same day, but he had sent me a confidential letter on the very day of the Soviet initiative).

I replied that the Soviets probably didn't want to permit the Reagan administration to score a success prior to the elections, but afterwards they were sure to return to the negotiating table. They, in fact, had an objective interest in opening negotiations on the issue of space weapons. "Your response," I indicated, was very useful in any case, and gave public opinion the feeling that the United States really wants to negotiate. Therefore, it is important for the administration to hold to this line, and continue to give a constant and consistent demonstration of the West's willingness to negotiate and the American will to explore all the possible negotiation pathways; if possible, as well, in an address to the United Nations by Reagan himself the following September.

"Besides," I concluded, "it is also possible that, within the Soviet leadership, there is still no clear vision of the line to follow with the West." President Reagan said he agreed with my appraisal of the situation.

Moving on to speak about the mines reportedly floating free in the Red Sea, I reported that the Italian government had received a request for assistance from the Egyptian authorities to conduct operations for the location and identification of those explosive devices. The government had decided to refer the matter to the competent parliamentary bodies with a proposal to accept the Cairo government's request, even though against a background where many things were unclear.

I expanded the scope of our discussion, and observed that still out-standing in the Middle East were all the problems due to the unresolved dilemma of Arab-Israeli relations, and that, at this point, a new attempt had to be made to unravel the situation. Perhaps it was possible to try and get the Arab countries to recognize Israel (with relative guarantees), quite naturally in exchange for what had to be concrete concessions for the Palestinians' future. Even moderate Arab leaders like King Hussein and Mubarak were in difficulty over the fact that the Israelis had succeeded in preventing any progress in resolving the problem of the Palestinians. It was to be hoped that a coalition government, able to make negotiations possible, could be formed in Israel. The problem could be solved only on the basis of mutual and simultaneous recognition by the two parties.

Reagan agreed on this point as well, and stressed that this had been precisely the position sustained by the administration and included in its own peace plan for the Middle East on whose basis, however, no progress had been made so far.

On the matter of Libya, I summarized Ghaddafi's message in the following fashion, making it quite clear that I was delivering it in good faith, but only as a "mailman," without any personal illusions about a possible and sudden change on the part of Ghaddafi. It was an opening, and, if there was a desire to cultivate it, in my opinion the results would be forthcoming, and never again would we have tragic episodes like the killing of the British policewoman in front of the Libyan Embassy in London.

Basically speaking, Ghaddafi had asked me to say two things: (1) He wanted Reagan to know he wasn't a Communist and fought against Marxism because his religion, his philosophical doctrine, and his vision of the world made him an opponent of Marxist materialism. From this viewpoint, he was on the same side as the United States, despite their mistrust of him. (2) Ghaddafi wanted to have a channel he could use for communicating with Reagan. He did not consider himself understood at all. He wanted to be "nonaligned" in the full sense of the word; he did not want to be considered at the service of the United States, but neither did he want to be considered at the service of others.

Before taking my leave, I spoke about the meeting the foreign ministers of the EEC member states were going to have in Costa Rica in September with the countries of the Contadora Group and the five countries of Central America. I expressed my strong belief that the European countries had to act in unison and concert with the United States, especially with respect to the problems of Central America, which was a region of such direct interest to the United States. On the specific topic of El Salvador, I noted that Congress had approved the appropriation of additional funds for the country precisely at that time, and I declared that Italy also planned to grant it substantial financial assistance in order to help Duarte in the difficult work he had begun to restore and consolidate Salvadorian democracy. President Reagan manifested his keen appreciation for the intention to contribute in that way to the stabilization of El Salvador. And I was pleased to hear it, because a few years earlier—hark, the awesome power of someone else's file cards— he had reacted against my praise of Duarte by saying the man was overintent on nationalization and, in that way, proposed to destroy the banking system and the coffee trade. On that occasion, I had urged him to obtain more accurate situation reports.

Among the many times I have had occasion to be received by Reagan, this one was the most significant. Maybe it was the atmosphere, or perhaps it was his euphoria over America's astounding success in the Olympics: I thought he felt somewhat cramped by the White House, but that in a short time he would certainly be reelected.

20 | *A Degree in Indiana*

The November elections gave Reagan a second term in office and I was happy George Shultz was to continue at the State Department, since by then I had established very frequent and productive contacts with him (in thanking me for the congratulations, he assured me he was "pleased to continue our close cooperative relationship").

I had seen him two more times after Los Angeles; on October 2 in New York, and on December 14 in Brussels where I filled him in on the visit I was about to make to Poland and, after my direct contacts with Riyadh, Cairo, Algiers, and Tunis, I expressed my opinion about a kind of progressive moderation on the part of the Arab countries which called for our swift appraisal of any possible positive implications.

However, besides the talks, we had a very intense exchange of correspondence throughout 1984. I will just quote some of the messages.

In February, in consideration of the fact that Ambassador Leamon Hunt (Sinai Peace Force administrative officer) had been murdered in Rome he proudly wrote: "The cowards who come out of the shadows to attack us shall not prevail." On March 27, after a visit to Washington by the Egyptian president Mubarak: "We have repeatedly expressed our willingness to undertake concrete dialogue with the PLO if it agrees with the terms we propose: acceptance of Security Council Resolutions 242 and 338 and recognition of Israel's right to exist." *May 3:* "While the president is on his way home, I want to share some immediate impressions on what I consider a very positive visit in China. Naturally, we will provide you with full details through the normal channels, but I wanted to send you my personal assessment immediately. The visit was a success."

June 1: "While the memory of our ministerial meeting is still fresh, I wish to tell you I found our discussions most useful, both here in Washington and in Wye. Such direct exchanges, without formal documents or speeches, are the best way I know to achieve a true understanding of international affairs. I hope there will be even more of these opportunities in the future. See you in London." *July 6:* "I know you followed closely the exchange of views we had last week with the USSR on the control of weapons in space. The Soviet reaction over the linkage with the discussion on offensive nuclear armaments has so far been negative, but not definitive. The meeting scheduled for September stands."

August 29: "The fact that Italy maintains discreet contacts with various members of the Palestinian community can be useful. Just as in other areas of sensitive diplomacy, the Italian efforts are important for us, and we hope this cooperation may continue."

September 10: "On the eve of your European meeting in San Jose, I would like to set out for you, as an ally particularly close to the United States, some of our major concerns."

October 5: "The almost nine hours of discussions with Gromyko offered us the opportunity to present quite sincerely the president's interest in *more stable and productive* East-West dialogue. . . . The discussions did not reveal any substantial relevant shift by Gromyko, but they did indicate a Soviet interest in *continuing* our dialogue, and perhaps in probing the ways such dialogue could be enhanced."

November 13: "We do not share King Hassan's optimism that their treaty of union with Libya could lead to concrete moderation in military behavior. Ghaddafi knows very well the position of the American administration: if Libya abandons its policy of support for terrorism and for the destabilization of other countries, we will recognize that such changes have really taken place, and we will be prepared to discuss the possibility of an improvement in our bilateral relations. . . . I attach the utmost importance to the continuation of our exchanges of views on these topics."

Moreover, I had had a significant display of the excellent political climate Italy enjoyed with the United States administration when, in Rome on November 17, I received a delegation of congressmen led by Dante

Fascell, the influential Florida Democrat who now chairs the Foreign Affairs Committee. On that occasion I made the acquaintance of some new parliamentary colleagues: Jack Brooks and Ronald Coleman from Texas, Lee Hamilton from Indiana, George Whitehurst from Virginia, Eldon Rudd from Arizona, and Gerald Solomon from New York. They no longer raised questions on the staying power of Italian democracy, and were prolific in their praise for our international consistency.

Vernon Walters was in Rome around mid-December, and his comments were also relaxed in tone. We spoke about aid to Ethiopia. It was right and just to give such aid, but its distribution within the country on aircraft with the Red Star had to be avoided. It was true that "U.S.A." was stamped on the bags and parcels, but not that many people know how to read. Vernon told me he was tired of being ambassador-at-large, averaging six hundred miles of air travel every day; he expected to be appointed either to the United Nations or to the embassy in the Federal Republic of Germany (both of which positions he filled, one after the other).

At the beginning of 1985 the conditions were ripe for a new trip to the United States by the Italian government. The visit was well prepared and without any difficulties, considering the prevailing political atmosphere (with a certain approval over there—once it had been established that the Socialists were not antimilitary—for cooperation between the Socialists and the Christian Democrats, since the pencil pushers on the Italy desk at the State Department had the habit of often repeating in their memos that, in 1922, such cooperation would have spared Europe the experience of fascism).

They were also quite courteous in setting the date so that Craxi could arrive directly from South America where he was going for the inauguration of President Julio Maria Sanguinetti in Uruguay. March 5 and 6 were two very intense days.

We went to the White House after a session with Shultz devoted to the preparation of the summit meeting in Bonn and to an update on Central America. The main issue was the space shield, unfortunately christened "Star Wars" by the press. Reagan expounded his thesis in these terms: for the moment, it was only a question of research and study; if the threshold of an authentic antimissile *defense* system were reached, the United States would stop, offering the USSR the choice between immediate negotiations on a massive bilateral dismantling of missiles or creating their own analogous system with the time required to do so technically. Reagan spoke about this with firm conviction in his voice. While the second hypothesis may seem quite paradoxical at first glance, it wasn't so; when the United States was the only one to have nuclear weapons for many years after World War II, it never took advantage of that fact to back its opponent up against a wall. In addition, the Americans were convinced the USSR would have assented to negotiations in order to avoid having to deplete its own resources in such an expensive competitive endeavor.

The Reagan administration was asking the Allies for adhesion to the plan, but mostly, I believe, in order to surmount obstacles in Congress. On the scientific level, Shultz was the one who explained why, in their opinion, government restrictions could not be applied to research efforts. And Europe was being offered a great occasion (my old friends in the Pentagon told me it wasn't true) to ensure the progress of its technology jointly with America, with fallout far beyond the military sphere alone.

When discussing Latin America I was struck by how emphatically Reagan ruled out, almost with indignation, the idea of armed U.S. intervention in Nicaragua. While not contradicting him, Shultz was more cautious, saying that a second Cuba in the area would not be tolerable. And therefore it was useful for the Europeans to work on Managua for a restoration of democratic liberties.

On the Middle East, we unfortunately had to note that there was nothing new, while plenty of time was devoted—also during the White House luncheon—to international trade (in view of the new round of GATT negotiations) and to the measures to be adopted against drug trafficking.

More thorough analyses were conducted during talks with Secretary of Commerce Malcolm Baldridge, Secretary of Agriculture John Block, Attorney General Edwin Meese, and Treasury Secretary James Baker. I also met with the president of the World Bank, Alden Klausen, to coordinate our efforts at cooperation in the development of the Third World with those of Italian consultants in the Bank as well.

We listened with special interest to the data on jobs. Out of the twenty-two million jobs created in the United States during the last ten years, two-thirds were created in small and medium-sized companies, and nine out of ten in firms with less than one hundred employees, while large industry created no jobs at all. In addition, more than two-thirds of the new jobs were in the so-called "services" sector, while half of the "advanced technology" was produced in small companies rather than in big ones. According to their experience, Baldridge told us, priority should be assigned to an analysis of how to stimulate entrepreneurship in small companies.

We fully intended to keep it in mind, but I was thinking about something rather contradictory: out of the thousands of products I had seen on sale in Los Angeles, not one of them was "made in America": practically everything came from Taiwan and Korea.

In comparison with the customary protocol of these visits, the great innovation was the invitation extended to Craxi to speak before a joint session of Congress. This invitation was promoted by 50 senators and 150 congressmen, and the White House had given its full support. It was a success.

Numerous members of Congress approached me to ask for an update on the negotiations for Spain and Portugal's entry into the EEC. Most of them were favorably interested in the political aspect. Some were worried about competition in the citrus fruit trade. These reservations did not strike home immediately, but later on—once the grueling yet brilliant efforts had brought the negotiations to an end—I was forced to register exaggerated American trade reactions. When I raised my objections, they told me that political problems and commercial ones follow different and separate tracks.

In one of the Kennedy Center theaters, the Washington program was also livened up by the projection of an abridged version (in comparison with the EPIC SIX-HOUR MINI-SERIES) of the movie on Christopher Columbus directed by Alberto Lattuada and featuring Gabriel Byrne, Rossano Brazzi, Virna Lisi, Oliver Reed, and Raf Vallone.

Despite the general expressions of praise and all the applause, I didn't have much luck because sitting next to me was a real bore who asked me the weirdest questions, like whether or not there were raincoats in Columbus's time. For reasons of unquestioned expertise in matters related to Columbus, I tried in vain to suggest he consult Paolo Emilio Taviani.

I met with Shultz once again on May 15 in Vienna where the CSCE was holding its closing session. This time too he had seen Gromyko for a six-hour meeting, but without making any progress; the general impression was that Gorbachev was still working on the Soviet strategy. Shultz summarized his thoughts on the existing situation in East-West relations as follows:

Positive elements: The fact that President Reagan's new term of office was just starting, and that the Americans had drawn up a complete and articulated global approach to disarmament problems; the fact that, at the same time, a younger leader was taking over in the Kremlin and that he had plenty of time in front of him.

Negative elements: Unforeseeable episodes such as the recent killing of an American officer in East Germany, as well as the contention between the United States and the USSR on human rights, on the problem of the space defense system, and lastly, on the issue of German reconciliation.

Shultz asked me to receive (two days later in Rome) his ambassador-at-large Richard Murphy, on his way back from the Middle East, for a detailed briefing on the mission Shultz himself was planning. Murphy explained their line of reasoning in brief: the United States cannot want peace more than it is desired by the parties directly concerned, but once everything was ready, the Americans would be willing to give their support.

President Reagan had authorized Murphy to meet with a Jordanian-Palestinian delegation during the mission in April. However, the PLO had hesitated, and had not permitted influential Palestinians who were not members of the PLO itself to sit down at the same table with the Americans and Jordanians. If King Hussein's visit to the White House were to produce the hoped-for results, the Americans were thinking about once again promoting a meeting between a U.S. representative and a Jordanian-Palestinian delegation.

Murphy is a very discerning and perceptive person, but I had the distinct feeling he would not be able to do everything he personally would have liked to do. I told him so, and he most likely reported it to George who wrote me a long letter on May 31 to reassure me that they were not going to desist in their quest for solutions. "In your turn, please reflect about what your government can do to further a valid process. It is my intention to keep in close touch with you in order to examine developments and exchange ideas on how we can translate the promises of the present into the reality of the future."

I made a rapid trip to the United States to go to South Bend (Indiana) to receive an honorary degree in law at the Notre Dame University, the prestigious "kingdom" of the magnificent rector, Fr. Theodore Hesburgh. My companions in receiving the same honor on that occasion were Napoleón Duarte and the Kentucky congressman Romano Mazzoli. If I am not mistaken, it is the only American university with a chair of *European Law,* and I used that as the subject for my short address to the patient students of that beautiful center for higher learning.

American citizens were taken hostage by armed Shiite groups, apparently in response to the transfer to Israel of Islamic prisoners captured in Lebanon. The United States had not been in favor of the Israeli decision, but had not been able to prevent it. Reagan instructed Bush to coordinate action against terrorism, especially airplane hijacking. The vice president also came to Rome, both offering and requesting extensive cooperation. In a sort of scale of responsibility in this regard, the Americans assigned first place to Iran and Libya, with a lesser share held by Syria and the Soviet Union. In our opinion, however, the problem was also a political one. The situation was at a standstill.

Craxi told Bush he was convinced that Arafat had long ago opted for negotiations, but so far had not been able to follow through due to the lack of clear signals from Israel.

Bush remarked that Gorbachev was involved in drawing a new map of power in the Soviet Union. I concurred with him and suggested that, in the speech Shultz would deliver at the ceremony to commemorate the tenth anniversary of Helsinki, it would be appropriate to consider that the Soviets were seeking to shift attention from individual rights to social rights. This attempt had emerged quite clearly in Ottawa with the Soviets' insistence on including the protection of individuals under major objectives such as peace, health care, and employment. All nations are concerned about safeguarding and pursuing these objectives, but that did not mean total silence about what for Westerners are the individual's civil and political rights. Furthermore, the Soviets were trying to boost the credibility of the other concept that, by forcing the Soviet Union to rearm for security purposes, the United States, and the Western world in general, were actually trying to hamper Moscow's planned economic development process. In that sense the Western countries came across as the opponents of social and economic progress in the Soviet Union. Bush acknowledged the soundness of these lines of reasoning, and said he would discuss them with Shultz. Upon his return to Washington he skipped the protocol channels and sent me a personal letter to thank me as well for the work done to make his visit "such a success."

On July 3 Shultz alerted me that the date of the Reagan-Gorbachev meeting was about to be announced in Moscow and Washington: 19 or 20 November in Geneva. And he said we had to work together on the preparations. A few days later he sent his congratulations on our semester as president of the EEC, and for the contribution given "to the realization of our common purpose of *close cooperation and broad partnership.*"

This sign of appreciation compensated me for the bitterness of the blaring contrasts over the Spanish fruit and the California walnuts: and I do believe that Ambassador Maxwell Rabb had also reached the point of not being able to stand even the mention of them.

Shultz and I saw one another during the UN General Assembly (I spoke on September 25, after Mubarak: I repeated from that rostrum that it was not possible to leave Syria out) and I mentioned to him what Shevardnadze had told me shortly before: "I am optimistic by nature, but at this moment I do not have the elements for being so. However, we are preparing for the upcoming meetings with the utmost care and we hope they will produce results."

When I said goodbye, hoping to see him soon, I could not imagine that a terrible mine was about to explode in relations between Italy and the United States.

21 | *The Achille Lauro Affair*

Achille Lauro, the brilliant commander who never became famous outside of Naples during his lifetime—he missed his chance in July 1953 when he didn't save the last De Gasperi government—did acquire world renown many years later as a result of a violent act of international terrorism which took place on the cruise ship bearing his name.

Such are the quirks of history. The now deceased monarchical leader justified his lukewarm feelings for De Gasperi by saying that a man who had not become wealthy by the age of seventy wasn't worth much at all. Yet his own vast riches had soon disappeared and, in that fall of 1985, his fleet was being administered by a government commissioner. Thus do worldly glories go up in smoke.

The evening of 7 October 1985, I was meeting with the Spanish ambassador, who had brought me the instruments ratifying his country's entry into the European Community and I was listening to words of renewed gratitude for the decisive role played by Italy during its term of presidency, when I received an urgent wire from our embassy in Stockholm. A radio ham had picked up a message from the *Achille Lauro* saying that the ship had been hijacked by a commando of Palestinians.

It was not an alarming message per se because in such cases errors in message interception are frequent, as are phrases with a double meaning (the enemy is on the doorstep may also mean that a husband has left the house and the way is clear), and quite often even facetious cranks. However, the direct reference to the Palestinians was disturbing. We had just concluded a parliamentary debate in which we had had to use strong language in commenting on an Israeli bombing which had caused a real massacre in the PLO headquarters in Tunis. Someone had judged our condemnation of the fact as excessive, but perhaps he would have changed his mind if I had quoted to him the reply of a Tel Aviv official to whom I had pointed out the disproportion of the retaliation: more than seventy civilians killed for the three Israeli victims of an attack in Larnaca. They had gone far beyond an eye for an eye and a tooth for a tooth. "We can't just go there every day," he said to me.

The hypothesis of an escalating vendetta could therefore be well grounded, and I immediately sought further information. There was no way to get in touch with the ship. We contacted Arafat in Tunisia, but he said he was not involved and was completely in the dark.

Shortly before 10:00 P.M. that Monday our embassy in Egypt confirmed the news. The ship had left Alexandria where most of the passengers had disembarked to travel to Cairo by land, and it had been taken over by a commando of—reportedly twelve—raiders. They were asking the Egyptians by radio to make *that fact* known and to obtain docking authority from other Arabic countries; in the meantime they were separating passengers according to nationality with the intent to kill those from less friendly nations. No one knew exactly where the ship was.

I telephoned the Egyptian state minister Boutros Ghali, who guaranteed maximum cooperation, as their defense minister was doing at the same time with our ambassador Giovanni Migliuolo. We also got in touch with Tunis, Riyadh, and Aden, informing the Quirinale and Palazzo Chigi as well. We were more or less prepared to cope with Arab hijackings, even though, in one case, when I had ordered the hijacker to be detained in Sicily, the reply had been that the local prefect, on his own authority, had already let him go. However, the hijacking of a ship was something new and, when there is no precedent our Civil Service is short on ideas. We had found that out on 16 March 1978, when Aldo Moro was kidnapped. Nonetheless, the crisis unit was organized at once to handle contacts, to field family inquiries, with Defense Minister Spadolini to coordinate possible military action.

We were soon in a position to have a clearer picture, as we compared the data fed to Rome by the government commissioner in charge of the Lauro fleet—the son of the late RAI-TV journalist Willi De Luca—with what we received from Migliuolo after a meeting of the Egyptian government in Cairo. There was a total of 370 crew members, of whom only 8 were escorting the passengers traveling overland by bus, and who, according to the Egyptians, amounted to a total of 676. Few passengers—perhaps only 8—had remained on board the ship, which was *believed* to be forty miles off Port Said. Shortly thereafter, the representative of the Lauro fleet in Genoa informed us, however, that the kidnapped passengers were reportedly 60—later he told us 80—20 of whom were Americans. Overall, the passengers belonged to many nationalities, with a prevalence of Austrians, French, and Swiss.

I don't know on the basis of which information, but at midnight the Egyptian prime minister told Migliuolo that we needn't worry because it would all be over the next day. It seemed that the hijackers, who had initially mentioned the liberation of Palestinian prisoners in Israeli hands, in their latest message were referring to 50 Palestinians in jail in Italy.

During the night, Craxi convened an emergency meeting where I was able to provide the aforementioned data. Spadolini and the military leaders (General Bartolucci, General Giannattasio, and Admiral Martini) briefed us on operational action which could be taken in the case of failure of the mediation of Cairo and of the help promised by Arafat, who reiterated that the PLO as such had nothing to do with the criminal deed. At any rate, the PLO representative in Egypt had made himself fully available.

We made a firm decision to demand an unconditional surrender. Two transport aircraft and four helicopters were transferred from Pisa to Gioia del Colle to be ready for action. The British immediately gave permission to land at their base in Cyprus, and the Greeks authorized use of their airports in Rhodes and Athens.

Until dawn and beyond, the phones in the Ministry rang off their hooks. Anguished inquiries flowed in from Naples (a good number of crew members were from Torre del Greco), but no less alarmed were the calls from families in Vienna, Bern, Paris, and even Johannesburg. Trusting in the authority of the Egyptian government, we evoked calm and optimism, but we were far from certain.

We were able to be a bit more precise around 4:00 A.M. when we received the data on the passengers traveling to Cairo by land: 221 Austrians, 80 Germans, 72 Americans, 71 Swiss, 42 French, 20 English,

15 Danes, 11 Belgians, 10 South Africans, 2 Argentinians, 2 Chileans, 2 Peruvians, 1 Greek, and 1 Norwegian. In addition, there were 83 Italian tourists.

By late Tuesday morning, the ship still had not been located, except for a generic reference to a "northbound course"; and I could not help but think back, with surprise, to the many briefings I had attended as defense minister, in which we were told how every inch of earth, sky, and sea was monitored twenty-four hours a day by extraordinary surveillance equipment. The Rome Center had intercepted a radio message by the captain of the *Achille Lauro,* Gerardo De Rosa, notifying us of the hijackers' request, that 50 prisoners in Israel belonging to the group of "the famous man of Naharia" be released. Besides the use of the English language, which might have been imposed by the Palestinians for their own understanding, our experts were very skeptical about the authenticity of the message.

The policy my colleagues and I decided to pursue was simple: since Arafat disclaimed involvement and was cooperating, we had to find out whether or not the Palestinians classified as pro-Syrian were willing to assume the same stance. In this case, political isolation would constitute the strongest argument to force the commando to surrender.

Monsignor Capucci—the bishop from Jerusalem under confinement in Rome following his notorious enterprises (a concession made by Israel after he was sentenced for the transport of weapons)—a *super partes* expert on Palestinian groups, came to offer his assistance. In the meanwhile, a PLO source identified the leaders of the commando: Talat Yacoub and Abdel Fatah Lahem, two dissidents who had supposedly escaped from Beirut. In a press release, Arafat repeated for the third time that "the PLO strongly condemns the operation against the *Achille Lauro* with which it has nothing to do." He had been pushed to take such a public stand by a recommendation we had made to him upon Washington's request. The Americans had asked this of Ambassador Petrignani. Arafat also informed us that he had sent two qualified leaders—Hani al Hassan and Muhamad Abbas—to Cairo to help out.

Shortly after midday, Migliuolo let us know that the Egyptians had located the ship eight miles out from the Syrian port of Tartus. This was confirmed five minutes later by the Foreign Ministry of Damascus: the hijackers were asking permission to dock and demanded a contact with the Italian and U.S. ambassadors within a few hours. Syria had not acceded to the request "also to mark its condemnation of the criminal deed" but it was ready to do so, if requested by the two governments concerned with a view to start negotiations.

The extreme difficulty involved in boarding a ship at sea made it more than desirable to have it dockside in a harbor. Bartering, of course, was out of the question, except perhaps for the symbolic release of the nineteen-year-old Palestinian Kalas Muhamad Abnam Zay Nab, who had been arrested in Genoa in the previous month of June under the simple charge of carrying two passports.

We all agreed on this approach, and I contacted the Syrian foreign minister Shara, former ambassador to Rome, who was on a visit to Prague. President Assad himself came to the phone and said to me: (1) Syria had already condemned the hijacking, even publicly; (2) he could guarantee that no group directly or indirectly connected with Damascus was behind it or in any way responsible for it; (3) not knowing who the hijackers were, he was unable to give us any advice, but he thought we should not refuse a contact, even if only for humanitarian reasons; and (4) he was ready to cooperate and expressed his full support.

Under these conditions, it would have been even more logical to have the *Achille Lauro* dock; and so we had advised our embassy. Unfortunately, however, the Americans were of a different opinion—and directly informed Damascus of this—and Craxi couldn't do anything else but accept it.

I could well understand the troubled mood in Washington, where the humiliating wound of the Tehran hostages had not healed, and still open was that of the kidnapped victims in Lebanon; but it was a mistake to place hopes in a naval operation, preventing the ship's entry into a harbor, an action which we considered to be much safer. Then again, Carter had paid a high price for having rejected the more than honorable contact with Khomeini's Paris lawyers, which had been offered to him through me. Rabb came to tell us that by now it was a known fact that two Americans had been killed on board (while the U.S. ambassador in Damascus doubted this was true) and informed us that the National Security Council had set the deadline for military action for the following day, and was ready to proceed alone should we disagree on the need for it.

It may well be—but this is pointless speculation—that if the ship had entered the waters of Tartus, even the murder which was committed in those hours could have been avoided. Furthermore, it would have been possible to note there were no more than four raiders, with the obvious consequences. The American position, at any rate, was unacceptable, and Craxi stood his ground. The ship was *Italian,* and we ourselves did not rule out boarding as a last resort, but not before having explored other possibilities which would not entail bloodshed, also considering the high risk to human lives in such an operation.

At 6:40 P.M. Ambassador Petrignani confirmed Washington's firm opposition to any negotiations. Eighty minutes later, however, the State Department, through Deputy Secretary Armacost, suggested the tactical move of proposing a contact in international waters, in order to avoid a final destination in Lebanon which would have really placed passengers and crew members in jeopardy. The Syrians assured us that they would do everything possible to prevent a docking in Lebanon, but they added that Talat Yacoub was not the only organizer of this misdeed; his name had been leaked in order to put us on the wrong track. In fact, his group was accusing the Egyptians of having allowed the armed terrorists, now in control of the ship, to board it in Alexandria.

The *Achille Lauro,* however, was once again heading toward Egypt, having obtained permission from Cairo to dock in Port Said, despite the Americans' objections. Foreign Minister Meguid explained that, in his opinion, the worst solution was to leave the ship adrift. Also on the spot, in order to try and convince the hijackers, was Abu Abbas, whom the Jordanians reported under PLO arrest in Tunisia as a traitor to the organization which was opposed to any hostile acts against Italy.

I spoke with West German Foreign Minister Genscher who was on a visit to Jerusalem. The Israelis had made no mention of the fact to him, and he promised to make inquiries. I told him clearly that, if the raiders had asked for acts of clemency from Israel, we would not even forward the request. The Germans offered us diplomatic or "otherwise persuasive" cooperation.

Our instructions to our embassy in Cairo were precise: "If the ship really approached Port Said, contacts with the hijackers were definitely authorized, not for negotiations, but only to find out exactly what they wanted."

Early the next morning, several official sources confirmed that the *Achille Lauro* was anchored twelve miles off Port Said.

The news of shooting between the ship and overflying helicopters was first reported as definite, and later denied.

There was a certain amount of confusion over the demands coming from the ship: the release of 500 prisoners in Israel and/or 21 Palestinians held in Italy; the presence in Port Said of the American and German ambassadors (later the Italian one as well); other than Egyptian ones, no vessels or aircraft were to approach the ship.

In close coordination with the Egyptians, the PLO representatives established contact with the ship, while feverish consultations took place between the foreign ministries. Bonn had heard that the hijackers were asking for a multinational safe-conduct; and that there was a willingness to issue a foreign ministers' statement to do *everything in their power* to avoid acts against the hostages. The Americans remained opposed to any approach; whereas the German ambassador was prepared to go to Port Said with Ambassador Migliuolo. Craxi had told the Egyptians that as far as Italy was concerned, they could count on a certain degree of flexibility in granting a safe-conduct to the hijackers, provided they had not committed any acts of violence on board for which they could be prosecuted under Italian criminal law.

At 4:00 P.M.—after informal advance notices, from Arafat as well— the Egyptian Defense Ministry announced that the terrorists had surrendered, were in custody, and that the ship was entering the harbor.

Twenty minutes later, the Italian Foreign Ministry succeeded in speaking directly with the ship's captain, and learned: the terrorists were no longer aboard the ship; *all* passengers had been well treated by the hijackers and were in good health; the ship was anchored fifteen kilometers outside the port awaiting instructions; they thanked the Italian government.

Why in the world Captain De Rosa should have said this remains a mystery, nor could there have been a mistake since the telephone conversation was amplified and heard by several Farnesina officials. Shortly before the hectic radio exchange with the Palestinian on land who was ordering the hijackers to disembark, De Rosa had said: "Everyone is in good health." At 6:30 P.M., speaking with Craxi, the same man said that an American passenger was missing and had presumably been killed;

while at 7:45 P.M. he specified to the Farnesina director-general Giulio Di Lorenzo: "No corpse has been found, but yesterday at 3:10 P.M. the terrorists gave me the passport of Leon Klinghoffer, an American citizen, saying they had killed him. As a matter of fact, Mr. Klinghoffer did not come to pick up his passport, and his wife is beside herself; and there are partially wiped-out stains of blood on the deck."

At the same time the U.S. naval attaché in Cairo was telling our ambassador that it seemed Mr. Klinghoffer had never boarded the *Achille Lauro*. In turn, when questioned by the Egyptians, the four hijackers declared they hadn't laid a hand on anyone.

Before leaving the ship, in their radio conversation with the PLO leader on land who was telling them to surrender, the hijackers had already said: "All the passengers are fine and have all they need; we give them food or tea, and they are free to go to the bathroom, stay in their cabins or play cards." And the leader had replied: "Apologize to the passengers, the crew and the Captain, and tell them that our goal was not the hijacking at sea, but exactly an act against terrorism and against hijacking."

While in doubt and awaiting the outcome of the investigation on board the *Achille Lauro*, we asked both the Egyptians and the PLO to detain the four Palestinians, reaffirming that what had been agreed upon beforehand still applied: a safe-conduct as long as it proved true that they had not inflicted harm upon anyone. The overhanging shadow of an assassination offset our relieved anguish over the lot of hundreds of persons. Then again, how only four terrorists could have kept an entire crew—who of course knew the ship inside and out—in checkmate for three days still remains a mystery for me.

At any rate, I thought I could finally get some sleep that night, heartened by the messages of congratulations coming in from almost all capitals and having been delivered from a distressful nightmare. That was not how it turned out.

The Americans had intercepted an Egypt Air Boeing 737, which they were almost certain had the four hijackers on board. Awakened by the White House, Craxi authorized both the Egyptian civil aircraft and the interceptors to land at the Sigonella Air Base in Sicily. What actually landed, however, were not the two American interceptors but two C-141 transports with fifty troops in full gear, who took position around the Egyptian airplane, which, in its turn, had been surrounded by an equal number of Italian soldiers for security purposes. The U.S. commanding general, in direct radio contact with Washington, said he had received orders "to take the terrorists."

The base commander, keeping his cool, invited the guests to abide by the law, and customary good manners as well, and refused to put up with any overbearing behavior. For a few moments the situation was very tense, only one step away from an irreparable exchange of fire. Later on, when I found out that the brains behind the adventure were the same Irangate muddlers, I no longer marveled over what had happened, but it saddened me to see how a great country could be swept into absurd situations by little men in undeserved positions of authority.

Reagan called Craxi a second time, while Shultz woke me up and Weinberger did the same with Spadolini. Our replies converged. We turned down the "wish" of the U.S. administration to transfer onto American territory those held responsible for Leon Klinghoffer's murder (it now seemed sure) for a regular trial, by countering with our legal position: crimes committed in international waters on an Italian vessel were to be considered as crimes committed on Italian territory. Our government could not, by its own decision, infringe upon the jurisdiction of Italian courts over those responsible for the hijacking of the *Achille Lauro* and the acts of violence committed on board.

President Reagan seemed to acknowledge this position, advising Craxi that the U.S. administration intended to request the extradition of the four terrorists pursuant to the existing treaty between the U.S. and Italy.

Directly thereafter, Palazzo Chigi gave instructions for the four hijackers to be taken into custody, while the two Palestinian leaders accompanying them were to be held as material witnesses, in order to acquire useful information for the trial on the hijacking.

On account of the specific status of the Egyptian plane, which was on a special mission on behalf of the Egyptian government and therefore enjoyed extraterritorial rights, the Egyptian authorities on board were informed of the Italian intention to take the four hijackers into custody with a view to indictment. This request was accepted. We also informed them that the two PLO leaders reported on board would be disembarked as witnesses and treated as guests by the Italian government. The answer was that the two Palestinian leaders, who were in Italy against their will, refused to leave the aircraft, and that, under such conditions, the Egyptian authorities felt they could not accept our request. Their suggestion was that we work out a mutually agreeable procedure for direct talks between a representative of the Italian government and the two Palestinian leaders.

In particular, the Egyptian ambassador in Rome formally advised that the two Palestinians on board the aircraft forced to land in Italy had to be considered guests of the Egyptian government which, therefore, considered itself responsible for their security.

The morning of the next day, Friday, October 11, the government was informed that the Syracuse district attorney claimed the right to proceed to the exact identification of the four hijackers of the *Achille Lauro*. This happened at the same time as the Egyptian government took official steps for the immediate release of the aircraft with all its passengers, except those responsible for the hijacking. The competent Egyptian diplomatic authorities, expressing understanding for this legitimate requirement of the Italian legal authorities, allowed the Boeing 737 to be detained for the time strictly necessary for the completion of identification formalities in the ways deemed appropriate by the Italian courts; with evident linkage, however, the *Achille Lauro* was still being held in Port Said by the Egyptian government.

Craxi sent his diplomatic adviser Antonio Badini to Sigonella to obtain precise testimony on the facts from Abu Abbas.

At 8:15 P.M. on Friday, having completed the procedures for the identification of the hijackers, the Syracuse district attorney felt legal requirements had been fulfilled and declared the plane was free to leave Sigonella.

As of that moment, there were no legal grounds for further detaining the Egypt Air plane and its passengers, except, of course, the terrorists already in Italian custody.

Nevertheless, the Italian government asked the Egyptian ambassador for the Boeing 737 to be transferred from Sigonella Air Base to the Ciampino Airport in Rome, in order to explore the possibility of conducting further investigations. This approach of the Italian government complied with Craxi's pledge to Reagan to provide the time required for the acquisition of evidence proving the involvement of Abu Abbas and the other Palestinian leader in the hijacking, as Washington assumed.

At 10:01 P.M. on October 11, the Egypt Air Boeing took off from Sigonella to Ciampino. Four Italian fighters took off at the same time from Gioia del Colle to provide in-flight protection.

At 10:04 P.M. an American military aircraft took off from Sigonella without authorization and tailed the Egyptian Boeing. The pilot did not respond to identification requests from our fighters and quite vulgarly told our pilots to stop busting . . . the reproductive organs that airplanes don't have. After this useless display of bravado, the aircraft dove to ground level and disappeared from the radar screens.

Around 11:00 P.M., the Boeing 737 landed at Ciampino, followed a few moments later by a U.S. T-39 which had declared an emergency, and which came to a stop only a few yards away. We immediately protested to Washington.

Until then, October 12 had been Columbus Day for all of us, but ever since 1985 we remember it for the hectic events which took place on that day.

At 5:30 A.M. Ambassador Rabb delivered to both the Prime Minister's Office and the Ministry of Justice (not to the Farnesina) a request for the temporary detention of Abu Abbas for extradition purposes, invoking the relevant treaty between Italy and the United States.

The case was now in the hands of the judiciary, with the sole request that it be examined without the customary red tape. As a matter of fact, Cairo was breathing down our necks. They would not let the *Achille Lauro* depart and threatened to take up arms if the two Palestinian guests were illegally forced to leave their airplane parked at Ciampino Airport (their consent for the four hijackers had been immediate). If our magistrates had ruled otherwise, even with ten armed Egyptian soldiers aboard the plane, we would have had to keep the situation on hold. But at the end of the morning the magistrates came to Palazzo Chigi to tell us (Craxi was ill and asked me to stand in for him) that the U.S. request for temporary detention could not be entertained because "elements of merit and substance compliant with the criteria imposed by Italian legislation for the acquisition and submission of evidence" were lacking.

At 3:00 P.M. the secretary-general of the Farnesina, Ambassador Ruggiero, informed the ambassadors of Egypt and the United States that there were no legal grounds for holding the aircraft and its passengers any longer. We had taken precautionary measures also in the form wisely recommended by Minister Spadolini, that is, for all intents and purposes, the four terrorists were formally identified by some passengers from the ship flown in to Rome.

The Egyptian ambassador confidentially informed us that, for fear of new interceptions, the two Palestinian leaders would leave Italian soil on a Yugoslav airliner. The transfer took place at Fiumicino Airport, after which the Egypt Air plane took off and the *Achille Lauro* was able to leave Egypt en route to Italy.

Upon leaving Italy after eight years of highly rated and intense diplomatic activity Ambassador Rabb declared that, with very few exceptions, his relations with me had been excellent. One of those few occasions was precisely that . . . Sigonella Day.

Rabb, who had had contacts with everyone in the previous days, except the Farnesina, was disconcerted by Ruggiero's announcement, the exact terms of which, moreover, must not have been quite clear to him. He had actually rushed out to the airport, only to find out that the Egyptian plane was already on its flight back. As a partial justification for his irritation I feel there must have been a mistranslation in the second telephone call between Reagan and Craxi. The latter had said that the two escorts would not be let free until the investigation was over. Perhaps due to inexact translation, Reagan had thought this would take a few days.

Rabb stormed into my office and launched into a tirade which I heard out without interrupting (and perhaps this "irritated" him even more). I replied that detaining the aircraft when the judiciary had ruled out any legitimate grounds for so doing would have been tantamount to unlawful seizure. We are a nation based on the rule of law, and we do believe in human rights, *erga omnes*. Furthermore, I was amazed that the Americans had not considered the offense they inflicted upon the Egyptian president, with the blow to his pride as a former Air Force officer; and this precisely when we were all endeavoring to help Egypt emerge from the isolation it had endured for having accepted the American suggestions at Camp David.

Rabb was deaf to reason and was astounded I would raise legal arguments while, for him, the problem was only one of accepting or rejecting a request from the president of the United States. Any political considerations on Egypt seemed out of place to him on account of the fraternal aid provided to it by the United States.

It was clear I couldn't follow him in this direction, and I just said that we were the ones who should be vexed over the arrogance of some of their troops; however, our joy for the swift end to the hijacking induced us to be very . . . forgiving. We shared their grief over the atrocious death of the late Leon Klinghoffer, by now confirmed, but, to be sure, the Italian judges would inflict the proper punishment upon the culprits.

We parted on an unusually cool note, while pouring in were unbelievable dispatches on the clamor the American TV networks were raising against us, almost as if we had been weak toward terrorists and hadn't done everything humanly possible to put a quick end to the commando's criminal deed.

This unfair uproar went on for a few days with no reaction from the U.S. administration in our favor. In his report to the Chamber of Deputies on the *Achille Lauro* affair, Craxi expressed "the heartiest and most regretful surprise, as well as feelings of bitterness, for a friendly government's failure to recognize everything the Italian government had done for the successful outcome of a particularly critical and sensitive situation: the hijackers' surrender and the rescue of both passengers and crew were obtained in less than forty-eight hours without firing a shot; a success unfortunately clouded by the discovery that an American citizen had lost his life in the course of the terrorist attack." And the prime minister was able to add with pride: "No free government in the world has been able to achieve decisive results in the fight against terrorism without destroying the principles and provisions of a state based on the rule of law, as the governments of the Republic of Italy have been able to do."

As far as relations between Rome and Washington were concerned, Craxi could only hope that past and future clarifications would be of such a nature as to restore full harmony between Italy and the United States once and for all. The two countries are friends and allies in a continuing and ever-growing relationship of joint responsibilities and intense cooperation, promoting the utmost consideration, friendship, and respect for one another's dignity and national sovereignty. Unfortunately, Italy's domestic climate was overcast not only because of American insensitivity, but also because the Republican party ministers distanced themselves from the government. I interpreted this, however, not so much as a consequence of the *Achille Lauro* affair, but as disagreement over the strong criticism Craxi and I had expressed after the Israeli bombing of Tunis. It was going to take Americans years to accept the idea that it is necessary to have a dialogue with the PLO and not fall prey to the possible criminal illusion of wiping it out with bombs.

Things were further complicated by the forthcoming select meeting in

New York called by Reagan to consult with the main allies on the eve of the Geneva encounter with Gorbachev. Considering the atmosphere in the United States, it was impossible for our government to attend, and this fact, together with the already announced French absence, would undoubtedly weaken the Western Alliance in the East-West negotiations. Fortunately, within a few hours I was going to see George Shultz in Brussels at the NATO Council meeting convened specifically in preparation for the Geneva summit, and I hoped we would find a solution.

It was a difficult encounter, but our mutual regard and cordiality served as protection against basic incomprehensions and prevailed over any formal acrimony.

I started off by saying that the two of us shouldered the grave responsibility for bringing immediate relief to a situation which, for the first time, had opened a rift in the traditional relations of friendship between the United States and Italy.

Shultz had a stern look on his face. The Italian government had released a notorious terrorist involved in the murder of an American citizen: this was inconceivable and inexplicable. He did not hide the fact that the U.S. administration was very upset.

I answered that in our system of government, such decisions pertain to the judiciary and not to the executive branch. The documents served by the Americans did not give us the right to detain Abbas forcibly, to say nothing about the complications with Egypt and the risks of a gun fight (the second one, I said, after the one miraculously avoided in Sigonella with the U.S. troops). The evidence submitted to obtain extradition was extremely general, and moreover was based on telephone taps of dubious origin, an element to which Italian judges ordinarily attribute little value, also considering how easy it is to fake them. In any case, it seemed out of proportion to me to focus on this instead of praising us for having succeeded, with the help of God, in resolving the act of piracy in such a short time, thus avoiding far more serious crimes.

Shultz, who had precise instructions, kept on repeating that the release was unaccountable and that Washington was very upset.

I patiently explained once again the separation of powers in Italy and stressed the political significance of the distressed appeals by Mubarak who said that the aircraft's forced landing was destroying, in his eyes, years of Egypt's policy of friendship. But Shultz turned a deaf ear. In fact, he thought it absurd that Cairo would expect apologies from the

Americans after having allowed a murderer to go free. At this point, so to say, I had to counterattack. I told him I had personally assumed the responsibility not to forward a formal note of protest for what had happened at Sigonella.

It was a very serious matter concerning a NATO base in Italy. When the Egyptian plane had been denied permission to land in Tunis, the Egyptians had asked that it be allowed to land in Italy: the government had agreed since this would have made it possible to arrest the four terrorists. We did not know there were other people on board. The American action forcing the airplane to land at Sigonella had been contrary to the agreements between the two countries: and the same applied to the landing of the Delta Force at Sigonella and its behavior toward the Italian forces, whose commander had fortunately displayed wise judgment and steady nerves. I ended by saying that the polemics over these events could risk affecting the *status* of NATO bases in Italy: I wondered whether the American administration appreciated the gravity of its decisions (supposing they were actually made by the administration) and of what had happened.

Shultz seemed calmer, and replied that the United States had never doubted that Italy would arrest the terrorists and bring them to court, and concurred that it would be wise to keep the polemics out of the media.

Then I added that Abbas had gone to Cairo because Arafat had been requested to expedite the terrorists' unconditional surrender: I pointed out that we had never asked Israel to release prisoners in exchange for hostages, we had only asked all countries to deploy persuasive efforts. Had the use of force been required to free the four hundred hostages, Italy would have done it, but it was far more preferable to avoid force in every possible way. Abbas had gone to Egypt upon our request, and had thus made it easier to solve the problem. I added that, if investigations were to prove the contrary, we would act accordingly.

Shultz hastened to say that there was no point insisting on our differences, although he could not mask the disappointment of the American administration, nor did he deem sufficient the reasons I had disclosed. However, the United States and Italy should keep on working side by side, and this was what mattered the most. The fact we disagreed over Abu Abbas's treatment did not mean we should not continue our efforts to maintain and strengthen the ties between our two countries. He concluded by saying that the American request for extradition stood: should Italy decide against trying the terrorists, she could hand them over to the United States where they would be brought to court.

I found this insinuation to be downright offensive and said so. Italy wanted to try the terrorists according to its own laws; should the evidence prove sufficient, even Abbas would be incriminated and, if appropriate, tried like any Italian citizen. Italy had waged its fight against terrorism, with well-known results, without ever violating its laws. We could not accept, I said, Ambassador Rabb's statements which seemed to cast doubts on our determination to fight terrorism or similar innuendos, no matter who made them.

The discussion with Shultz had taken place upon our respective arrivals at the NATO headquarters, and the other colleagues were waiting to begin the session. At this point we had to stop, and it was a good thing. When we met again at the end of the plenary session, George was much more relaxed and let me know he had been struck by what I had told him about Abbas's role as a *negotiator,* following a precise request from the Italian government, and with the assent of the Egyptian government. It was a *political* fact which, at least in part, could explain our government's conduct. He suggested, therefore, that in our contacts with the media we use a common language based on these points: (1) Abbas's special role as a negotiator, and the need for the Italian government to honor its commitments; (2) assurance that the Abbas episode would not constitute a precedent in the implementation of the extradition treaty between the two countries; (3) the determination to take legal action also against Abbas if sufficient evidence became available; and (4) the episode was over, and the friendship between Italy and the United States was not affected.

I immediately agreed in principle, but I had to point out once again that Abbas's release was based on legal grounds. It is true, there were also political considerations pointing in the same direction, but they alone would not have been sufficient to allow him to leave Italy.

Shultz proposed that the State Department counsel, Dr. Sofaer, and Italian experts work out a document reflecting what had been agreed. I accepted and I appointed, for the Italian side, the director-general for political affairs, Ambassador Biancheri, and my chief of cabinet, Minister Cavalchini, to negotiate with the American counterparts.

George and I parted with the customary (restored) cordiality.

Unfortunately, the hardliners in Washington were still on the warpath. While George was still on his return flight, the reasonable text drawn up jointly by our experts and Dr. Sofaer in Brussels and faxed to Washington for higher-level approval was not deemed suitable (by whom in the White House, I do not know).

Times like this call for action out of the ordinary. I phoned my old friend Vernon Walters, who as U.S. ambassador to the United Nations was a cabinet member, and told him that if Washington did not change its attitude immediately, neither Craxi nor I would attend the meeting with Reagan. Walters realized we were dead serious, and asked me for time to consult with the White House. In no time he called me back to ask if Craxi would be willing to receive Deputy Secretary of State John Whitehead who would be bringing an "adequate" letter from Reagan. I said yes of course, and the distinguished special envoy immediately took off for Rome. America owed us apologies and we got them.

Shultz's deputy brought an entirely satisfactory letter from Reagan to Craxi, and delivered it on October 19 in terms which respected the truthfulness of the facts, and adding that if the American people had had the information he had now received, they would have acted in a different way. The president of the United States wanted to let us know that, in New York, not only would we find no animosity toward Italy, but that he himself would make "a special effort to show that the friendship between Italy and the United States, and the personal one between the two heads of government, is very strong." Whitehead felt there were some lessons to be learned from the events of the previous week.

1. First of all, it was necessary to have better coordination in our commitment against terrorism, not only between Italy and the United States, but among all Western nations. We had to be a step ahead of terrorism and not allow it to create friction among us. We could think in terms of a treaty or a code of conduct. Italy could be of great assistance in the fight against terrorism.
2. In the second place, Whitehead acknowledged that the conduct of the U.S. armed forces on Italian bases had to be reexamined after the events in Sigonella; steps would be taken to make sure that such events would never occur again.
3. Finally, Whitehead observed that disagreements like the ones the

previous week benefited neither Italy nor the United States. Therefore, the incident was to be filed away as quickly as possible.

I thought Maxwell Rabb looked the most relieved of all; while those
who believed that the government crisis which had ensued as a result of
the affair could definitively sink the Craxi government were perhaps
quite surprised, for, on the contrary, it was immediately reconfirmed.

Thus were we able to go to the meeting in New York on October 24.
I went ahead of Craxi and, at a meaningful banquet hosted by Italo-
Americans, I had the opportunity to realize how much the Italian gov-
ernment's firmness and dignity had been appreciated.

The hijackers were tried by the Genoa Court of Assizes and, on 10
July 1986, were sentenced to prison (two of them for life); and even Abu
Abbas, on the basis of information which came to light *later on* and
indicated his grave responsibility in the affair—he was considered the
one who started the fire and doused the flames—received the maximum
sentence provided for by Italian criminal law. However, while the four
are in prison, the ringleader is still at large, pursued in vain by our
international arrest warrant.

Unknown to Arafat, and indeed in order to damage him (this seems
to be a sure thing), Abbas had planned a blitz to show that, at least in
ports, Israel was not inviolable.

Time, however, is a great healer. I recently saw Mr. Whitehead, who
told me quite cordially that we were far removed from the difficult
moments of the *Andrea Doria*. He had even forgotten the ship's name!
Indeed, on 13 April 1988, the official spokesman of the U.S. administration declared: ". . . In Italy, Abu Abbas was tried 'in absentia' and
sentenced to life imprisonment. We applaud the firmness displayed by
the Italian government in taking legal action against Abu Abbas *after* his
responsibilities *came to the surface*."

22 | *Paper and File Cards*

Reagan had wanted a consultation of the Western countries, and it took place at the U.S. Mission to the United Nations. Our host was Vernon Walters who was very expansive with us.

The president invited Shultz to deliver a detailed introduction on the preparations for the meeting with Gorbachev, and immediately after that, provoking obvious suspense among his aides, he said he had spent the weekend all alone and had summed up his reflections on a slip of paper which he proceeded to read. Before our consciences and before history, not only were we to refrain from hindering Mr. Gorbachev's efforts, but we were to foster them, leaving the verification of whether or not he was serious (as Reagan hoped) to "afterward."

I thought of how effective Reagan would have been if he had acted and spoken more often without a script. Between his rigid file cards and this tiny slip of handwritten paper there was an abyss. The support for President Reagan's position was unanimous, not only from us Europeans, but also from the Japanese, Australians, and New Zealanders.

Once we had weathered the *Achille Lauro* storm, the relationship with Shultz continued to develop quite intensely. By way of support for the American position in Geneva, we also held a ministerial meeting in Rome of the Western European Union, reaffirming the indivisible nature of the Allies' security. Despite my personal perplexities and information, we also encouraged the Americans on the Strategic Defense Initiative (SDI), promising to sustain it in the Italian Parliament, and to maintain close contacts with the Germans for an appropriate common position. No matter what might be the future developments, I was pleased to see that the Geneva agenda included the idea of a joint East-West research project on nuclear fusion. I had spoken about this topic at the Erice Conference in August with the scientific adviser to the U.S. administration, Professor Edward Teller, within the framework of the vast movement *for science without secrets and without frontiers,* where I am active along with Professor Antonino Zichichi and which has led to the creation of the World Lab, an excellent tool for peace. It was not by chance that we set up the World Lab in Geneva, the early site of the League of Nations, the headquarters of the large CERN research center, and, in 1985, the place of the encounter between Reagan and Gorbachev of such great historical importance.

Along with the major international issues, foreign ministers also have to deal with matters of ordinary administration. While in no way comparable with the *Achille Lauro* affair, also troublesome was what we considered the arbitrary retaliation decided by the Americans against the EEC trade policy, and applied in the form of a surtax on the imports of "pasta" products for human consumption, which particularly affected our food industry. Shultz sent to Rome Reagan's personal delegate for GATT matters and the like, Mr. Clayton Yeutter. He couldn't help but note how odd it was for them to unleash upon our exports their reactions over a presumed European damaging of their fruit market, since we had all but disappeared from the external market in that sector. We also discussed the incomprehensible delays in "reopening" to Parma ham. On the other hand, we noted the American administration's intention to resist the pressures for protectionism, which would have been detrimental to some of our important products like footware and textiles. Yeutter is a very skillful negotiator and is secretary of agriculture in the present cabinet.

I had gone to Warsaw in December and returned with the firm belief that things, even though very serious (there was great emotion over the assassination of Fr. Popieluzko), would develop in a positive way. General Jaruzelski's position was more open than it ordinarily appeared to be, and, in our embassy, I had been able to meet with the leaders of "Solidarity" (including the present prime minister) without any objections. I let Shultz know what I thought about the situation, and he assured me that, if the program of assistance to the farmers through the church organization were to start, America would have contributed to it. This program got within an inch of becoming operational, but was never able to take that last, tiny step.

At the very outset of 1986, however, there was another difficult moment with Shultz (when you come right down to it, two in six years is not a bad record; quite the contrary). The United States continued to focus its concerns over the potential dangers of terrorism on Libya, and felt that we Europeans were not sufficiently convinced and alert. Therefore, Deputy Secretary of State Whitehead was sent on a visit to the various capitals to display the evidence of Ghaddafi's terrorism.

Craxi and I received him together, and he gave us a file attesting to the fact that the colonel had been informed of an airplane hijacking to Malta before it took place; the file also referred to other similar connections. As chance would have it, the only *proof* we were able to cross-check turned out to be nonexistent. It was alleged that the terrorists arrested for the attack on Fiumicino Airport had been carrying *Tunisian* passports stolen from the workers who had recently been sent back to Tunisia from Libya. Since I had closely followed the relevant investigation, I was able to rectify that immediately: the passports were Moroccan. And when one of our guests' aides interrupted me to say I was doubting the word of the president of the United States, I ironically replied that I would never dare do that, I was just pointing out a mistake made by a State Department typist.

We once again clarified the fact that, even more than the Americans and others, we were the ones most directly concerned about Libya not instigating terrorist activities because of the limited distance between our countries. In force for some time was an embargo on military supplies as well as a decision to reduce our presence in Libya quite drastically, much to the detriment of Italian workers and companies. Just like others, and even more so, we were prepared to deal with any subversive activities the colonel might want to sponsor. The only thing we could not accept was "signing on the dotted line" under information from the intelligence services which, as far as we knew, did not correspond to the truth (and I recalled the mystery of the mines in the Red Sea which no one had found but whose origin had been ascribed to Italy by the CIA). As a matter of fact, we recommended the careful screening of such intelligence in order to avoid endorsing stratagems or falling into the trap of misinformation.

Rabb had told me that John Whitehead was not very pleased when he left Rome, but when I spoke with one of the prime ministers and with colleagues visited during the same *tour,* I noted how astonished they were over the weakness of the "proof" which had been so solemnly announced. Shultz wrote a few days later (January 26), in view of an upcoming EEC Council meeting, informing me of public opinion's growing perception of a serious disagreement between the United States and its allies over the gravity of the terrorist threat, the central role played by Ghaddafi, and the nature of the measures ("peaceful measures") which we could adopt individually and collectively to counter it. We should not allow our common front against Libyan-assisted terrorism to be transformed into a cause for debate and division within the Alliance. Shultz wrote me:

John placed the accent on our concern that the Community's statements during the meeting of the foreign ministers not weaken our common efforts in addressing this problem of ever-increasing gravity. I am quite frankly worried that this would occur if the ministers were to come up with only a mild resolution denouncing international terrorism in general, and without a specific reference to the central role of Ghaddafi and Libya in recent acts of terrorism.

Moreover, I think it would be equally sterile to confine oneself to a discussion on the efficacy of the sanctions against terrorism or not to succeed in defining the measures which have been, can be, and should be adopted to force Ghaddafi to abandon his present policy of state terrorism.

The ministers of the Community reiterated the commitment against terrorism but, in the absence of evidence, did not name Libya in the official communiqué. Shultz was disappointed, but he thanked Craxi in writing for having spoken about it.

I had not had, nor did I expect any response to the *feelers* I had transmitted from Ghaddafi to Reagan, since the Americans could use many channels. However, the tone of George's letter was quite explicit: Ghaddafi continued to be the "current demon" since he had taken over from Fidel Castro and was yet to be replaced by Ortega and his Sandinista comrades.

And yet, was Ghaddafi really "excommunicated" by the Americans? Some time earlier, the American ambassador to the Holy See, Bob Wilson, had asked me to let Tripoli know he wanted to visit the colonel, and this was done; and since Bob Wilson (I myself had seen in California just how popular with and close he was to President Reagan) certainly hadn't gone to visit the Sabratha excavations, in my incurable optimism I could also think that something good was under way. The ambassador to the Holy See, and former *personal* representative of the president, could perhaps enjoy more freedom of movement than his own State Department.

At the same time, I was very pleased George had agreed to come to Rome over Easter for political talks and also to satisfy the long-cherished wish of his wife, a Catholic, to attend the Easter Mass celebrated by the Pope.

In the meanwhile, unfortunately, the American people suffered an immense collective blow over the loss of the crew on the space shuttle *Challenger* which exploded shortly after takeoff. On that occasion Ronald Reagan's enormous prestige and consummate skill were evident. Not only were no accusations launched against the administration, but the president uplifted spirits and generated enthusiasm by going on TV to exalt the contribution which America, even at the cost of grave sacrifices, had always given to the cause of science and progress. Shultz as well, in his reply to my message of solidarity, wrote the following words: "We will long remember these seven courageous Americans and will draw inspiration from their example in pursuing a vigorous program, continuing to cooperate in the broadest possible way with other nations in our space efforts."

George and Obi Shultz spent three days in Rome. Even though other issues were discussed as well in the talks at the Quirinale Palace, Palazzo Chigi, and Villa Madama, the overriding problem was Libya, not least because dissenting views over transit in the Gulf of Sidra had already caused a clash. The Americans claimed freedom of navigation on the basis of a general principle: the Libyans, evoking as well a different and specific U.S. stand during the monarchy, maintained they were territorial waters. The risk of an escalation in the dispute was far from imaginary and in the background, quite evidently, was the negative assessment of Libya as a party without any respect for lawfulness in general.

The fact that it was a question of principle was also revealed by the Americans' simultaneous demand to be able to navigate without permission or advance notice in the Gulf of Taranto. The difference of views with us was resolved by submitting the legal case to a study group (also because we insisted that their "libertarian" thesis ended up by extending the same possibility to the Soviets, Albanians, and everyone else; while in practical terms, and with due reciprocity, we were prepared to exempt the Allied fleets from the advanced notice requirement); nonetheless, a proposal of ours to call upon the International Court of Justice at The Hague to interpret the status of the Sidra waters was ill viewed by Shultz.

Libya and the price of oil seemed to be the only topics of interest to Shultz during his talks in Rome. On other topics he looked distracted and at times even nervous, like at the Quirinale where President Cossiga energetically illustrated our invincible will to do our utmost in preventing any criminal acts by terrorists, no matter what their nationality or ideology. I have no idea how the cool climate of those talks ended up in the newspapers.

Everything went well with Craxi as long as discussion focused on East-West relations (Shultz reported on his meeting in Stockholm with Soviet Prime Minister Ryzkov) and on the downfall of dictatorial regimes in the Philippines and Haiti. However, when Craxi said (while touching upon the Mediterranean area, and even deploring Ghaddafi's alleged right to use weapons against the entry of foreign ships in the Gulf of Sidra) that more intense political-diplomatic initiatives were the best way to discourage factors of instability, our guest's reaction was ice cold.

And the temperature dropped even further when Craxi added: "It is especially the force of law and morals that must be opposed to the illegality of terrorism, in order to isolate politically all those who protect, encourage, or merely tolerate the organizations of violence and subversion." At Palazzo Chigi, on the other hand, the Americans immediately expressed strong confidence in the handling of monetary problems by the Group of Five or Group of Seven, where some European "friend" was trying to downclass Italy, pretending that the United States was the one in favor of the smaller groups.

I had noted that outside of the talks, whose contents were scrupulously recorded by the respective précis writers, Shultz was more at ease, more talkative. I therefore tried to understand why, on Libya, he was so edgy all the time. I found the answer, at least I think so, while he was leaving Rome.

During the round of talks at Villa Madama I had tried to adopt a more acceptable approach. I assured him that we were on our guard against all possible international acts of terrorism. Libya wasn't the only country which might want to "punish" us for our friendship with America and the good relations with Israel (we were openly reproached for the fact that in the EEC we were among those who did not tie economic concessions in favor of that government to a change of policy in the occupied territories). Other nations were also opposed to our policies: Iran, for example—even though dialogue was open—considered us responsible for Western support to Iraq; groups of Palestinians plotted to release many of their fellow terrorists who were in our prisons and we did not know for how long Arafat, bereft of anything like an open ear on the international scene, could continue to keep them at bay.

Even cutting down to size the multicontinental horizons in some of Ghaddafi's proclaimed intentions, the fact that Libya constituted a threat to the stability of Chad, Sudan, Egypt itself, and perhaps Indonesia was accurate. However, we should not overestimate its military power, and other means had to be sought to bring it back to a policy of respect for the international rules. We had indicated one way with the embargo on the sale of weapons and cutting back on trade relations. Other countries, perhaps praised as honorary anti-Libyans, were making more money than ever before.

Italy, I continued, had no sympathy at all for any nondemocratic regime. Toward its neighbors, however, it had always strived to practice a policy of dialogue and strengthening of relations, no matter what the respective political systems might be. When the South Tirol terrorists had found asylum in Austria, we never interrupted our effort at mutual understanding; and when there were many psychological motives for dissent and tragic memories with Yugoslavia, we likewise made sure that what prevailed were notions of wisdom and understanding. Firmness and patience: along these two tracks we had constructed and defended peace. And we continued to act in this way as well toward all the countries on the other shore of the western Mediterranean, never indulging in the classical inhuman heritage of *divide and conquer*.

In this framework I repeated the suggestion to defer the Sidra controversy to the International Court of Justice at The Hague which would have had the joint effect of pushing Ghaddafi toward respect for lawful procedures. In this, I said, the International Court at The Hague is worth more than the Sixth Fleet. I also referred to its usefulness in past disputes: between Libya and Tunisia, in the North Sea, and even between the United States and Canada over a bay in Maine.

Shultz heard me out, but dismissed this last proposal as "not appropriate." And with a note of irony he expressed a wish: "I wish the Italian government good luck in its attempt to bring Ghaddafi back to reason with good manners."

However, he did consider of great political acumen a reference I made to the political consequences of the decrease in the price of oil (which certainly brought relief to the Italian budget). In particular I was thinking about U.S.-Soviet relations and the worsening of the Soviet foreign currency reserves, since gas and oil represented 80 percent of their exports to the West. The fall in the price risked having negative effects also on Saudi Arabia, I added, including a cut in aid to poor countries and therefore a reduction as well in major public works and in investments in general in the Third World. I asked Shultz what he thought about it.

He replied that he too had tried to analyze this problem, but had not come up with a convincing response. What could be done was to draw up a list of the winners and the losers. The losers were the Soviet Union, Saudi Arabia, Libya, Indonesia, Ecuador, and Mexico, perhaps more so than anyone else. The winners were Italy, Germany, Japan, the United States, Brazil, India, perhaps China, and Argentina. Saudi Arabia didn't have a large population and could withstand the blow. Jordan, Egypt, and Morocco were suffering from the decrease in remittances from their immigrant workers in oil-producing countries.

On the other hand, however, the drop in the price of oil kept inflation under control. In the United States, the cost of money in real terms had finally been reduced. Despite the negative effects, in the final analysis the fall in the price of oil was a stimulus for the economy and its impact could be considered positive. "What we don't want," continued Shultz, "are pendular movements: but how to address this problem and where the price will stop is difficult to say. Maybe at fifteen dollars, as the experts say? It is a topic that should perhaps be studied at the Summit Meeting of the Seven Most Industrialized Countries in Tokyo."

I concluded the lengthy dialogue with a remark I considered appropriate. With the United States, Italy had a much more solid relationship than in the past when we were the only side to believe in it and had to cultivate it in a very harsh situation of opposition. I recalled the state of siege in Rome during the visits by General Ridgway and President Nixon.

In St. Peter's Square, Shultz would be able to see that *everyone* was pleased by his presence in Italy.

Shultz replied: "Italy is a great partner of America and I am ready to say it on any occasion. Our dialogue is frank, we see one another often, and we have a good way of discussing things."

Two hundred thousand people in St. Peter's Square on Easter morning not only gave an edifying religious example, but were also excellent input for the American reporters in Shultz's party who might amend certain articles on a terrorized and frightened Italy. George, and even more so Obi, were in seventh heaven. At that moment Ghaddafi's shadow was far away in the distance.

But it came back immediately and I found—at least I think so—a key for interpreting the rigidity I had noticed in George. According to the original plan, at the end of the Mass and after paying their respects to the Holy Father (he had received them in a private audience the evening before), the Shultzes were supposed to go to Ambassador Wilson's residence for a light luncheon, and then depart from Ciampino Airport at 2:00 P.M. This suited me perfectly because it also allowed me to make at least a token act of being present with my family. However, I had just arrived home when I was informed that George was already on his way to the airport. I sped on my way (Minister Ferri had yet to set his speed limits) and reached the airport seconds before he did. Sullen looks between Bob Wilson and the secretary of state, perhaps not exactly to the regret of Max Rabb, cleared up the situation for me. An American friend who was there told me in a whisper: "Bob still reports to Mac-Farlane and not to the State Department."

23 | *George's Easter*

Confirmation of the fact that the outcome of Shultz's trip was good reached me in the form of a note delivered on the very evening of Easter Sunday:

Dear Giulio,

Before leaving Rome I want to thank you for everything you did to make my visit a success. Our talks were useful and productive. . . . I feel that the partnership undertaken by the United States and Italy over the last few years to control crime, drug trafficking, and terrorism serves as a model of cooperation also in other fields . . .

Affectionately yours,
George

Mrs. Helena (Obi) Shultz had also written to my wife in enthusiastic terms, with words of praise for my granddaughter ("a charming young-ster") who had been seated next to her at the Mass; it was enchanting the way she described the city of Rome at Easter time.

The press had exaggerated in focusing the contents of our talks on Libya alone. We had also spoken at length about a subject very dear to Shultz, and which he intended to dwell upon with the NATO ministers in a sort of informal seminar: the relationship between technological development and guarantees of freedom. These, however, are not imme-diately newsworthy subjects.

The Sidra issue, nonetheless, continued to be a cause for concern. To demonstrate their point, the Americans announced plans for further navigation in those waters, and Ghaddafi kept on saying he would use every possible means to prevent it. In the EEC we were all worried, and felt there was something explosive in the air.

The evening of April 14, Ambassador Vernon Walters was sent to Rome (as well as London and Paris) to convey urgent messages. He had the formal meeting with Craxi because I was abroad, but I returned to Italy immediately and, in the presence of Rabb, we spoke at the airport. I was struck by how my friend Vernon repeated three times that he was only an envoy *(nuntius)*.

The American administration was notifying us that, since the EEC had not approved economic sanctions, the second hypothesis indicated by Whitehead in January now applied, and that was the adoption by America of "other means." Reagan informed us that the Libyan responsibility for the attack against a Berlin nightclub sometime before had been ascertained, and that another "Libyan" attack against the American Consulate in Paris had been foiled by the French police. Furthermore, a total of thirty-five American targets were being kept under observation by the Libyans. Therefore, according to Washington, the time had come to launch an attack against the terrorist bases in Libya, being very careful to avoid harm to civilians. If the United States did not take action, the Americans would be looked upon as cowards. Unfortunately—and I don't know on what grounds—they felt that, while they were prepared to defend the lives of their allies' citizens, we Europeans did not harbor the same concern for American citizens; and American public opinion was in an uproar. They didn't expect assistance for the operation in Libya, but only hoped it would not be condemned.

Under the mistaken impression it was a consultation and not an act of notification, Craxi had replied that he considered military retaliation to be a grave error (Walters said Chirac was of the same opinion, but Thatcher not entirely so). We had our *suspicions* about the Libyan matrix behind acts of terrorism, but no proof. It was necessary to multiply the political and diplomatic efforts, but it was not right to resort to military action, thereby triggering off a chain of unforeseeable reactions. In response, Vernon Walters had told him that, at the Security Council, a Soviet-sponsored resolution condemning navigation by American ships in the Gulf of Sidra had been backed only by Bulgaria, and therefore, the isolation of America portrayed by Craxi certainly did not exist. Public opinion in the United States would not have condoned it if the administration did not defend the lives of its own citizens and left the way open for Ghaddafi to kill them. "If one of your cities were to be attacked, what would you say if the American Congress were just to vote a resolution of condemnation?" He referred to a figure of 67 percent (the wondrous power of opinion polls) of Americans in favor of action.

In Palazzo Chigi, and later on with me at Ciampino, a very resolute Vernon had nonetheless promised that, the next day, he would report to President Reagan on the Italian position which he had found similar to that of the other European leaders. I have to believe he had no idea American aircraft had already left England and were heading toward Tripoli to bomb the general headquarters of Ghaddafi, who escaped death because someone (I don't know who) had warned him in time. However, there were numerous victims, including women and children.

It was a very sad moment, even if the fears of a much vaster conflict came to nothing in light of the passive stance assumed by the Soviet ships anchored in Libyan waters; a clear sign that the U.S. attack had not taken Moscow by surprise.

Since this episode also gave rise to divergent appraisals within Italy, it would be useful for me to include the full text of a letter I sent to Craxi at the beginning of April.

Dear Craxi,

A detailed report on Shultz's visit is being prepared by Ministry staff, but I would like to anticipate a point for your information (I have already mentioned it to Spadolini).

If the element of freedom of navigation is truly important, once the United States has "de facto" claimed the waters of Sidra to be international, it would be necessary to obtain an international legal sentence preventing the risks of further ad hoc military maneuvers. The right place is the International Court of Justice in The Hague. I am well aware that Washington-Court of Justice relations are tense and that, vis-à-vis Nicaragua's suit on the mining of its ports, the United States already declared that was a political issue, not a legal one: therefore, it does not acknowledge the Court's jurisdiction.

I certainly did not submit formal Italian proposals to Shultz, but I did explain:

1. In August 1984, Ghaddafi had proposed a sort of arbitration with the United States, and with the arbitrators selected by Reagan. The proposal was not accepted.
2. The Hague has already ruled on maritime matters, including even a U.S.-Canadian dispute over a bay in Maine.
3. Appearing before The Hague today would do away with accusations that the United States ignores international fora, thereby attenuating the "Nicaragua" impact.
4. IF GHADDAFI DOES NOT ACCEPT RECOURSE TO THE HAGUE, the psychological advantage for the United States is obvious.

Shultz said immediately that Ghaddafi is an outlaw. A disquieting answer. I replied that with the early-style Tito (massacres, Stalinism, etc.) De Gasperi had taught us to work patiently: the outcome was excellent. Besides, what is the alternative? And doesn't the evident Soviet acquiescence in this regard also entail alarming implications, besides being a guarantee for grave and immediate complications?
I hastened to write to you because I know that yesterday—and it is correct—you told the secretaries of the coalition parties to ignore the "proposal," which really isn't one at all. During a meeting it is normal to look for possible solutions without the solemnity of negotiation proposals.
What hurts us with the Americans and with others is the considerable amount of speculating they can do on the divisions—all to be demonstrated—among Italian political forces. In this way, we don't help them to reason in a less emotive way without haste.

> Regards.
> Giulio Andreotti

At the Summit Meeting of the Seven Most Industrialized Countries which took place a few weeks later in Tokyo (May 1986) Italy firmly raised the issue of the *seven* and not five-member composition of the meetings of finance ministers, and scored a victory. It was a very unruffled summit meeting: reaffirmed positions in the fight against terrorism; relief over the Baker plan for the public debt of the poorest countries;

hopes for increased cooperation, after Chernobyl, for the safety of nuclear installations.

The fact that the Soviets had not reacted openly to the bombing of Tripoli had kept that issue off the Summit's working agenda; unfortunately, however, we were once again in a rather delicate position over Libya.

As part of the customary U.S.-Italian bilateral talks, Craxi and I went to see Reagan who was assisted by Shultz, Baker, and Admiral Poindexter who had taken over on the National Security Council from poor MacFarlane who was ruined in the "Iranian" affair. Everything was going very nicely until the president read out the usual file card of recommendations on behavior toward Libya.

We could not refrain from stating our viewpoint, and I said to the president that, as he would recall, we had practically reduced Italian presence in the country to zero and had reduced, by more than half, our exports, which excluded weapons in any case. "It was rather unusual that the American oil companies were still there, despite announcements to the contrary."

Reagan was quite taken aback and turned toward his cabinet members who assured him that they were taking a close look at the legal aspects, but that the policy line had been adopted. Everything would have ended there, if Admiral Poindexter hadn't interjected: "We're talking about something which perhaps is already past history. As of this morning there is shooting in the streets of Tripoli and, at this moment, who knows where Colonel Ghaddafi has ended up."

I will just quote what I said then: "If you are referring to something as recent as this morning, I apologize. But already last week your intelligence people had told us the same thing and, by calling our embassy, we found out it was completely untrue. I wouldn't want one of your informers—maybe because you pay them well—to be feeding you *welcome but false news*, and you, *unintentionally*, to be misleading the president of the United States."

I knew very well that by mentioning the American oil companies I was not increasing my popularity with the members of the cabinet, and that by refuting Admiral Poindexter I was doing something of even less . . . personal gratification. However, I have never been able to stand pregnant silences. Besides, the news on turmoil in Tripoli turned out to be entirely unfounded, as I had been able to deduce.

Despite Reagan's cordiality toward me that evening (also because I was the only one at the dining table who knew the meaning of the equestrian term, Caprilli's jump), I had to find an early opportunity to clear things up with his entourage. And I found it by accepting an invitation in June to speak in Philadelphia to the World Council on Foreign Affairs, followed by talks in Washington with Shultz (I did the round trip from Canada where I was accompanying President Cossiga on a state visit; it was exhausting, but most useful).

I set the tone for my speech in Pennsylvania by recalling that Eisenhower's legitimate dissent in 1956 with the French and English allies, who had resorted to the use of weapons in the Suez Canal zone, had in no way affected relations within NATO or in general; the difference of opinions on the American move in the Mediterranean against Libya was certainly to be considered in the same way. In a global perspective, much more than that was required to be able to set a "treacherous and Machiavellian" Europe against America, "strong in its principles which we all respect." On the contrary, we had to live together in peace, avoiding a mad arms race and adapting ourselves to "the duties prescribed by existing treaties." Once again I praised the "policy of contacts and weapons reduction, a policy in which we firmly believe."

The most noteworthy development in the talks with Shultz was the positive reaction to my proposal for a stable and structural form of contact between the United States and the European Community, both with the ministers and with the EEC Commission. We had to make sure that individual problems that arose in time did not project the image of a constant skirmish, while in terms of global policy we certainly would have been able to highlight our converging views on major predominant issues. Shultz had already shown his receptivity to this idea by paying a visit to the EEC Commission when he went to Brussels every December for the NATO Council meeting. On the Middle East, I was told about possible action on the part of the Holy See (Msgr. Silvestrini) in Lebanon, which I considered rather futile, because of the divisions, too, among the Christians; I ventured to suggest that we all push on Gemayel and the others so they would not think they could establish domestic peace between Christians and Muslims (and within the respective communities) by beating on the poor Palestinians. We discussed Egypt and I suggested the idea of choosing Rome—and possibly Professor Ago as arbitrator—to settle the dispute between Egypt and Israel over Taba, which also stood out as a negative example of true peace not implemented between the two countries. George also spoke to me about the terrible nuclear accident at Chernobyl: perhaps Russia would now be convinced that the necessary technical and scientific cooperation in this field as well would be entirely to its advantage. But there was even more; the impact and panic felt throughout the world would have helped to make progress in negotiations for nuclear disarmament.

Besides the specific and quite significant issues discussed, that round of talks in Washington was one of the most positive and thorough I have ever had. Shultz also let off steam with me over some of Congress's cuts to the budget; there is really an astounding similarity, I observed, in the problems we have to face as ministers. We parted on that note.

Early in September I received a visit from Vernon Walters whom I had not seen since the famous evening of the bombing of Tripoli on April 14. The president had sent him on a new tour to heighten the awareness of all governments about the threats of terrorism which the United States saw lurking even in the offices of airline companies. In Washington they had the feeling that the USSR was now more cooperative in this field. Even though Vernon knew it well, I reiterated my line on Libya: if we were attacked (Craxi had said it quite clearly) we would respond but, for our part, we avoided worsening the crisis by trying to maintain, obviously not *at any cost,* a logical *modus vivendi* between neighbors. The United States had placed an embargo upon any imports containing even the slightest trace of Libyan oil: it was their right, as they had done for Cuban nickel. But the more I had to do with oil, the less its "trade routes" and its links with politics and diplomacy were clear to me. Now that the Sidra storm had blown over, wouldn't it be wise for the Americans to reexamine the possibility of a different relationship with Libya? Were they really sure that, if Ghaddafi were ousted, he would not be replaced by a militant pro-Soviet leader or an Islamic fundamentalist, with even more problems for security in the Mediterranean?

On the subject of South Africa, Walters said that, in his opinion, an EEC embargo on coal would be a mistake, (we were meeting then in Brocket Hall to address the issue) because we would cause the unemployment of fifty thousand black workers. Evidently in the United States as well there were several schools of thought on this sensitive subject.

I asked Vernon how his lobby was going in the Glass Palace. The year before he had come to see me in Merano where I was on vacation, and had shown me astounding figures on the almost customary practice for many countries of casting a vote at the United Nations different from U.S. positions. He told me there was some improvement and promised to send me the statistical report submitted by the U.S. Mission to the State Department every year. There was a precise purpose behind my question: to highlight how, as a rule, Italy voted with the United States, even though American public opinion was not always led to acknowledge that fact.

I have heard from many ambassadors that Vernon Walters has always been very good at personal relations, paying calls to all his colleagues and always being quite open in his relationships. The number of votes coinciding with those of the United States at the UN, however, did not improve (except for a few percentage points on the part of Malta and Angola). I believe Walters could have obtained far better results, if at the same time there hadn't been a widespread feeling of hostility against the United Nations in Congress, to the point of even raising the possibility of moving the UN out of the United States. The country which votes the most with the United States is Israel (89.9 percent) while Canada, despite its closeness and customs union, stands at 72 percent. Among Eastern European countries, Rumancia leads with 16.8 percent.

Again in September I met with Shultz in New York and received further confirmation that the expedition into Libya had not jeopardized U.S.-Soviet negotiation contacts. Back in August he had written me a long letter with full details on a meeting of experts about to take place in Moscow, and filled me in on the instructions given to Paul Nitze. Other meetings of U.S.-Soviet experts the month before had addressed individual items on the agenda drawn up for the formal resumption of negotiations scheduled for September 18 (chemical weapons, exercise for disarmament in the CSCE, and Mutual Balanced Force Reduction talks). Nitze himself had come to Rome to show us a very constructive letter written to Gorbachev by Reagan. To both Nitze and Shultz I was able to express Italy's *deep satisfaction* over the course of events. And I repeated this to George himself during those talks I had with him in New York on September 24.

A complication in the U.S.-Soviet relationship arose with the case of an American journalist arrested in the Soviet Union on charges of espionage. If he were not released immediately, the summit meeting would be cancelled, since American public opinion (or the opponents to détente?) was once again up in arms. However, I had the distinct impression that an exchange of true or alleged "007s" was simmering, and therefore there was no reason for alarm. I dispelled George's worries over Jaruzelski's scheduled visit to Rome, telling him we had requested and obtained one hundred acts of clemency linked precisely to the trip which, in addition, served the no less important purpose of a visit to the Vatican which was supposed to be a prelude to a journey by the Holy Father to Warsaw. The rigid American stance toward Poland—prompted perhaps by the Polish communities in the United States—seemed out of place to me. I confirmed my impressions based on the days spent in Warsaw in December: the General was not only acting in good faith, but also as a constructive element in a tacit evolution under way. The trial of the killer-policemen in Torun could not be underestimated.

We then discussed UNESCO. Even if the Americans had withdrawn from the organization, I considered it important to find out if M'Bow's possible reelection might preclude their return which I deemed indispensable. Ambassador Gerard had been quite drastic on this point. What did George think of candidates like Enrique Iglesias, the foreign minister of Uruguay, Boutros Ghali from Egypt, or the Nobel laureate Abdus Salam? Even though interested in the subject, Shultz told me that the State Department had not taken it under study.

Referring to terrorism, I told him we had proposed to our European colleagues the use of metal detectors on diplomatic pouches at airports, but they were not enthusiastic about it. The British, who had been the first ones to denounce the misuse of pouches as a way to transport even weapons, were invoking the Geneva and Vienna Conventions, and were also afraid that such a waiver would provide a way for Eastern European countries to get into the classified information of Western embassies. Unfortunately, when the time came to replace the theories with concrete action in the fight against terrorism, all we got were sophisticated objections. This measure, which we were going to apply in any case, struck Shultz as a sound idea. He also expressed satisfaction on the buy back of FIAT stock from Libya, a decision made in Turin in order to abide by the same policy line, and suffer no setbacks on the American market. At that moment he did not react to my rather ironical remark that there was reason to envy Ghaddafi if all punishments inflicted upon him were like that, because he had made a net profit of 1,000 percent on the buy back. A few days later someone in Washington had second thoughts about it, but the shares had already changed hands.

Shultz congratulated me on the honorary degree in law bestowed on me two days earlier at St. John's University following the proposal made by my old friend Professor Edward Re.

It had been a very moving ceremony on account both of the hospitality of the president, Fr. Joseph Cahill, and of the awarding at the same ceremony of an academic Ph.D. to 491 students, some of whom had come to St. John's for that purpose with an M.A. from other universities. I was impressed by the large number of Italian last names among them, which stood out as a significant index of the improved standing achieved by the families of Italian immigrants. Many bear an American first name (Joseph Fonte, Richard Lo Russo, Marilyn Chiaromonte, Debby Romanello) but others—perhaps from families who have immigrated more recently to the United States—left no room for doubt: Sandra Bertolotti, Laura Giovannini, Romana Mattia, Angelo Ciminera, Carmine Esposito, Salvatore Incardona, and even Laura Mussolini.

We celebrated in a new Italian restaurant called Il Palio, decorated with the distinctive colors of the Siena boroughs. Yet, this is the work of the South Tirolean Andreas, a well-known restaurant owner from Merano who, on account of the many Italian Americans in New York, wisely decided to drop the final *s* from his name.

The summit meeting between Reagan and Gorbachev took place in Reykjavik in October. In addition to the information supplied to the Atlantic Council through Paul Nitze, Reagan had made it a point of advising the Allied countries in writing of the four points he was going to raise, underscoring *above all* his continuing commitment toward ironing out differences with the USSR: human rights, reduction of armaments, "regional" problems, bilateral issues. And George Shultz came directly to Brussels from Reykjavik to brief us on the tempestuous and turbulent meeting.

The late-night news had spread pessimistic feelings in our countries and I had left Rome in such a frame of mind. I ran into George at the entrance to NATO headquarters and he flashed me the OK sign. He told us that, when the working groups were unable to come up with any results, the summit was about to be adjourned without a conclusion when the two leaders decided to have a one-on-one meeting, with only the interpreters present, in an attempt to avoid failure. And the consensus had been found. George voiced—and I thought without any disrespectful innuendos—his admiration for Gorbachev and Reagan who, without the assistance of their respective staffs, had even tackled problems with which they were not quite familiar. I recalled De Gasperi who, when he had to make a decision, would hear out the experts and all others, but in the end always found the ways by himself.

The Soviets had even accepted a point which seemed impossible to us: the changes to their criminal law, which the Americans had requested in order to put an end to the ambiguity of actions contrary to human rights but formally lawful (e.g., the procedures for forced admission to insane asylums).

When Shultz returned to Belgium two months later for the ordinary session of the Atlantic Council, his mood was dark grey, and not over international problems. The polemic over the scandal of American arms secretly supplied to Iran was on again and in a bad way, and George felt particularly ill at ease since he had always taken a drastic stance in reprimanding the allies who were allegedly breaking the embargo, and in maintaining that negotiations with terrorists are out of the question, not even for the release of hostages. With a frenzied cross fire of denials and explanations—all different—the White House had put itself in a difficult position; to further complicate the issue, that very morning of the Council meeting the news spread that the arms supplied had been *temporarily* taken from NATO stocks. The sensitive nature of the issue was clear to everyone even from this perspective, but the worst part was the clash with Congress, because the money made on the illicit sale had reportedly ended up in the hands of the anti-Sandinista guerrilla movement precisely to make up for the funds not approved by Congress itself. Furthermore, rumors had it that Colonel North (the man of the Sigonella affair again) had made a mistake on the number of the Swiss bank account, thus sending astray both those funds and the generous contributions of an Asian sultan who had also been solicited to step in for the financial aid to the "Contras" in Nicaragua denied by Capitol Hill in Washington.

In my opinion, however, Reagan was so popular that it was in vain for reporters to call the affair "Irangate" in an effort to stir up memories of "Watergate." Luckily so; if a crisis had exploded at that time, negotiations with the USSR would have stalled, and perhaps run aground forever. I openly expressed this concern—taking advantage of my position as chairman *pro tempore* of the Atlantic Council—along with encouragement not to succumb to the mood of a scandal which was liable to take the limelight off the much more important issues of world peace and disarmament.

On the side we had arranged a working breakfast together at the Hyatt Regency Hotel because I had to lodge a protest about the nth meeting which had been held in London under the standard label of the Western powers occupying Berlin (the United States, United Kingdom, Federal Republic of Germany, France) and reopened the loathsome dispute over the "directorate." I hated having to raise this point when Shultz's mood was focused on quite other matters. And he actually did appear impatient, and he tried to say that the talks had already centered on Berlin (for two whole days!).

There was also another complaint on my list and it had to do with the solemn celebrations on the centennial of the Statue of Liberty when there had been awards for Americans of all origins, and none for an Italian. Thinking I would sweeten the pill, I said I was pleased because, at long last, an "Italian," Antonin Scalia, had been appointed to the Supreme Court, thus fulfilling an intention manifested by previous presidents but never enacted. But I had put my foot in it. I quote from my notes on the unexpected minor storm which ensued.

SHULTZ: This I cannot accept. Frankly, I don't think it is up to you to tell us who should receive an award and who should be appointed to the Supreme Court. In our country, this is not done on ethnic considerations, but on the basis of merit. I consider this interference in our domestic affairs.

ANDREOTTI: It is clear that there is no intention whatsoever on our part to interfere. At least three American presidents, on their own initiative and without any urging from me, had occasion to let me know that an American of Italian origin would be appointed to the Supreme Court. President Reagan did it. I think it is logical to be pleased. By the same token, I am pleased when I happen to see many Italian names at university graduations. This means a step up in the quality of Italians in America. Witness to this effect is also provided by the presence on the American political scene of men like Mario Cuomo and Alphonse D'Amato, no matter to which party they belong. And Lee Iacocca, who for some time chaired the committee for the Statue of Liberty celebrations, is of Italian origin as well.

I'm well aware that in America merit is not assessed on the basis of ethnic considerations; Kissinger was a foreigner when the war broke out and he became secretary of state. This is part of the great American dream.

But going back to our type of politics, I would like to remind you, by way of example, that in the whole Iran affair we have been more careful than others in maintaining an attitude of discretion. We have issued no statements. We are a serious ally.

SHULTZ: I know Italy is a serious ally.

The discussion continued at length on other subjects without any more sharp displays of nerves, even if my counterpart was clearly quite tense. We spoke about EEC agricultural policy, Central America, Lebanon in ever-mounting difficulties, South Africa, and the ineffective nature of the partial economic sanctions imposed by the EEC (not on coal exports), King Hussein's plan for the West Bank which we were willing to support but on which I was somewhat skeptical. I strove to take George's mind off the somber thoughts of those days by telling him about an exchange of views I had had in Florence with Soviet Deputy Minister Adamisin, with whom I had agreed on the policy of not allowing prejudicial conditions to stop U.S.-Soviet contacts. I had had the impression that the space shield would not be an insurmountable obstacle, and that perhaps a solution could even be found to the dispute over the limits to research. I took the opportunity to add a few words once again about the advisability of meetings between scientists (Shultz immediately said: "Open labs"), suggesting that if Teller and Velichov got together, they certainly would come up with a formula, and better than us politicians.

I really felt sorry for Shultz. He did not want to expose the president or disavow some of his staff, but he had every right to be furious over Irangate if no one had kept him informed at the proper time. That is why I took no umbrage over his reaction on Italian Americans. Besides, a short time later American Ambassador Abshire went to see his Italian colleague Fulci to tell him that George, *a posteriori,* had deeply regretted his outburst.

Shultz notified me that Bob Wilson (I called him "the Libyan resignee") would be replaced in Rome, at the Holy See, by the U.S. ambassador to Lisbon, Frank Shakespeare. The State Department had taken its revenge.

Another year full of events, emotions, joyful days, and hours to forget, was coming to an end. At some times it had been difficult for me personally to maintain an objectively firm position, without letting myself be influenced by some Italian domestic currents of thought, whose good faith I do not question, but who are wrong in believing that it isn't possible to argue with Americans; it can be done as long as it is done honestly and not through the media or by sensational announcements. Halfway through the year I had been very pleased to notice that an idea mentioned by Craxi to Paul Nitze, concerning a method for jointly evaluating security in the Mediterranean and not deciding under the pressure of events, had been picked up by Reagan who sent Deputy Secretary Armacost to discuss it in depth. With him he brought a letter from Reagan himself which spoke of "the specific duty to work side by side"; it declared that "history and geography give Italy a unique view of the entire area"; and it recognized that Italy had "confronted the terrorist challenge with success."

And Shultz had assured me that we would spend Easter together in Rome again.

24 | *Visiting the Jews in New York*

The American colleagues of the Interparliamentary Union invited us to the United States in January 1987, and I led a delegation representative of seven parties (Adolfo Battaglia, Gianfranco Conti Persini, Antonio Guarra, Antonio Rubbi, Egidio Sterpa, and Saverio Zavattini).

The earlier political reservations were now a thing of the past, and there was no need for dual programs. We had very important meetings, with exchanges of views always open and, at times, lively. From Vice President Bush to Secretary of State Shultz, from Supreme Court Justice Scalia to our old friend Edward Derwinski, who had become undersecretary for security, science, and technology; and with a large number of very influential senators and congressmen: the speaker, Jim Wright, the majority and minority whips in the Senate, Robert Byrd and Bob Dole, as well as the chairmen of the Foreign Affairs Committees, Dante Fascell and Claiborne Pell. Our political escorts were Senator Robert Stafford (Republican, Vermont, who is now retired and sent me a beautiful farewell letter) and Congressman Claude Pepper (Democrat, Florida), who was later our host in his home state. Among the many colleagues we met, Senator John Danforth of Missouri praised the cooperation between Aeritalia and McDonnell-Douglas, whose main plants were in his constituency.

Once again, and all together, we served our nation well, displaying substantial consensus on problems, not weakened by the logical differences dictated by respective party membership.

In Florida we went to the capital, Tallahassee, where we were received by Governor Bob Martinez and by Jeb Bush (George's son), the state secretary of commerce. Chief Justice Benjamin Overton hosted a working luncheon for us, and then we had the time of our lives on a visit in Orlando to the Magic Kingdom and the Epcot Center, two Disney creations on the Atlantic Coast.

The illustrations of what agriculture should be like in the year 3000 are fascinating, but I confess that I enjoyed the pranks of the seven dwarfs who came to enliven lunch, and all the more so since we were in the restaurant opened by the owner of the famous Da Alfredo in Rome. It never hurts to let your hair down.

The next morning we were able to visit the Space Center at Cape Canaveral, which is now dedicated to John F. Kennedy. These visits are also very useful for learning about the enormous amount of experimental work being done by the Americans in the field of missiles for civilian purposes.

From Florida to New York with a program that was punishing, but in an intelligent way; a very warm welcome at Columbia University where President Mike Sovern and Maristella Lorch, a very dynamic professor, expressed the desire for a greater presence of the Italian language and culture in this most prestigious center for higher learning. On this same subject, a seminar was then held there to discuss new ideas and new ways for *increased presence* as further development for what was already a very serious and extensive program. This was evident from the intense schedule of activities planned for that period: lectures by people like the Neapolitan biologist Professor Aldo Moretti; Rosella Mamoli Zorzi, Daria Parocco, Renzo Bragantino, and Giorgio Padoan, from the Faculty of Letters in Venice; Sergio Zatti from the University of Pisa; Enrico Malato from Viterbo University; then there was the noteworthy presence of Alberto Moravia and the authors Maria Luisa Spaziani and Letizia Cravetto; on top of that, Vittore Branca from the Cini Foundation, Alberto Conte the mathematician, and Franco Ferrarotti the sociologist from the University of Turin. Also scheduled for springtime were the historian Gilmo Arnaldi from Rome; Franco Fortini and Ginevra Bompiani, authors from Siena, and Professor Joselita Raspi-Serra from Salerno.

All of us were very impressed by the visit to Columbia. We promised to promote the bolstering of its "Casa Italiana" and, in general, of the activities organized by the Italian Institute of Culture in New York. From there we went to the Council on Foreign Relations for an exchange of views on the prospects for security and peace after Reykjavik.

I then gave some free time to my colleagues who did not know New York (then again, who ever knows it completely?) and I took the opportunity to have lunch with Vernon Walters in the beautiful official residence he has in one of the Waldorf Astoria towers. Before our departure we were received with extraordinary warmth by Governor Mario Cuomo. He even told us—and someone interpreted this half-serious quip as the start of an electoral campaign—he was sorry we hadn't spoken about policies in Washington, because no one was making policies at that time in America. Mario, however, in very touching terms evoked his Italian origin of which he was very proud. Fortunately, he didn't mention Irangate which would have made us feel uncomfortable (even though it wouldn't have had the same effect on Congressman Pepper and the other Democratic colleagues).

However, in an interview with *Le Monde,* the person who did speak about Irangate during those same days was George Shultz. In response to the reporter who asked him how people from the National Security Council had ever been able to do what they did without his knowing about it, he said:

The president had declared publicly that he considered it important to establish contacts which could help bring about a change in Iran's conduct, with evident strategic importance, and on this I am in agreement with the president who has, here too publicly, made it known that *he made the decision* to show our good faith with the *signal* of a small shipment of arms.

In the following months correspondence with Shultz intensified on some specific topics, notably the discussion in Geneva on the alleged Cuban violations of human rights, and the opposition to the introduction of an EEC levy on fats and oils. To avoid the levy, I maintained, America would have to show greater flexibility in trade negotiations in general, and, despite the administration's claim that it was often difficult to parry thrusts toward protectionism in Congress. And Congress was the direct source of the damper on European expectations to obtain interesting technological contracts for the SDI system.

While Senator Nunn was working hard on bringing allied cooperation in the defense sector to a higher level, Congressman Les Aucoin pushed through an amendment stipulating extensive restrictions to foreign participation in research on the Strategic Defense Initiative. Shultz wrote to me immediately (May 25) expressing his regrets and the administration's intention to mount opposition; unfortunately, he was afraid Senator John Glenn, who was moving in the same direction as Aucoin, would score a similar success, with the consequent victory of a policy line totally opposed to the spirit and the objectives of the agreement for equitable foreign participation in the program. In effect, Glenn won and not the administration.

It wasn't doomsday for me, but certainly one of the best arguments our government had used in persuading Parliament to support SDI no longer applied. Nonetheless, most interest at that time was focused on the push toward a positive conclusion in the negotiations to dismantle medium-range missiles in Europe. In this matter Italy made a substantial contribution, helping to overcome the legendary impossibility of true verification.

In Moscow they kept on thinking that the verifiers were none other than spies; and in Washington the granting of an *entry visa* to a Soviet was still frowned upon by the bureaucracy. We invited scientists from the opposing fronts to Rome, being careful to choose them not only for their unquestioned scientific renown, but also for their personal potential of direct access to their respective heads of state; the outcome was a model for contacts which, in practical terms, turned out to be very simple and without drawbacks.

Before the Atlantic Council in Reykjavik, we had Reagan, Shultz, and Baker in Venice for the Summit Meeting of the Seven Most Industrialized Countries. Senator Amintore Fanfani had become the head of the Italian government after a dispute between the political parties over the construction of nuclear power plants, which had even led to the dissolution of the Senate and Chamber of Deputies. A useless dispute because the ambiguous referendum on the issue was not avoided and was actually moved up to immediately after the elections, thereby preventing even the newly elected Parliament from exploring temporary solutions. At times it is difficult to explain the "ins and outs" of Italian politics to foreigners, especially when there are not reasonable ways to do it.

The summit meeting was held at the Cini Foundation on the island of San Giorgio where the 1979 session had taken place. Reagan was always

in excellent spirits; evidently in his own heart he had more than surmounted the polemics over Irangate, and also because public opinion
was so much on his side that the Democratic party had never seriously
considered an attempt to involve him in person. The change in the head
of the White House staff (Howard Baker had taken over from Regan)
seemed to have turned things around and restored uncontested popularity.

During the breaks the president willingly entertained the other participants by drawing from his repertoire of jokes, to which he had recently
added a whole series of funny Russian ones. I wrote down four of them
which, he said, he had also shared with Gorbachev, except for the
second one.

Brezhnev dies and appears before St. Peter asking to be let into Paradise.
With his record, the request is denied and he is only offered the choice between
the Communist or capitalist hell. "No doubt, I'll take the first one," replied
Comrade Leonid, "because there the heating certainly doesn't work."

Curfew time in Moscow. A patrol stops a man who is killed outright. The
partner of the policeman who fired the shot took him to task over it, and said:
"Why did you do it? There were still 15 minutes left before curfew." "You're
right," said the other one, "but I know where he lives and he never would have
made it home in time."

Brezhnev and Carter are discussing freedom, and the American president, to
demonstrate the extreme liberty in his country, says that any citizen can stand in
front of the White House and cry out "DOWN WITH CARTER" without
anyone stopping him. "In the USSR too," replied Brezhnev, "every citizen can
cry out 'DOWN WITH CARTER' no matter where he is and for as long as he
wants."

A group of friends are trying to decide what is the oldest profession in the
world. The first one says it's doctors because Eve came out of Adam after an
operation. The second sides with engineers because the universe was created
according to a plan. The third said: "In the beginning there was chaos, and that
means a lot of lawyers."

In addition to the little official gifts exchanged on these occasions,
Reagan also received a fine copy of the Statue of Liberty made by the
Venetian sculptor Gianni Visentin. Once it was clear that the present
was for Ron Reagan and not for the American president as such, he

assured us he would keep this souvenir even after 1988, without violating the strict laws on those matters.

In view of the looks of admiration it had caused, I also ordered another slightly smaller copy for George Shultz and his delightful wife.

The talks in Venice went smoothly, more or less according to the customary pattern. Nor was there any change in the somewhat Byzantine habit of issuing unbelievably lengthy joint statements which no newspaper in the world could publish word for word. Six documents were approved, where the only new point was the pledge to cooperate in research on AIDS, just like we had done for cancer in London and for drugs in Bonn.

In the statement on East-West relations, Mrs. Thatcher did not object to the introduction of a favorable reference to the efforts being deployed by the United States to reduce nuclear weapons (besides, the principle of deterrence was reiterated, since NATO had decided that for the *foreseeable future* it was to be that way). Shultz, however, was very concerned about the Anglo-German disagreements over the negotiations on the "medium-range" missiles, which had come to the surface in preparation for the Atlantic Council meeting in Reykjavik where we were to go directly from Venice.

We met for a round of talks at 7:00 A.M. in the setting of the Hotel Cipriani, such an ill-suited place for talking about missiles. I reassured George about our utmost Italian commitment so that the Council meeting would conclude in such a way as to bring the negotiations into the last straight and heading toward the finish line. I had seen Genscher and we agreed with one another. The point to avoid was the British request to set a fire break, below which further reductions in nuclear armaments were no longer to be considered. Shultz felt there was still quite a distance between the German and British positions, and hoped Italy would be successful in bringing them closer together.

A second problem that was difficult to solve seemed to be the issue of conventional stability. Despite the efforts of the State Department, the differences between the United States and France were still outstanding and Charles Thomas was sent to Paris for a last try at negotiations.

George then asked me a direct question concerning the Persian Gulf: "The other day you told me Italy would not be able to take part in any joint initiative in the Gulf since the present government has not received the approval of Parliament and is therefore not in full possession of its powers. On the American side, therefore, there has been quite a demonstration of flexibility. But what do you think the prospects are as regards the Italian government's position after the elections to Parliament?"

I replied that any movement in one direction or another was impossible during an election campaign. As far as the future was concerned, in my opinion it was necessary, in any case, to give priority to political initiatives within the United Nations. A resolution had to be adopted, and sanctions had to be applied to whichever side did not respect the cease-fire. Were all of that to produce no results, other initiatives connected with security in the Gulf could be explored. Political action, however, had to take precedence over everything else; moreover, it seemed to me that such action had started off on the right foot.

I recalled that as chairman of the Foreign Affairs Committee I had had to work very hard to help Minister Colombo obtain approval from the Chamber of Deputies for sending our ships to Lebanon. There has always been very strong resistance to the involvement of our troops outside our own area: this is not out of pacifism, but out of fidelity to the primacy of the political ways so deeply rooted in us. No one could misunderstand this spirit. There has been no real opposition to the deployment of the cruise missiles in Comiso precisely because of this recognized Italian equilibrium. Patience and tenacity were also required for Iraq-Iran; and we would be successful.

Shultz registered this position, predicting that Iraq would accept the Security Council resolution, but not Iran. I was less pessimistic.

In Reykjavik, as a matter of fact, hesitant voices were raised over the nuclear agreement (France and the United Kingdom were, and remain, pensive whenever reduction or replacement options appear on the scene), but we won the day. George very much appreciated the firm Italian support, together with the push toward having the one hundred Soviet missiles aimed toward the Far East removed as well. This was a show of solidarity due to Japan and other nations. Once home, George wrote to tell me he had reported *our success* to the president, and to thank me for my *wise advice*.

We were then faced with two huge issues: the conclusion of the missiles agreement and the situation of the Iran-Iraq conflict, ever on the verge of expanding the war zone. With utmost commitment, and maintaining frank and frequent contacts with the two contending parties, we sought to assist Secretary-General Pérez de Cuéllar in his fervent efforts. And naturally we maintained intense contacts with Washington and frequent ones with Moscow.

Shultz was just about to leave for Moscow when I met with him over dinner in New York on September 23, also in view of our upcoming chairmanship of the Security Council in October. He was very kind to send me the following note the next morning: "Thank you for the exquisite and gracious hospitality yesterday evening. You know how to produce the proper blend of cuisine, sociability and substantive discussion. It is the Andreotti technique, in both Venice and New York."

During these same days I had a unique opportunity thanks to two of my Jewish friends, Leon Tamman, the president of the Union of Arab Jews, and Raffaello Fellah, the president of the Jewish Refugees from Libya. I received an invitation to attend a luncheon in the large building of the Jewish Anti-Defamation League, which is right across the street from the UN headquarters.

They had even invited prominent people from outside New York, and they invited me to expound on my thoughts. I abridge them as follows:

The defense of the security—and not only the existence—of the State of Israel is sacred for us, but we also adopt the same commitment of solidarity toward the Palestinians in order to obtain legitimate political normalization for them. It is necessary to get out of the closed circle of preconditions and accept the simultaneity of satisfactory declarations and commitments. It is certainly not possible to improvise a conference or impose it upon Israel. However, a minimum amount of *"preparatory preparation"* has to begin. I am in a position to inform you that Arafat, aware of Shamir's firm hostility toward the idea of a conference, has expressed to me his willingness to explore other formulas.

At the end of my presentation, and during the question-and-answer period that followed, all I received was a display of respectful courtesy. However, a relationship destined to develop in a useful way was established with Dr. Abraham Foxman and other leaders.

In October I returned to the United States to attend the annual banquet of the National Italian-American Foundation (NIAF) in order to receive from them a sign of distinction awarded to me by Jeno Paolucci, Frank Stella, and John Volpe for—how good of them—my contribution to harmony between the United States and Italy. I readily admit how pleased this made me, also with respect to some of our local mudslingers who every so often kept on insinuating that, on the other side of the Atlantic, I didn't always receive a warm reception (and who were really irritated when I would reply that friendship with the United States is to be lived "at ease" and not "at attention"). My joy was further increased by Shultz's invitation to make the return trip this time on his airplane in order not to miss the NATO meeting in Brussels to assess the state of the U.S.-Soviet negotiations which were proceeding smoothly, but which demanded constant vigilance to avoid last-minute developments to the contrary. In talks with George during the flight, I had an opportunity to reassert the extent of our commitment in contacts with Iran and Iraq to bring about a cease-fire.

Meanwhile, the situation in the Gulf was becoming incandescent. On October 19 Reagan had informed Craxi that U.S. naval units were destroying an Iranian military offshore platform at Rashdat in retaliation for a missile which had hit the U.S.S. *Sea Isle City* three days earlier in Kuwaiti waters. If the U.S.-Soviet summit-level agreement hadn't been in the making, this could have triggered rather serious complications.

I went to refer this to Pérez de Cuéllar the next day, before taking my return flight at the end of a lightning trip. We considered the method of retaliation to be lethal, and maintained our trust in consensus; at times, I pondered in the depths of my heart whether or not I was a dreamer, but I persevered.

Three days later Shultz informed me ahead of time about the visit Shevardnadze was about to make to Washington to deliver a letter from Gorbachev. "In the preparations for this meeting, what will be most helpful to me, as in the past, is the firm support I have always been able to count on from you and the other allies."

By now the negotiations on the European missiles were very close to the finish line. The Soviets were only afraid there might be some final hitch. I let George know this, calling his attention to a letter of mine in February on the dangers of a declared speeding up of the SDI which might imply an interpretation of the ABM Treaty (how many initials!) different from the one so far accepted or, even, an early jump ahead in the deployment of the antiballistic defense systems.

However, everything went very well. The two foreign ministers met in Geneva on November 23 and 24, and on November 25 Shultz came to Brussels to announce that the final meeting between Reagan and Gorbachev was to take place on December 7 in Washington.

In my statement during that special session of the Atlantic Council, I expressed gratitude to George Shultz and his staff for "the tenacity shown in these negotiations, with the support of full agreement from our side, and with exemplary consultation among allies at every stage." And I was able to say: "I never had doubts about this auspicious conclusion, even when we had to register the very real risks of a breakdown in negotiations." But Shultz looked at me with gratitude in his eyes when I said that our communiqué had to express not only our full adhesion, but also our exhortation to all to immediately ratify the agreement which would be signed. In fact, he was well aware of the clouds still in the skies above the Senate in Washington. And he knew those opposed to it would have used the argument of presumed doubts and hostility in European countries. I was able to say that in Italy, we were ready—government and opposition—to undersign what concerned us (removal and verification) and to ratify the agreement with no delay.

Shultz informed us that the Soviets were about to announce the date of their withdrawal from Afghanistan. This was another sign of changing times.

In the atmosphere of joy over the agreement to be signed for sure on December 8, the Italian government received an invitation for a visit to the White House by the new president of the Council of Ministers, Giovanni Goria. Quite significantly, the date was set for December 16.

I was very pleased about it because Goria's first encounter with Ambassador Rabb had been a stormy one. Goria wanted to take the trip, and Rabb had practically made it conditional on a swifter and more decisive Italian stand in responding to a request for sanctions against Iran.

In our will to involve the International Court of Justice in The Hague, the EEC, and the United Nations in seeking solutions to the crisis, Rabb saw what he considered a lukewarm stance. And we found this quite disconcerting because it certainly wasn't the ambassador's viewpoint (nor even that of Reagan or Shultz). The situation, on the contrary, called for a good dose of patience and moderation since Velajati's deputy, Larijani, had voiced an open outlook in New York, and now was not the time to abandon the path of wisdom. Goria acquitted himself quite well in the talks with Rabb.

I had the impression that the very kind chief of protocol, Ambassador Roosevelt, was smiling as I led the way into the White House for the new Italian prime minister (he was not to be the last one!). Informal diplomatic forecasts had twice surmised my return to Palazzo Chigi, but —I explained this to a few friends over there—in the relay exercise Craxi had forgotten to hand over the baton, while the secretary of my own party held a grudge against me over an election poster; and yet its sole purpose had been to attract young people away from the Socialist sirens and get them to vote Christian Democrat. This friend told me that George Shultz had told Reagan how pleased he was not to have lost me as an ally at NATO Council meetings. During this trip I also saw the new chief of the National Security Council, General Power, who made a very good impression on me after the sad experience with Admiral Poindexter. In a lengthy article, reprinted by the Italian newspapers, the admiral gave a patriotic version of Irangate, maintaining that the United States shouldn't have left Iran adrift, and also considering the recovery of its important position on the oil market.

During our meeting Reagan was overjoyed. He told us about his very recent talks with Gorbachev, and was also optimistic about the 50 percent reduction in strategic missiles. However, he did insist on the SDI program to which his file cards ascribed utmost importance. Goria replied that, were there to be a further decrease in the opponent's threat potential, it would also be to the benefit of defensive systems.

Secretary of Defense Carlucci came into the discussion on the Persian Gulf and praised the efforts of the Italian navy. We then talked about Central America and I considered the importance Reagan and Bush attributed to the testimony of a Sandinista, Major Miranda, to be somewhat exaggerated. He had defected to Managua and didn't believe in any substantial changes by that government, even though Gorbachev had announced his intention to no longer supply arms, and to support the Arias Plan.

Goria described our framework agreement for assistance to Argentina and, with respect to Central America, also voiced the support for the Arias Plan which had developed in relations between the EEC ministers and their colleagues from Central America and the Contadora Group. I took advantage of the discussion to underline the importance of close Euro-American cooperation also within the post-Helsinki CSCE process.

At this point Goria raised our concerns about what was happening in Israel, and referred to an international conference as the only possibility for negotiations. President Reagan replied that he had tried to persuade the potentially interested parties to convene the conference, but his efforts had been to no avail because Israel was worried about being relegated to a minority position and isolated by the other participants. The Americans were not opposed to an international conference, as long as the conditions existed for its successful outcome.

In my turn, I repeated how urgent it was to find a solution. It was dictated by the constant increase of the Arab population in Israel itself, whereby, in a few years, we would be faced with an unbearable situation.

Carlucci supported the prospects of an increase in the emigration of Soviet Jews to Israel, but they were precisely the ones who left the USSR and, instead, wanted to go to the United States or to Canada.

Vice-President Bush informed us that King Hussein did not think he could do what Sadat had done, and therefore looked upon an international conference as a sort of "umbrella" for bringing the positions closer together. Hussein, however, was to be encouraged to embrace what Sadat had done, also in light of the running disputes among the moderate Arab leaders.

I recalled that if Sadat had been able to accept Camp David, it was because he had obtained the Sinai in exchange, and was able to stand tall as a patriot able to expand the country's borders and not as someone who had sold out the nation's best interests. It would have been disastrous to push King Hussein without at least a glimpse of a possible solution to the issue of the occupied territories. I reminded those present that a year before I had asked Shamir about the possibility of Israel withdrawing from the occupied territories, but he had answered me with a resounding no. Nothing in my possession seemed to indicate that, in the meantime, the situation had changed to any substantial degree.

Vice-President Bush insisted on saying that the real key to a solution lay in direct talks between King Hussein and Shamir, in order to set up a confederation of the Palestinians with Jordan.

Deputy Secretary of State Whitehead raised anew the Israelis' suspicions about a conference and their fears about ending up in a minority position; this was why they clearly preferred direct contacts and negotiations. I felt it necessary to stress that, in the absence of any solution on the horizon, direct bilateral contacts were considered potentially dangerous by the Arab side; on the other hand, I pointed out, the conference in itself represented not a solution, but only a possible way to seek a solution.

On the Middle East, unfortunately, there wasn't the slightest gleam of even a beginning in the quest for a valid procedure to unravel the situation. And I was sorry because in the next few days I was to accompany President Cossiga on a state visit to Jerusalem, and I would have liked to bring a word of hope from Washington.

The situation was to change not long afterwards, but at the very high price of the "Intifada," the silent revolt of the hopeless which, put down at times in a cruel way by the occupying troops, set off a widespread wave of reproach after being reported on American TV.

On the visits to Congress, we highlighted Europe's satisfaction over the December 8 agreement and the need for rapid ratification. The Soviets were very worried on this point. Even though some time had gone by—and they had told us this—they still couldn't understand how come Carter had signed the SALT II Agreement in Vienna and then been soundly disavowed by his Senate. A possible repetition of such a downfall would have swept away forever any possibility of agreement between East and West.

Bob Dole and others filled Shultz in on our firm position, and he came to our embassy in person to thank us and to underscore the *extreme usefulness* of the Italian visit to Washington at this time.

As I said, since I had to accompany the president of the Republic on his visit to Israel, I had to leave Goria who received an honorary degree from Georgetown University and then went to see Pérez de Cuéllar in New York.

In Jerusalem there was a very big stop sign in front of all the possible openings. We did not point a finger to reproach the soldiers who answered the stones by shooting; once again, we sought to convince our counterparts that this could not go on, and that solutions not sought in a hurry are, at a certain moment, imposed by violence and the lack of reason. Far removed from politics, however, something was afoot. From an old classmate of mine who has been living in a kibbutz for forty years, I heard sincere and heartfelt hopes for coexistence with the Arabs. And I took what he said to heart.

Entirely different in nature, however, was the personal satisfaction brought home from that trip to Israel: hearty congratulations for the International Fiuggi Prize whose jury I had chaired and which had been awarded to the American professor Paul Lauterbur who had discovered the use of nuclear magnetic resonance for diagnostic imaging.

At times, we who live in the world of active politics make the mistake of believing that political facts are the only ones with a true meaning and a . . . resonance.

25 | *The NATO Train*

The big sculpture I had been awarded in October by Jeno Paolucci's Foundation, which I had shipped to Rome by sea so that exorbitant airfreight charges would not dampen my joy over this distinction, reached me just on New Year's Eve of 1987, and I saw this as a good omen. Those who give awards, and gifts in general, do not consider that the homes where most people live hardly have enough room for anything more than the inhabitants and basic furnishings. This, however, is not meant as a criticism of the NIAF, to which I will always be most grateful.

With Prime Minister Giovanni Goria and a group of qualified businessmen, we devoted the first week of 1988 to a thirty-thousand-mile journey in the Far East. We visited Kuala Lumpur, Singapore, Djakarta, and New Delhi, with a technical stopover in both directions at Muscat, where I had already been for the celebrations to mark the fifteenth anniversary of the sultan of Oman's reign, in a dreamlike atmosphere created by millions of lights imported from Hollywood for the occasion. With Goria we verified the effectiveness of ASEAN, an alliance quite different from NATO, but in which the United States also plays the unquestionable role of a binder. Will American attention shift decidedly from the Atlantic to the Pacific? This question keeps surfacing in countless discussions, in literature, and in market projections. In India, however, we got a first glimpse of the policy trends of the nonaligned countries in a world no longer marked by head-on confrontation. We were happy to meet Rajiv Gandhi's wife who comes from Orbassano in the Piedmont region. From close up she betrays her Italian roots, whereas during the mournful ceremony around the funeral pyre of her mother-in-law Indira, I had noticed that her "Indianness" was faultless.

During the closing months of 1987 I was under the impression that the State Department was planning to undertake new initiatives to resolve the increasingly tragic situation in the Middle East brought into their homes by the alarming and sometimes cruel scenes broadcast every day by American TV networks. While in the past it would have been risky for the administration to show the slightest signs of openness about justice being done for the Palestinians as well, this time, in election year, the opposing party could successfully play the card of criticizing a passive attitude on that issue. But this was not Shultz's motivation, as he was not planning to stand for election as the number one or number two man on the ticket for Reagan's succession; in fact, he did not hide his intentions of going back to California after the elections. In his remarkable moral rectitude, George suffered over the situation in the occupied territories and wondered whether favorable opportunities to avert what was now taking place had not been missed.

Washington's diplomacy devoted all of January 1988 to the Middle East, holding meetings with many Arab leaders, to the point of creating some apprehension in Jerusalem. In a letter dated February 6, Shultz wrote me that the status quo was not an option for Israel or for the Arabs; and that the situation which was taking shape as a consequence of the breakdown in the peace process and the widespread frustration over the prolonged *occupation* saw all leaders "more open to new ideas." Speaking of the difficulties inherent in the "International Conference," he lingered on various alternatives for a schedule of bilateral negotiations in preparation for the conference itself, saying:

> Your support for our efforts will be crucial in the coming days. I trust that in discussion with King Hussein you will underline to him the urgent need to make progress in the peace process on a realistic basis, and will inform him of your support for peace in the Middle East.

I felt it necessary to respond to George's invitation in a thorough manner and, even at the risk of weighing down the description of events, I will quote my letter of February 9 word for word.

Dear George,

I received your letter on the eve of my departure for Bonn and at the end of a week especially dedicated to the Middle East with visits to Rome by the King of Jordan, President Mubarak, and the distinguished member of the PLO, Mr. Kaddoumi. I fully share your opinion that lack of political initiative could worsen a situation which is already so tense and sensitive; and that the status quo is unacceptable. It is also correct to believe that it is important to have clear ideas on the possible contents of negotiations before dwelling on form and procedures. Too many disappointments have marked past decades; too many plans have been drawn up and not applied; too much friction and rancor has been allowed to accumulate, even knowing all too well that the passage of time would not resolve but only deepen the problems.

What has been taking place in the occupied territories since December now calls for bold decisions, without stopping any longer to look back on missed opportunities, beginning with the unwise difficulties raised in 1948 by some Arab states against the birth of a Palestinian nation alongside Israel, as conceived by the United Nations.

Since you're asking for my opinion, I'll try to summarize it as follows:

— Without further delay, it is necessary to give those populations a clear sign that work toward a solution is under way, thus putting a stop to the escalation of a revolt which is all the more dangerous insofar as it began spontaneously—as everyone recognizes—and therefore cannot be controlled by any organization.

— The idea of an International Conference cannot be discarded, all the more so since, beginning with Shimon Peres, it has numerous supporters in Israel itself. Without even mentioning the wishes expressed by the Arab Conference in Amman, and the EEC Council before that.

— Any other initiative—diplomatic or psychological—should not be looked upon as an alternative, but as *preparation* for the Conference, considering that it would be most serious if two precise commitments were not undertaken by all parties concerned: (a) recognition by all of the right to life and security for all; and (b) the willingness to *return* the occupied territories.

— There are three possible ways to meet the request of the Palestinian people in distress: independent state, confederation with Jordan, union with Jordan.

The Conference should select the proper option, or else call for direct consultation between the parties concerned.

— Possible border changes to make the countries more secure should not be ruled out.

— If the platform for negotiations rests on the Security Council, the problem of restoring diplomatic relations between the USSR and Israel will come to the forefront: such a development *(strictly related to the Conference)* should go hand in hand with a substantial liberalization in the exodus of Soviet Jews from the USSR. This might constitute the key element for removing Shamir's prejudicial hostility.

Looking back over past events, it must be recognized that lack of global negotiation was the weak point which caused the failure of every attempt at solving the Arab-Israeli conflict. Bilateral agreements are not the answer. Camp David bore the important positive fruit of the return of Sinai to Egypt, but it did not bring about true peace between that country and Israel, while the Arab world harbored the suspicion of having been outwitted by the old "Orazi and Curiazi" stratagem [known to Romans since the Republican period, by which a fighter arranges to fight his enemies one at a time rather than all at once.—EDITOR]

The Lebanon-Israel agreement was denounced even before it came into force. People have to realize that bilateral agreements are not a viable answer.

I was deeply encouraged in hearing from King Hussein the heartfelt words used by President Reagan in displaying to him his determination to devote even the last year of his political mandate to the quest for a breakthrough in the situation. The king of Jordan, who had already informed us in Rome, dwelt at length on this subject in the meeting he had with the twelve EEC ministers who were favorably impressed.

In our own little way, we will endeavor to bring persuasive words to bear even on Shamir, whom we have invited to Rome on February 15–16, and at the same time, as we intensify our aid to the populations of the West Bank and the Gaza Strip, we will use that opportunity for contacts in order to appease troubled spirits. I will act along these same lines when I visit Damascus and Riyadh in a month's time.

The crucial point is that all parties gain, or at least do not lose, confidence in the ways of negotiations.

I will be truly delighted to hear from you on the developments of your initiative and on the outcome of Mr. Murphy's mission.

With warm regards and best wishes for all the work you are doing at such a complex time,

Yours truly,
Giulio Andreotti

Murphy toured the Middle East capitals, and saw interest even in Syria and Saudi Arabia (Shultz's letter of February 20) "for the renewed emphasis we are placing on the search for peace": so much so that George decided to go there in person, directly after a meeting in Moscow and a briefing he came to give us in Brussels on February 23. In a long private meeting between the two of us, I had the opportunity to congratulate him on the almost scientific way he was conducting negotiations with the East. I renewed the invitation to him to come to Rome for Easter, and he accepted; and I told him, but he knew it better than I did, that the Soviets had no intention of putting things on hold while waiting for the next president. In fact, if some new result were not achieved in the near future, they were afraid we might be heading toward six months of international stalemate.

Back in Rome, I met with the governor of Florida, Martinez, who was promoting development programs for his already well-advanced state. Hearing him praise small and medium-size enterprises and their ability to create ever-new and more numerous jobs, I felt a certain degree of irritation for our school of economic pseudo-science which distracts us with economies of scale and other theories like that.

By a quirk of scheduling, I was in Damascus the day before Shultz's arrival; and I was able to leave him a note on my talks with Assad, Khaddam, and Shara, indicating by way of introduction that I had observed satisfaction for his visit to Syria at the initial stage of his field consultations. It turned out to be a very good round of talks, and I believe it benefited from what I had been able to tell the Syrians about the excellent unfolding of U.S.-Soviet dialogue.

It was also thanks to Italy's contribution in solving a sensitive problem which had arisen between the United States and Spain that difficulties in this dialogue were averted. In negotiations over the U.S. bases, the government of Felipe González needed some cuts in total numbers since —with a remarkable sense of responsibility—the Socialist party had set aside the hostile positions it had assumed prior to the elections and had handed the decision over to the voters in a referendum, while pledging full support for NATO policy (for reasons of domestic fronts, the non-Socialists took the opposite stance, thereby placing upon Felipe's head the halo of the first begotten son of the United States). A certain number of NATO aircraft had to be removed from Spanish soil, and in their technical evaluations military experts were concerned about the unilateral imbalance this would create. This led to our accepting the invitation from Brussels to base them in Calabria.

Meanwhile, the U.S.-Soviet negotiations at summit level were progressing. Reagan came to Brussels on March 2 to brief us during a joint meeting with heads of government. The process hadn't faltered.

Murphy arrived in Rome on March 12 to report on Shultz's trip. Murphy had been very active during those weeks and seemed optimistic, but reminded me of Penelope's weaving. The framework was perfect: negotiations between Israel and *each one* of its neighboring countries would begin in May on the basis of acceptance of the famous Security Council Resolutions 242 and 338. It would all be preceded by a solemn conference to lay the foundations which, however, would not have the power to impose solutions or veto any agreements reached. The Palestinians would participate as part of the Jordanian delegation.

Murphy had also been in Bonn and told me he had been received very warmly. That was easy for him personally, but what guarantees did he have that Israel would accept his plan? That hadn't been his impression at all from the talks with Shamir. I thought Murphy was as convinced as I was that more had to be done, but it was not up to him and, as I said, he felt that only Shultz's personal commitment could produce results.

Members of the Soviet Plenum, who were our guests at that time, maintained that perhaps even *with* them the solution would be difficult, but *without* them all efforts expended on Jerusalem and the surrounding region were to no avail.

I even encountered interest in the Palestinians and emotion over the "Intifada" in Beijing, where I made a lightning trip to inaugurate the medical facilities supplied by our Department for Cooperation to Development; they also included an emergency surgery center for injuries incurred in automobile accidents, linked up by a telematic system to a perfect network of ambulances with intensive-care equipment on board.

I resumed my efforts at détente with the Chinese, who were still irritated with the Americans because of U.S. accusations that they had sold weapons in the Persian Gulf. They firmly denied it, and were annoyed over the alleged photographic evidence. Scientific and university cooperation with Italy is quite intense, both bilaterally and in the World Lab. During the Tiananmen Square crisis, it was this sound intellectual bond which made it possible not to regress by decades.

In that same month of March Shamir went to Washington, where he had three days of talks, but left—as Shultz wrote me—after having "voiced reservations on various aspects of the American plan," which also met with a negative reception from the Islamic Conference in its session at Amman. It was a tiresome ping-pong game, while unfortunately the Intifada went on with its daily toll of victims. I was becoming increasingly convinced that only the simultaneous development of new positions could open a way out of the ever more entangled knot; and I was pained to see all the efforts of Shultz and his people fall through.

Meanwhile I had gone to Geneva together with Genscher to try and speed up the proceedings of the Disarmament Committee on the banning of chemical weapons. Along the lines of what we had done for nuclear arms, we were thinking of arranging a seminar in Rome of scientists from all over the world to study valid models for agreement verification. George thanked me for my "priceless contribution" and promised to have our ideas examined. The seminar did indeed take place and with good results, even though the subject is more complex and intricate than nuclear weapons.

George and his wife Obi were happy to return to Rome for Easter. Because of the inclement weather, the solemn Mass was celebrated inside St. Peter's Cathedral; this afforded them an opportunity to observe yet another version of the impressive Vatican liturgies, while also admiring (after the Pontiff had greeted us with special warmth) the large crowd which, heedless of the rain, had packed into the square for the blessing of the Pope and his wishes expressed in virtually all the languages of the world.

Now that he has returned to private life, I hope Shultz will be able to come and spend at least another Easter together with us. George is a man whose value is measured by his own merits, and not by the positions he holds. And he deserves the highest esteem and friendship.

This time, his talks with Cossiga were most cordial and free of any misunderstandings. During the visit he spoke mostly of his meeting with Shevardnadze a few days earlier, largely taken up by the problem of Afghanistan. Among the issues to be resolved was the suspension of Soviet and American aid to the opposing sides. The proposal for a moratorium had been rejected, but possible solutions continued to be explored. The Pakistanis were attaching special importance to being protected by the Americans, and were willing to continue providing them with the necessary logistical support. The Americans would consider a unilateral declaration on the right to resume supplies to the Afghan resistance movement, were the Soviets to continue supplying the government forces. "Perhaps the Soviet Union will in any case proceed to withdraw from Afghanistan, even without an agreement or special guarantees, but they would certainly prefer that the withdrawal take place on the basis of an agreement providing for a more orderly and dignified solution." In brief, this was Shultz's report.

Although no agreement had been reached on this and other issues, it was already something positive that "regional" problems had been discussed. Quite interesting was the Soviet pledge not to allow any acts of North Korean terrorism which could jeopardize the games in Seoul ("Our athletes will be there too," Shevardnadze had said). Noteworthy as well was an overture on southern Africa: the United States was willing to work on Savimbi and use their good offices on the Republic of South Africa, if the USSR undertook to conduct parallel action with Angola for the withdrawal of Cuban troops.

In addition to direct news, the evening before I had heard clear statements from the Iranian foreign minister Velajati, who was passing through Rome, on the Soviet will to withdraw from Afghanistan. I did speak to him as well about Shultz's idea for a sixty-day truce between Iran and Iraq, along with the broader commitment not to use chemical weapons and not to bomb urban centers.

The problem of the PLO hung heavily over the Middle East. Shultz recognized that neither Shamir nor Peres was able to sit at the same table with leaders from the Palestine Liberation Organization without running the risk of losing the elections. Perhaps this was due to an overdemonization of the PLO, but it was nonetheless an undeniable fact (Shultz mentioned Israeli reactions to his meeting with two Americans of Palestinian origin). The Israelis were making a mistake and—because of the *partial* analogies—should have remembered the precedent of the French who expected people not even to speak with the Algerians, until the day they gave in on much more radical positions than the ones they had so rigidly precluded beforehand.

I reported the opinion expressed to some of our visiting deputies by the Latin patriarch of Jerusalem, according to whom "no problems are solved without speaking to the PLO"; and on the similar position voiced by the president of the World Union of Arab Jews (Leon Tamman), who had said the same thing, specifying that he personally had always voted for the Likud, but had now become convinced that nothing could be done without the PLO.

What could be done during the transition stage, in addition to the meritorious work being carried on so capably by the secretary of state? On a strictly personal basis, I aired a hypothesis which I would not present in public until the Americans deemed it appropriate: it had to do with two separate declarations which would make it possible to overcome the present impasse, in which the Israelis object to the article in the PLO Statute denying their very right to exist, and Arafat claims recognition prior to any territorial solution. The possibility could be considered of placing "into neutral hands" (possibly the secretary of state himself) a PLO statement committing the organization to consider as obsolete the contested article in its Statute; and a parallel declaration from Israel undertaking to discuss with the PLO until there was a more representative body.

We spoke at length about the Palestinian issue and concluded that a huge amount of work still had to be done quietly on both Israel and the PLO. I remember telling him that this was silent work which reaped glory for no one, but there was nothing else to do if we were aware that solutions could not be *imposed,* and all the less so from one day to the next. "Nobel prizes can also be won without solving problems, but it is preferable to endeavor to achieve results."

I didn't want to discourage him as he prepared to return to the Middle East, but I considered it right to remind him that he didn't have enough playable cards in his hands. He confirmed this himself both in his report on the visits, which he sent on April 18, and when we met in Brussels five days later. Since he felt that neither Shamir nor Peres could make concessions, on account of understandable preelection fears, I told him that, if this were the case, they should be pushed to hold the elections earlier.

On that same day, April 18, a new complication had come up in the Gulf. Convinced that the Iranians had laid mines of their own making in the waters of Bahrain, the Americans attacked and hit Iranian targets, invoking the right to self-defense sanctioned by Article 51 of the United Nations Charter.

I once again asked myself what would have happened if the United States and the USSR had not been in a phase of open dialogue at that time.

Yet, ratification of the December 8 agreement was slow, even though numerous congressmen passing through Italy kept telling me it was only a matter of procedure. The Soviets were starting to get nervous, and when two of Reagan's appointees to the Supreme Court were not confirmed by the Senate, they raised worried questions, through us as well. Shevardnadze had said it directly to Shultz in Geneva on May 13. We learned it from him the next day in Brussels.

I, therefore, took advantage of a session in Parliament on the ratification of our parallel agreement, on dismantling the missiles in Comiso and accepting the verifications, to send a message to the U.S. Congress. I immediately received congratulations from Shultz ("While the Treaty is under discussion before the American Senate, I take this opportunity to tell you how much I have appreciated everything you have done to make the INF Treaty become a reality").

American ratification finally came through, and in such a way as to confirm that the delays had not been due to dissenting positions. Shultz sent me a very flattering message:

Dear Giulio,

The vote, 93 to 5, approving ratification of the INF Treaty, indicates the broad support of the Senate and in the United States in general toward the Treaty. This positive result is the consequence of major efforts deployed for many years, and shows what we can obtain when we have strong determination and cohesion. You and many other members of your government have contributed to this process; among other things, I recall your firm statement of support during the Senate debate on the Treaty. Please accept the expression of my highest regard and esteem for everything you have done, and my thanks for all the help and good advice you have given me.

Sincerely yours,
George

In early June, with the treaty ratified at long last, Shultz went to Moscow. Those who expected more were disappointed, and placed the accent on Gorbachev's complaint that Americans were giving priority to human rights over disarmament. On the basis of George's briefing at NATO—which, as always, coincided with what the Soviets were also telling our government—it was nonetheless certain that the new course was under way. And I was able to speak about "small steps in a well-defined process."

This successful line also defined our policy in defense issues. The Italian Parliament approved the deployment of the U.S. 401st Air Wing transferred from Spain, and George, overdoing it as far as I was concerned, but not for Italy, wrote me: "Italy has once again shown its deep commitment to NATO's security. All the countries of the Alliance should appreciate your commitment and sense of responsibility for the common good. Your leadership constitutes an admirable example for the entire Alliance. I hope our excellent dialogue on arms control and other matters may continue in the months to come."

In a round of contacts in preparation for the Summit Meeting of the Seven Most Industrialized Countries in Toronto, De Mita also went to Washington. And he did so at a most appropriate time, because Reagan had just returned from Moscow, and was able to give him firsthand details confirming Gorbachev's "good intentions." The occasion also served to reiterate the dangerous nature of those isolationist trends which recurrently surface in the United States, but are countered quite effectively by the White House. Election years ordinarily accentuate these thrusts; and between primaries, mid-terms, and the lengthy preparations for presidential elections, every year is practically an election year in the United States. Of late, in order to exorcise such trends more effectively, we have to add reassuring words on the *open* nature of the European Community, which—to catch people's imagination—is frequently forced to repeat that it does not want to be or become a "fortress."

We marked our presence at the Canadian summit with concrete proposal on specific issues: environment, drugs, and differential reimbursement methods for Third World debts according to the individual countries' degree of solvency. In general, more than a cut in absolute terms, in our opinion it was necessary to work out acceptable deadlines and reasonable reductions in interest rates, with an initial period of grace.

Reagan, and Shultz as well, followed the Toronto proceedings with their customary attention, taking part in all discussions and showing no signs of emotion over their forthcoming departure from public life. Outside the sessions we Italians had the pleasure of seeing and pointing out how many Canadians of Italian origin had attained—quite a number in just a few years—outstanding positions in business and society. Even on the City Council there are many "Italians," and we greeted them with feelings of legitimate pride.

Before parting, the seven delegations agreed on a precise timetable to enhance the fight against drug trafficking. I wondered, hopefully, if this would be the time we would really hit the nail on the head. In the past I have often feared that not enough was being done in this area, and that some highly suspect countries were basically left undisturbed when they gave no cause for military-related concerns. And yet, the link between drugs and terrorism is no figment of the imagination or of suspicion.

Would we be able to register some success at the next summit meeting in Paris? Judge Giuseppe Di Gennaro, who, from Vienna, coordinates the United Nations activities in the fight against drugs, told me many times in the past (things have improved now) that he did not receive full support from all countries. And he also explained to me the contradiction between two methods tested in Bolivia. The field agents for the United Nations Fund For Drug Abuse Control (UNFDAC) *persuade* the farmers to uproot drug-producing plants, encourage and fund substitute crops, and help them to withstand the threats of the drug traffickers. Others use the blitz method: they burn the plantations and dry out the soil, but the farmers are left without any income and are forced to move to new land to start growing the same vicious crop again.

Some time before he presented his candidature for the presidential election and was then compelled to withdraw it, the influential congressman

Gary Hart had agreed to come to the regular meeting organized in Rimini by the Pio Manzù Center. Once the storm broke, without even having to "chercher la femme" because this woman Donna was on the front pages of all the newspapers, the organizers asked me if they should cancel the invitation. Naturally, I replied no. And Hart came, delivered his speech, and only suffered the nuisance of a few extra photographers covering his every step.

We had breakfast together and I found his knowledge of international affairs much more profound than was normal among the colleagues of his I knew. On the Middle East as well, he had realistic ideas, and did not conceal the fact that it was necessary to inform and educate public opinion without being its subservient prisoner.

He did not speak about his "adventure," nor did I refer to it. Otherwise, I would have said to him what was written to me in a semi-ironic way by a Republican senator pleased with this adversary's disappearance from the opposing ranks: "Gary has displeased everyone; temperate people because he was unfaithful to his wife, and the *nonconformists* because the girl stated they had slept under the same roof, but in separate rooms. Luckily they only blamed him for lying, if not, the poor guy would also have risked making an *unnatural* name for himself; that would be too much for him . . ."

In the United States polemics on personal issues before elections or in view of some appointment are much more ferocious than in Italy. The recently elected George Bush had to swallow a bitter defeat at the hands of the Senate which did not ratify the appointment of Senator John Tower to the office of secretary of defense, where perhaps Frank Carlucci would have remained with no hurdles and to the satisfaction of all.

The reasons for not surrendering in the tug-of-war with the White House had nothing to do with Tower's lawful connections with the weapons industries; quite on the contrary, they heightened his professional skills. I don't know if smoking came into the picture, but the Senate charged that a fondness for wine and women was a shortcoming in a member of the cabinet.

In effect, it wasn't a bankable asset for someone who is also at the head of a navy where the strictest prohibitionism still applies. Nor can the secretary indulge in what Winston Churchill did on a visit to an

American aircraft carrier: he showed up with a doctor's order prescribing alcoholic beverages for medicinal purposes. I myself saw this historical relic which the ship's captain had kept and framed.

On September 26, I was at the UN when President Reagan delivered his address. It sounded like a farewell speech as well as a message to the American people; he was pleased with the steps toward progress, but recalled that history teaches us to be prudent, and that the possibilities of failure are always high. Were we to fail, however, we would bear the brunt of the just anger of future generations.

The first time I had heard Reagan speak at the Glass Palace, I had been impressed by the precision of his language and by the fact that, without reading, he never had a moment's hesitation and never made mistakes. But he was reading. Before his speeches a crew of workers sets up a small podium with an arrangement of mirrors allowing him to see the written text from different angles. The optical illusion is perfect.

An Iranian civilian aircraft, full of passengers, was shot down over the Gulf by the U.S. Navy because of a deplorable error caused by high technology. Confusion in the reports added to the sense of dismay, because Washington came up with three versions in the course of one afternoon: (1) it wasn't true; (2) it was a military aircraft; (3) correction: it was a civilian aircraft flying in a corridor reserved for military traffic.

Fear of retaliation and the return to "square one" of the arduous negotiations for the cease-fire with Iraq gave rise to peaceful steps. Velajati sent his bright deputy Larijani to see me in Rome, and I was able to inform Washington that there were possible ways to offset a deterioration in the situation. According to Larijani, the United States was to refrain from attempting to put a stop to a fair debate in the Security Council and to a reasonable resolution objectively illustrating the facts, making explicit reference to the need for preventing the recurrence of similar incidents, as well as providing for suitable indemnities.

Regarding the procedure, Larijani favored an initiative on the part of countries not overly involved in the conflict, and expressed the wish that a joint effort by the Federal Republic of Germany, Japan, and Italy could bring forth open proposals liable to meet with a broad consensus.

On the Gulf, Larijani repeated that Iran was prepared to take part in a plan that would lead to a global cease-fire, and that could come out of a meeting of the Gulf countries. The presence of the fleets could be decreased *gradually* and safe navigation guaranteed by political means.

Before meeting with Larijani, I had received a message from Armacost in the State Department asking us to encourage the establishment of a direct Iran-United States channel. Larijani told me that the Iranian government had received a Japanese proposal aimed at fostering the resumption of dialogue between the United States and Iran, and pointed out that, at least in the beginning, it was preferable to open an indirect channel. To that end, he asked for assistance from Italy, even suggesting how it could be done.

These good offices inspired by caution were in conflict with the American frame of mind, more exalted by the blow inflicted upon Iran than saddened over the loss of human lives which had been caused—unwillingly, for sure. As a consequence, despite tentative acceptance, Armacost's request was dropped by the Americans themselves. With this impression in mind, I sent a telex to Shultz the evening before the UN vote:

Were there to be a request to withdraw the fleet from the Gulf, or other similar measures, there would really not be room for a reasonable text tomorrow at the Security Council. But if it is a matter of repeating what you have already declared, that is that error was the cause of that grave incident, adding the U.S. intention to pay an indemnity to the families of the victims—even from a humanitarian viewpoint—I think we would be on the right path. On the other hand, I recall President Reagan himself, in relation to the events connected with the supply of weapons to Tehran, which caused so much grief to you and the State Department, wisely mentioned his concern not to push moderate Iranian leaders out of the picture.
As regards the "unofficial channel" between the United States and Iran, I urged its creation because of a specific U.S. request. Suggesting that Italy act as an intermediary, Larijani told me he intended to respond to the U.S. proposal which he had also received through the Japanese. If the U.S. prefers Japan or another country, and agrees on it with Iran, we certainly will not mind, because it is a "service" we would accept only if useful, and with all the consequent political risks.

The problem of the safety of the Olympic athletes in Seoul was back on the table at the Toronto meetings. Since I was going to see President Samaranch (his son was getting married in Rome), I promised George I would keep him posted. And I was able to reassure him. Samaranch had just returned from a meeting with the president of the German Democratic Republic, Honecker (who had been one of his go-betweens with North Korea). Although the door had been left open to Pyongyang, even after the deadline for registration had expired, the general impression was that the North Koreans were not going to change their negative attitude, even though they would not indulge in violent forms of boycott. The North Koreans were disappointed over the massive participation announced from all over the world (with only four exceptions: Albania, Cuba, Ethiopia, and Nicaragua), but it was unlikely they would defy the reaction of China, the Soviet Union, and other countries by harassing both athletes and spectators. In any case, it was felt that, if any disturbing action were to be taken, it would occur before and not during the Olympic Games.

On the subject of the Seoul Games, I had also received a visit in Rome from a personal representative of South Korea, who had come to Europe to extend invitations and renew assurances: former Foreign Minister Kim Yong Shik, currently mayor of the Olympic Village. Not only had he confirmed what I said above about almost universal participation, but he had added that there would be six hundred people in the Soviet delegation and a more or less equal number in the Chinese one. Such a signal should dispel any pessimist's persisting doubts.

On September 27, after addressing the UN General Assembly, I met with Shultz who was just back from a visit to Bolivia where, together with his wife, he had fortunately emerged unscathed from an attempt on his life. When I congratulated him for having escaped the peril he rejoined: "Those who made such an attempt know we are winning and don't like it." I found him more determined than ever in carrying on the fight against drugs and terrorism; with regard to the latter, he underscored the threats inherent in the production of chemical weapons which, according to his sources, Libya was preparing to embark upon. However, he sidestepped the subject when I hinted at the positive expectations aroused by Deputy Secretary of State Whitehead in Bulgaria (I had been in Sofia the week before and had been impressed).

His reference to chemical warfare made me urge strong action to achieve a total ban. As long as Western countries continue producing such weapons for defensive purposes, any effort to dissuade other countries is much less effective. It seemed important to me that the conference proposed by Reagan and Mitterrand for the early part of the New Year in Paris not just be a series of fine speeches, but of concrete commitments. No progress was being made in Geneva. It was important for Libya to participate as well, because it was much easier to make nations accept dismantlement measures or . . . vows of chemical chastity on international models, than it was to point an accusing finger at an individual country.

Algeria has suggested a wise solution for dealing with this Libyan factory under construction, which the Tripoli government says will be devoted to medical products, while others suspect or declare it will turn out toxic gases: extend ownership to companies from several nations in order to guarantee that production will be confined exclusively to medicines. However, it is really necessary for all nations to ban these arsenals.

Along with political and diplomatic contacts, I used my week in New York for other purposes. I was invited to Columbia University and to the Metropolitan Museum, with the very kind French director, Philippe de Montebello, as my guide. I visited the impressive exhibition of Umberto Boccioni's works. One of the experts there told me something rather curious. As a reaction to Italian racial laws, all the work of Italian futurists had been boycotted by the important Jewish trade channels, who saw in Marinetti and his "school" an expression of fascism, even if this movement had started up earlier. This may be, but perhaps the thrust behind recent commercial reappraisal came from the great success of the exhibition on futurists held at the Palazzo Grassi in Venice. The expert sadly showed me Boccioni's largest painting, purchased a few years earlier by a private collector for one thousand dollars; it had also been offered to him, but he had turned it down.

Boccioni had died at a very young age and I did not know he had started as a figurative artist and had later returned to that style. The last two paintings in the New York exhibition faithfully testified to this fact. In London, as I admired a large painting by Balla at a Royal Academy exhibition, I learned from its owner (Gianni Agnelli), who was also there, that the painter had depicted the March on Rome on the back. Quite appropriately, the painting was not hung with both sides visible because it would have stood out in the exhibition; however, on second thought, the Jewish dealers were not entirely wrong in attributing deep political roots to those artists.

I spent a delightful evening in the dream world of Atlantic City, a thirty-minute helicopter ride from New York, where gambling, entertainment, and nightlife evoke the frenzy of Las Vegas. The only thing missing is the astounding sight of thousands of lights in the middle of the desert, as in Nevada. On my way to the airport, I didn't miss my stop at Belmont Park for the races. For years I saw General MacArthur's widow there at the same restaurant table; I imagine she was a regular patron. And forgetting the horses for a moment, I am led to think how deeply indebted contemporary Japan is to the gruff insight of this American general.

With Reagan's strong backing, George Bush easily defeated the Democratic candidate, Governor Michael Dukakis. To tell the truth, foreign policy, as usual, was not a major theme in electoral speeches. Positions for or against the death penalty were given much more space than the crisis in the Middle East or the Iran-Iraq War (in fact, there was a sort of patriotic understanding to leave out the latter issue). Perhaps in the hope of attracting Jewish votes, Dukakis announced that if he won, he would move the American Embassy from Tel Aviv to Jerusalem: something not even Shamir was asking for at that time. But this statement didn't have much of an impact.

Bush carried the election by a wide margin of votes: the majority system applies in all states, and therefore the difference of even a single ballot is enough to give the winner all the electoral votes of a state (in theory, a difference of fifty votes could carry all the "electors" who, practically "pro forma," elect the president). Only two states and the District of Columbia voted for Dukakis; the Republican candidate swept all the rest. However, less positive elements were to be seen between the lines. That same night I heard some interesting comments and wrote a few more down during the following days:

— For the second time since 1920 when women obtained the right to vote (the other time was during World War II with millions of Americans abroad), the total number of voters dropped in absolute terms with respect to preceding elections, and despite an eight million increase in the number of those eligible to vote for the first time;

— Of those with the right to vote, the 27 percent who went for Bush was the lowest in the history of the United States;

— Except for the South, it was the lowest voter participation since 1824;
— The decline has been steady since the peak of 62.8 percent in 1960. Since then, only in 1984 was there a 0.5 percent gain. There has been a 20 percent drop in the total number of voters since 1960;
— Voter registration has also experienced a parallel decline since 1960, dropping from 83.4 percent to 70.5 percent;
— There has also been a decrease in ballots in states like North and South Dakota which do not require registration, but not of the same order as the national average;
— In Wisconsin and Minnesota, where voters can register at the polls, participation today is below the level of 1984, when that change was introduced to make things easier for voters;
— There was a marked drop in voter participation in 46 states and in the District of Columbia, less so in Colorado and Nebraska; there was an increase only in Nevada (1.9 percent) and New Hampshire (0.7 percent). In the national capital only 36.57 percent of eligible voters went to the polls;
— Interest in the presidential candidates was so low, that in twelve states fewer votes were cast for them than for candidates to the Senate.
— Compared with 1984, voter participation among Republicans dropped sharply (5 percent of the national average). Among Democrats it rose slightly (0.9 percent).

In November, on the eve of the PLO National Council (convened in Algiers, quite wisely *after* the elections in the United States and in Israel), we increased our efforts to help the top leaders seize the favorable moment and take intelligent and courageous action. The sacrifice of the people of the Intifada had by now given rise to a wave of empathy in the world on which a political breakthrough could be built at long last. Arafat had always maintained that he could not *give everything* while receiving nothing or almost nothing in return; but here was precisely the new factor to be introduced into the equation: that is, remove any elements of suspicion from the minds of the adversaries and the doubtful. Closely monitored by the Algerian president, the Council, explicitly specifying that the minority in opposition would also comply with the decision, painstakingly approved a document covering the three famous points: (1) rejection of violence; (2) respect for the security of Israel; and (3) acceptance of the UN resolutions.

With a view to setting an acceptable framework for this evolution in their positions, the Palestinians issued a declaration of independence (however, without forming a government in exile as some would have wished), and this was the point used by all those who still insisted on their opposition to the PLO. Shultz wrote this to me on November 28, acknowledging the progress achieved, but judging it insufficient. Unfortunately, the fact that Abu Abbas *(Achille Lauro)* was a member of the National Council was very disturbing for us as well. I tried (on 1 November 1988) to induce the State Department to consider the Algiers vote in a more open way, as we had done in the EEC Council, by highlighting that: (a) they had not formed the feared government in exile; (b) they had cited the 1947 resolution, thereby also acknowledging the birth of Israel; and (c) they had spoken of borders to be negotiated, taking, therefore, no rigid stand. And I also asked if there might be a glimpse, however dim, of Israel's willingness to negotiate, or if the Shamir government did not intend to return the occupied territories, no matter who the Palestinian interlocutors might be.

Shamir himself had told me this quite frankly a few days earlier in Jerusalem. No matter what Arafat wrote or said, he could not believe him. It was to no avail that I had quoted the Bible: "I seek not the sinner's death, but that he be converted and live."

Arafat had asked to go to the UN to explain the Algiers conclusions, but the American administration—violating UN prerogatives—denied him an entry visa, setting off a real wave of international reaction. When the decision to hold the session in Geneva, in order to uphold the invitation to Arafat, was put to the vote, it was approved by 151 votes; two countries (United States and Israel) voted against and one abstained (United Kingdom, despite having approved Algiers at the EEC).

I expressed my regret in a letter to George: "I am sorry that precisely you, who have done so much to resolve the problems of the Middle East, must appear as the one responsible for the impediment. I hope you will devote the weeks that still remain before the Inauguration to the problem of the Middle East; I believe there are concrete possibilities to start up a platform for the peace process." And I called his attention to an important fact revealed to me in person by Chadli, the Algerian president. After the PLO Council, Egypt and Algeria had resumed diplomatic relations as part of a trend toward reconciliation in the Arab world, which, I wrote, had to receive continuing encouragement.

Gorbachev addressed the United Nations early in December, and met with Reagan and Bush at a working luncheon. The political continuity in the American administration was not displeasing at all to Moscow (De Mita said that Gorbachev had confided this to him a few days before the elections) and the meeting in New York made it possible to draw up a program for the uninterrupted development of the major negotiations.

George came to Brussels to brief us on that meeting, and summed up his policy achievements in a way which aroused our enthusiasm. Not only had substantial progress been made along the road to disarmament, but of the six hundred political prisoners in the USSR, only a few were still in confinement and they were about to be released.

We were all touched when we said our farewells: it was the last time he attended a NATO meeting. We gave him a model train, immediately dubbed: THE NATO TRAIN. Quite different, however, was the source of my deep feelings that night. George had given me a verbal answer to my letter, saying that I would soon have reasons to be pleased. And it was true. On the occasion of a press conference that Arafat was holding in Geneva (actually to say nothing more than what he had declared in Algiers), the announcement was made that the United States had decided to establish contact with the PLO and that the first meeting would soon take place in Tunis where the PLO has its general headquarters.

While the other European ministers had taken their leave of Shultz in Brussels, I had another opportunity to see him when I accompanied to Washington Prime Minister Ciriaco De Mita, who had taken over from Giovanni Goria.

The decision to set up contacts with the PLO "insofar as the *three conditions* had been satisfied" was the core of Reagan's briefing, where he stressed his personal satisfaction at having been able to help achieve concrete progress toward the goal of a global peace among all parties concerned. The president outlined for De Mita the results of his meeting with Gorbachev, which I had heard about at the Atlantic Council meeting. Reagan's plan for conventional disarmament—agreed upon with the Soviets—was flawless: (1) a census of the forces; (2) reduction to positions of parity; and (3) further balanced reductions.

We also discussed Namibia and Central America, but I found it quite striking the persistent way everyone on the American side spoke to our prime minister about the choice of Italtel's partner in the electronic telecommunications programs, exalting the superiority of the American option.

For my part, I advised Shultz to devote his last five weeks in office to Lebanon, about whose future I was rather pessimistic.

During a luncheon with the president-elect, we spoke in depth about the fight against drugs, and we were pleased to note Bush's impassioned dedication to this issue. This was also a sign of continuity, because in May 1985, Mrs. Nancy Reagan had made a special trip to Rome to bear solemn witness to the significance of the war against drug traffic. She did this by visiting Fr. Mario Picchi's rehabilitation center, which benefited from the exemplary involvement of Ambassador Rabb's wife.

On the subject of military issues, Bush said quite clearly that his policy coincided with Reagan's, but that he needed time to think before resuming the negotiations. Shultz and Mrs. Ridgway were present at the luncheon, but I had the impression they were kept somewhat in the background. I recalled what I had heard years before from an old senator in Washington on the marginal role of vice presidents, and how irritating this was, not so much for them as for their staffs. Now that Reagan's number two man had been "promoted," perhaps his staffers were showing their teeth. I wouldn't rule it out.

With Brady, we spoke about his debt relief plan for the poorest countries, which he had drawn up after replacing James Baker when the latter moved over to the White House to coordinate the Republican electoral campaign. Baker was the sure choice as the new secretary of state.

I did not know if I would accompany a fourth prime minister to the White House. By now I knew the protocol inside out and would have no problems.

Bush promised De Mita he would soon come to Italy.

26 | *Pro-Perestroika*

The present pope, by returning to chant the *Te Deum* in the Roman church of "Gesù" on New Year's Eve, has restored a tradition so dear to Pius IX up until the breach at Porta Pia [by the Italian army in 1870 that separated the city from the Vatican state.—EDITOR] When I am in town I like to attend this ceremony because the ancient flavor of such moments enchants me, and it is also an opportunity—in the midst of collective meditation—for personal stocktaking of the high points and low points of the past twelve months. As 1987 drew to a close, I was grateful for the constructive agreement between Reagan and Gorbachev of December 8, and prayed to God that, in the wake of this fundamental international achievement, the coming year would register more progress in the same direction. If he hadn't been slowed down by the Democratic "majority" for electoral reasons, Reagan certainly would have wanted to put a crowning touch upon his two terms of office. For his part, it was entirely in Gorbachev's interest to speed up the pace of the new course of events even though foreign diplomacy was not the sole concern of the Soviet leader, who was so deeply absorbed in the problems of nationalities and, worse yet, those of economic and productive shortages. However, even if nothing spectacular had happened, the détente process had made progress. *Te Deum laudamus.*

What was not being enforced, however, was Resolution 598 of the UN Security Council, adopted on July 20 after such arduous efforts. Much to the gratitude of the secretary-general Pérez de Cuéllar, we kept up our contacts with Iran and Iraq so that, by honoring the cease-fire, they would face up to negotiations for peace. The point of friction blocking everything (including the return of territories and prisoners) was whether the formation of an impartial body charged with attributing initial responsibilities for the war should be a *preceding* or *concurrent* factor. At the UN Security Council I had jokingly observed that it would have been enough to buy a back copy of the *New York Times* reporting Saddam Hussein's statements, but the Iraqis claimed that the decision to attack had been preceded not only by provocative acts in general, but also by repeated military action.

Negotiations between two-and-a-half parties (the two countries and the UN) have been going on for some time in Geneva, but so far the good offices of Pérez de Cuéllar and his representatives have not succeeded in removing the hurdle. In any case, the guns are silent, but the horizon over the Gulf is far from cloudless.

On the other hot spots around the world: no end in sight to the Intifada, since no substantial progress has been made on the Palestinian issue; in Cambodia there are signs of a breakthrough, promoted by Prince Sihanouk amidst serious difficulties; less tense are positions in Central America, with sure disengagement on the part of the USSR and Nicaragua looking forward to veritable elections; and some signs of a drop in tension in southern Africa, where moderate whites have gained ground. In the final analysis, 1988 hadn't been a bad year.

Even the tone of a letter of good wishes I received from George Shultz appeared quite symbolic to me:

The "NATO train" is a big hit here. I enjoy it a lot and so do all my colleagues in the State Department and in town. The other evening I was at the White House and I saw an electric train running around the president's Christmas tree. When I inquired, I discovered that the President was also interested in model trains. So, the other day, when I went to my usual private meeting with the president, I brought along the "NATO train." He was fascinated by it and we ended up spending an inordinate amount of time playing with it. You will enjoy the enclosed picture. With my thanks for your friendship and your support.

George P. Shultz

If they are playing with model trains in Washington, it means the barometer is pointing to good weather.

The easing of tensions in the world has had enormous repercussions on relations between African countries and the United States. In the trip with President Cossiga to Kenya, Zambia, Mozambique, Zimbabwe, and Somalia, I noticed how people were using a new language in this regard, even though positions on some issues—the policy toward South Africa, for example—are still rather distant. I will also remember this trip for reasons far removed from politics. Between different customs and impossible schedules, my migraines became so much worse that I had to take massive doses of painkillers. This determined a violent attack of labyrinthitis which literally made me collapse at Madrid Airport where I had flown directly after the African journey to attend an EEC Ministerial Council meeting.

The Italian Christian Democratic party had organized, in the United States, the celebrations for the fortieth anniversary of the Marshall Plan, and it was my job to deliver the main address in New York, which, as I have already mentioned, had to be canceled because of Nixon's absence. The leadership of both U.S. parties was represented on the organizing committee, and (even though the whole event was later canceled) this gave me the opportunity to make the acquaintance of Mr. Farenkhof, chairman of the Republican National Party Committee. Basking in the success of the November election and approaching the end of his term of office, he explained to me how the American electoral machine works, dwelling at length on the complex integration of black citizens, which, in his opinion, would keep the Democrats out of the White House for a long time to come. In November of this year, in New York, the Democrats discovered just how well grounded such a forecast was.

A delegation of American Jews came to Rome to attend the World Conference of Israeli Refugees from Libya, most of whom live today in Israel, but who are also numerous in Italy where their president, Raffaello Fellah, also resides. The discussions were responsible and constructive, while surprisingly, among the photographs on display in the hall of the Hilton Hotel, there was an almost nostalgic commemoration of Italo Balbo and Mussolini himself who, despite having called himself "the sword of Islam," must have treated Jews in Tripolitania and in Cirenaica with due respect (even after issuing racial laws), perhaps on the basis of the "divide and conquer" principle.

In my address I restated my position of solidarity with the Palestinians to whom we were just as committed as we were to persecuted Jews. And I received the assent, also in writing, from the American delegates. Perhaps times change, even at the slowest pace. However, messages from Lebanon and from Iran-Iraq were not encouraging: this was painfully confirmed in discussions I had in Rome with Jumblatt and Aziz on the same day.

With the secretary-general of the Foreign Affairs Ministry, Ambassador Bruno Bottai, we paid a call on the king of Afghanistan, in exile in Rome, to wish him a Happy New Year. It seems to be the fate of the kings of Kabul to come and live in Italy when deposed. When I was a boy, one of the current king's august predecessors already lived in exile in our capital; I remember this because he lived in the Prati section of town, across the street from the gym I used to go to; at times we were admonished if we made too much noise and disturbed His Majesty.

The present King Zahir has chosen a small house far from the city center and there he leads a dignified life "not making any claims, but ready to return to his homeland if the people so desire." The bad habit of attaching a label to everyone has ascribed international left-wing leanings to this king (or former king, as you like) only because, way back when, he had turned to the East when he couldn't obtain defensive weapons from the West. In this, as in other audiences, I found him to be a man of great fairness. And many months later, I was glad to learn that he was being consulted not only by the Soviet negotiator of peace in Kabul (which to date still remains unattained) but also by the American ambassador.

The early months of this year, along with legitimate curiosity about the appointments and trends of the new American administration, witnessed the development (albeit at a latent state) of a dangerous polemic between the Federal Republic of Germany and the United States on the strategic debate within NATO. Even those who were least versed in the relative technicalities grasped the heart of the matter: was the security of the most exposed European country being reduced or not?

Perhaps—and this is certainly not a personal merit—out of long-standing familiarity with the life of NATO, I was not at all concerned. I considered it a mistake to insist on having the spring session decide on the sensitive issue of short-range missiles whose practical effects would only be visible years later. Why such haste? To complicate matters even further, super-sophisticated commentators kept saying that a decision had to be made at once because, if the majority in Bonn were to change after next year's elections, the new leadership could perhaps accept commitments already made, but certainly not new ones. Genscher and Kohl's concern, on the other hand, centered on the objective terms of a doctrine whereby the potential targets for the new missiles would not be in the Soviet Union, but in other Warsaw Pact countries, beginning with East Germany. Then, for everyone, there was the problem of making public opinion understand the need for heavy expenditures (to pay for new generations of missiles) at a time when a reduction in the risk of confrontation was in the air.

With James Baker, who visited Rome in February, we shared our concern that the fortieth anniversary of NATO might be improperly minimized by such polemics. We would miss an opportunity to exalt the decisive role of the Atlantic Treaty even as a logical premise for later thawing in the East and with the East.

Baker agreed, but the issue did not disappear from the international press. On the contrary, it received increasingly colorful headline attention, overshadowing all the rest. I insisted on this point again with Baker when he invited me to lunch while we were both in Vienna for the beginning of negotiations on conventional weapons. As the Brussels meeting approached, we were happy to welcome both Bush and Baker to Rome. We had the opportunity to stress, with great calmness, that suspicions about German steadfastness in the common defense were groundless. Not that the American administration had any doubts about it, but this climate had been building up in the press, and President Bush himself had to acknowledge its determining influence. In these talks, I greatly appreciated the concise wisdom of the new head of the National Security Council, General Brent Scowcroft (one of the three wise men who had investigated the "Iran-Contra affair"). As for Baker, his prevailing background in economic and financial affairs was obvious, but fortunately, as secretary of the treasury, he had had frequent occasions to deal with the Alliance.

Quite objectively, I attribute concrete importance to the talks in Rome for the success of the Atlantic Council. And both parties acknowledged it.

The restatement of the commitment to ban chemical weapons was a feature of the talks with the Americans and in the Brussels summit documents, which made a passing reference to the Paris conference that Mitterrand had organized in January—on a suggestion from Ronald Reagan—and which had been quite successful. Perhaps it would have been enough to give a little more thrust to the proceedings in Geneva; however, it could not hurt to have an *ad hoc* session, to mobilize public opinion in a more solemn fashion. I took the floor during that session, left, and then returned four days later to underscore the importance Italy attributes to these negotiations. Unfortunately, its conclusion is still to come, and it may well be—judging from Bush's latest proposals to the UN—that the United States and USSR prefer to settle it as a two-sided affair, *open,* however—and it could not be otherwise—to all other nations. And yet, the absence of a conclusion justifies continued production, and, at least in the Middle East, fearful stockpiles are growing in size. I said this with some distress to George Shultz when he notified me of Whitehead's replacement by Eagleburger and Vernon Walters's appointment as ambassador to Bonn. Jokingly, he asked me to endeavor, using, as he said, "your somewhat mysterious but effective methods," to encourage Greece and Turkey to adhere to the Vienna conclusions, surmounting bilateral concerns.

I did not mind returning to the Paris conference a second time, however, because I was on my way to London, where the Royal Academy was opening a huge exhibition of twentieth-century Italian art.

The solemn concluding session of the Conference on Security and Co-operation in Europe (CSCE) was held in Vienna on January 19. And it also afforded the opportunity to renew my regard and appreciation for George Shultz, this time in front of a larger audience.

I made my round trip to Austria as quickly as possible because I did not want to miss a meeting for peace organized at the Rome City Hall by the Italian Catholic Action movement. Whoever, like me, comes from those ranks, feels proud to have been able, later on in life, to make his own little contribution so that peace, whose dominant values were instilled in us by popes of extraordinary personality, can first be safeguarded, and then gradually strengthened and rendered, I hope, everlasting.

In this way I was able to comment immediately upon Vienna, saying that a very good rapport now existed both between East and West, and with the neutral and nonaligned countries which had played an effective role as mediators.

The agreement focused on the following five points:

1. The duty of each nation to provide, at the domestic level, adequate legal guarantees for the respect of human rights; among other things, these guarantees are explicitly to cover the publication and accessibility of legislation relative to individual rights, availability of procedures for recourse against any abuse of authority, the power of appeal to second-degree judicial and administrative bodies, public trials, as well as the timely and formal communication of decisions handed down by appeals courts.

2. Focus on the freedom of movement, defined as the ability to move and set one's residence in one's own country and freely to return there.

3. A precise definition of what is meant by religious freedom; in this regard, it is the duty of each nation to foster a climate of religious tolerance, to eliminate any form of discrimination against believers, to refrain from denying to various communities of believers the status provided for them by their respective national constitutions; furthermore, to guarantee the possibility to have places of worship, to organize their own hierarchy, and to select their own "ministers"; to respect the right of each person to deliver and to receive religious instruction, individually or collectively, and to run seminaries.

4. Specific attention to the rights of national minorities, geared to clarify the duty of nations to take the necessary measures to protect and promote ethnic, linguistic, and cultural identity.

5. An explicit recognition of the role which may be played by private individuals, institutions, and organizations to promote implementation of the CSCE commitments, with the consequent pledge on the part of governments to remove any obstacles to their activity.

The text on the principles was supplemented by some references to:

— the need to continue in the search for effective methods to settle international controversies in a peaceful way (for this purpose, a meeting of experts will be held in Malta in 1991);

— the continuing commitment to fight terrorism, both by means of national measures and through increased international cooperation;

— a certain degree of recognition, even by nations still applying the death penalty, that, in any case, it would be appropriate not to rule out its abolishment.

A most important and entirely new element is the institution of a diplomatic mechanism assuring the effectiveness of human rights measures, and the actual implementation of the relative CSCE commitments. Each of the signatory states has the right to:

— request and obtain from the others information on individual cases of human rights;

— hold bilateral meetings in order to consider and resolve such cases;

— discuss cases and the outcome of bilateral meetings in the CSCE plenary sessions.

I have already mentioned the May Atlantic Council in Brussels in which Bush's package of proposals was approved, with a strong American undertaking to stimulate us Europeans on universal disarmament, where a 20 percent American cut was matched by a Soviet reduction ten times higher.

In those days I had to speed up my working pace because I had agreed to run as a candidate in European elections in a constituency different from my customary one, very large and politically diversified: from Emilia and Romagna, a Communist majority region, to the Veneto where the Christian Democratic party prevails. I took pleasure in pointing out in the Veneto, and specifically in the Province of Vicenza, that not only had the strong presence of NATO units not curtailed industrial development, but that in the area there is full employment and a highly efficient network of small and medium-size businesses.

Being a member of the European Parliament is incompatible with a position in national government. Was I only running out of party solidarity, ready to resign once elected as I had done in 1984, or was I planning to move to Brussels to devote myself to full-time European parliamentary life? I will admit that I was seriously considering the latter hypothesis as well. Politicians are frequently reproached that they don't know how to step down at the right time, when the going is good. And

I was going through a good period, with the added satisfaction of seeing some of my former critics correct their negative or dubious judgments on my firm positions (global détente, peace in the Middle East); and some of them were fair enough to even recognize it in public.

When I went to Paris with De Mita for the Bicentennial of the French Revolution and the Summit of the Seven Most Industrialized Nations, many people asked me this question about my intentions, all the more so since we were in the throes of yet another of our recurrent government crises, and the newspapers were mentioning my name among the candidates for succession. I replied that I couldn't tell what I would decide, but no one believed me.

Bush, Baker, and Brady (B.B.B.) participated in all the discussions and ceremonies, conclusively confirming their continuity with the Reagan administration. Further support to this also came in the form of a long and cogent message from Gorbachev to François Mitterrand, as chairman of that session. Starting with the consideration that "perestroika" is "inseparable from a policy tending toward full and complete participation in the world economy," and that "the rest of the world can only benefit from initial steps in the direction of the world economy by a market like that of the USSR," Gorbachev stated his willingness to engage in constructive dialogue and cooperation, identifying similarities and complementarity in respective approaches to world problems and particularly those of the Third World's indebtedness.

Upon our initiative, the Seven Nations once again addressed the threat of drug traffic and agreed upon new forms of cooperation. Bush did not conceal his distaste over the situation in Panama and also over the lengthy period when previous administrations had closed their eyes to drug trafficking in certain countries. Noriega was challenging the prestige of the United States, despite almost unanimous opposition to him on the part of the Organization of American States. The European Community had also expressed solidarity in condemning Noriega, but he was still in the saddle.

The new American president, however, mostly concentrated his attention on events within the Warsaw Pact countries, especially Poland and Hungary, which he would visit immediately afterwards. I was able to say something appropriate in that regard, because I had been monitoring developments in that area for some time. I recalled that when I had gone to Warsaw in 1984, I had felt the need to provide concrete forms of encouragement not only to Solidarity but also to General Jaruzelski; but it had taken Washington over two years to lift the sanctions. I was grateful to President Reagan because, skipping protocol, he had informed me of this in a personal letter, with the hope that the true national reconciliation I had talked about would actually take place in Poland. The visit in May of this year, accompanying the president of the Republic, Cossiga, and chairing in Warsaw the Colloquium of the Center on Ciceronian Studies, had given me the joy of seeing real changes under way and the atmosphere of authentic democratic commitment. Now we all faced the urgent and awesome duty of assisting Poland and Hungary (in addition to the USSR, of course) even materially, with the methods which would appear most effective. I took the opportunity to notify Bush that the next Colloquium of the Center on Ciceronian Studies would be held—in 1991, I believe—at Columbia University in New York.

During the breaks, the president returned to the subject of "open skies" which he had mentioned at NATO. This is an old idea which Eisenhower, president from 1952 to 1960, had proposed at the Geneva Conference (18 July 1955) of the four Heads of Government: the United States, USSR, France, and the United Kingdom. It involved a detailed exchange of data on respective military equipment, with recourse to aerial photographic verification to be conducted using aircraft supplied by the inspected party. Through Bulganin, the Soviets had immediately rejected the plan. Counting on the change in the international climate, Bush intends to sustain it anew. Our General Defense staff had already ascertained that we would have no objections, and we were able to say so to Baker and to Bush.

Entirely different in nature was a discussion we had at the dining table, which stemmed from a question someone asked. Was it true that Reagan or his friends had thought about a third election, and would that have been possible under the Constitution?

In this way I learned that a third term of office would today be possible only by amending the Constitution, whereas Roosevelt had been able to govern until his death, even beyond the twelfth year of his presidency. An amendment in force since 1951, which was approved in 1947, but was ratified only four years later by the individual states, only allows for one reelection. Before Roosevelt, the limit of two terms in office had only been a question of practice since there was no reference to it in the Constitution, reportedly because of George Washington's wish to "reign" for a longer period of time.

Circumstances decreed that I should be the one, after all, to preside over the five-party coalition which formed the new government, so that I had to leave the Foreign Ministry after six years. There is certainly plenty of work for my successor, Deputy Gianni De Michelis; however, the grand international policy of détente and dialogue is now deeply rooted and relations with the United States constitute the pillar around which our system of alliances rotates, not at all in contrast with Italy's marked European vocation.

CSCE negotiations in Vienna on the reduction of conventional weapons have not proceeded at the fast pace we would have liked, due to the difficulties encountered by the sixteen Western countries in agreeing on a common platform. The agreement was finally reached on September 20, and, at least on paper, the rest should not take an exceedingly long time. I feel it should be emphasized that the *pro tempore* chairman who presented the document to the Eastern countries was the Canadian representative, Mr. Peel. This is the great value of the Helsinki formula: Canada and the United States of America *are* Europe.

During those same days, Shevardnadze had long talks in Wyoming with Baker, who said the following when assessing the domestic situation in the USSR:

President Bush has made it quite clear that we have a deep interest in what takes place in the Soviet Union. He has reaffirmed our *commitment* and our *desire* to see the success of perestroika. He has indicated that he believes the USSR has been moving in a very responsible and balanced way with respect to the changes which are taking place, not only in the Soviet Union, but in Eastern Europe as well; and he has expressed our hope that we may see this type of attitude continue. With regard to the hypothesis of American aid to perestroika, one thing is a stable international environment, and another is assistance for their economic problems, all the more so since today's meeting confirmed that the Soviets are not asking for aid, but for technical advice on how to deal with their economy.

On the thorny issue of the ban on chemical weapons, aside from the aforementioned announcement of possible reductions agreed upon between the United States and USSR, a new element was the "Governments-Industries" Conference held in Canberra in September and divided into three working groups. The Arabs once again proposed a linkage between chemical weapons and nuclear disarmament; and the Americans insisted on having a small team of experts backing the negotiators in Geneva. If the procedure followed had been the one we started —a seminar of scientists working out an effective verification model— as we did for nuclear weapons, more progress would have been made. But I am convinced that the problem does not reside in a shortage of formulas, but rather in the lack of a widespread and true political will to reach a conclusion. And this worries me.

Max Rabb left Rome after eight years at the head of a far-from-easy embassy in which he had set himself the daily target of enhancing Italy's already excellent political standing in the United States. Some of his outbursts—actually rare—were due precisely to his frustration when faced with the risk of seeing the Italian *primacy,* which he proudly said he had brought about, challenged again.

In the realm of personal relations, I appreciated two acts of courtesy he extended to me: in April 1983 when my friends celebrated—without sending out invitations—the forty years of my public life, Max came to the Adriano Theater and I was happy to see him. Six years later, on my seventieth birthday, I received from him—on a day when my vanity was put to a hard test, what with a message from Gorbachev and a phone call from John Paul II—a long, handwritten letter overflowing with friendly words, concepts which he reiterated in his letter bidding a final farewell to Italy.

The choice of his successor ran a controversial path which someone attributed to the wish of Rabb's many friends in Congress (he was once called to Washington to convince some reluctant senators to approve the sale of AWACs to Saudi Arabia, and succeeded) to have him leave Rome after and not before Bush's visit.

The mechanism of Senate ratification of appointments is rather merciless. Not only is the candidate submitted to stringent questioning, even with snares at times, but the media play it all up, frequently using offensive and derogatory language for effect.

The choice of the fifty-year-old industrialist Peter Secchia, originally from a Piedmont family, is certainly due to the decisive role he played, in its widest sense, in Bush's victory in Michigan. However, since the prevailing practice is not to appoint career ambassadors, I don't see why people should underestimate his degree in economics and his skill in bringing his leading company to achieve gross annual sales of $400 million. In fact, in the wake of Bush's defeat in designating Power as secretary of defense, some senators—even though they were not pursuing a second defeat—wanted to keep Peter hopping on the burning coals, feeding material to the scandal press to elaborate on his eating and drinking habits; on his not always Victorian language; on his behavior with women. Someone even criticized us for our immediate "agrément" and even wanted us to withdraw it. The end result was only a few isolated hostile articles in the papers. I knew Peter Secchia was highly appreciated by President Gerald Ford (I had first met him at a reception hosted by Ford), and I never attached much importance to the clamor raised on Capitol Hill and which ended by being much ado about nothing, as was right, and with ratification of the appointment.

I received him for the first time on July 4, the morning of his first Independence Day in Rome, and we had an interesting and concrete exchange of ideas. That afternoon I went to the reception at the embassy and met his wonderful family. I see he is working intelligently and in harmony with the embassy staff, beginning with Minister Counsellor John Holmes, who knows Italy very well and is respected by all. During the summer he worked actively on the preparations for the visit to the United States by our president of the Republic.

A minor storm was about to break out during Peter Secchia's early days in Rome over a statement he made against the possible entry of Italian Communists into the government. His was a habit that American ambassadors had long since ceased to manifest, and there was an initial controversial reaction from the party in question. Quite wisely, however, Achille Occhetto understood that he risked nullifying the effect of his very recent trip to America; for his part, and with an authentic interpretation, Secchia acknowledged that this is a subject pertaining exclusively to national jurisdiction. This way, to everyone's satisfaction, after the early thunder, the rains never came.

With regard to the trip of the Italian Communist leader to the United States, duly assisted by our embassy, some critical voices were raised, but they were completely out of place. Perhaps people of my generation —who suffered the consequences of Togliatti's bravado ("made in Moscow"?), when he accused the Americans of being stupid, while De Gasperi was over there seeking help for the survival and the reconstruction of Italy—are more aware than others of the positive importance of such a different attitude, also by virtue of the great international changes.

I certainly do not fear domestic "competition" from the Communists in this field. What worries me is precisely the opposite; that bourgeois neoradical ideas—forgive me the expression—may challenge the achievements of 1977, when the parties underwrote and approved, all together (or almost) the solemn declaration upholding the Atlantic Treaty and the European Community.

On that day, so replete with parliamentary significance, I thought of the joy De Gasperi would have felt (I use the words "would have" because I don't know if they are still interested in earthly matters up there). The same thought came to my mind when reading about the visits to Washington and New York by Achille Occhetto and Giorgio Napolitano. In the great book of history everything always comes out even. Perchance, at the slowest pace.

Index